ORTHODOX WAY
a Catechism for for Seekers

by Deacon Charles Joiner, PhD

2025

Copyright © 2025 by Charles W. Joiner, PhD

ISBN: 979-8-218-60470-7

All rights reserved. No part of this book may be reproduced in any form or by any electronic or mechanical means including information storage and retrieval systems without permission in writing from the publisher, except by a reviewer, who may quote brief passages in a review.

For permissions contact Father Deacon Charles Joiner at cjoiner@mac.com.
Saint George Greek Orthodox Cathedral
Greenville, South Carolina

Printed in the U.S.A.

Table of Contents

Introduction
    Embracing the Journey of Faith. 7

Chapter 1 A Sacramental Worldview. 9
  What is a Worldview?
  Core Elements of the Sacramental Worldview

Chapter 2: The Orthodox Church: Preserving the Apostolic Faith Through History. 15
  Brief History: The Orthodox Church and its Claim to be the True Apostolic Church
  Apostolic Foundations of the Orthodox Church
  Timeline of Church History
  Holy Tradition and Its Relationship with Scripture
  The History and Canon of the New Testament
  Critique of Sola Scriptura: An Orthodox Perspective

Chapter 3 Faith as a Living Relationship: Embracing the Orthodox Way to Theosis. 45
  Faith is a Lived Relationship with God
  God Dwells in Us
  Awakening a Living Faith
  Grace, Synergy, and a Lifelong Journey of Salvation
  Life in the Church and the Sacraments
  Theosis: The Ultimate Goal of Faith

Chapter 4 Creation. 79
  The Six Days of Creation
  The Creation of Humans

Chapter 5 Ancestral Sin 93
  The Fall and the Concept of Ancestral Sin
  The Problem of the Western View of Original Sin
    and Doctrine of Guilt

Chapter 6 The Path to Salvation. 105
  God Prepares the Way

Coming of Our Savior — The Incarnation of God
How Christ Saves Us
General vs. Personal Salvation
The Church and the Nicene Creed: Doctrine on
the Nature of Christ and the Holy Trinity

**Chapter 7 Preservation of Apostolic Doctrine
in the Orthodox Church.** 133
Apostolic Foundations
Defending the Faith from Heresy
Schisms and Divisions
Other Innovations introduced in the Roman Catholic Church
since the Great Schism
Innovation Introduced by the Protestants in the Reformation
Other Factors in Preserving the Truth

Chapter 8 Orthodox Way of Life: A Life of Repentance. . . 161
Repentance (Metanoia): The Foundation of the
Orthodox Christian Life
Nature of Our Spiritual Being
The Nature of Passions that Cause Sin
Spiritual Disciplines: Tools for Transformation and Growth

**Chapter 9 Orthodox Prayers: A Journey Toward
Communion with God.** 175
What is Orthodox Prayer?
Stages of Prayer: From Oral to Noetic Prayer
Jesus Prayer
When Do We Pray?
Where Do We Pray: Create a Quiet Place
How Do We Prepare for Prayer?
How Do We Pray?
Establishing a Rule of Prayer

**Chapter 10 Fasting in the Orthodox Christian Tradition:
A Spiritual Discipline.** 203
Nature of Fasting
How to Fast

Table of Contents

Chapter 11   Orthodox Worship: A Comprehensive Overview. 213
  Worship a Participation in the Divine Life of God
  The Liturgical Cycles
  The Divine Liturgy: Heaven on Earth

Chapter 12   Repentance: A Journey Back to God. 227
  Need for Repentance
  The Parable of the Prodigal Son
  The Way of Repentance
  The Preparation for Confession
  The Act of Confession

Chapter 13   Death and the Final Judgment. 247
  The Spiritual Realm
  Understanding Death
  Paradise and Hell
  The Second Coming of Christ
  The Universal Resurrection

Appendix A: Ten Questions Inquirers Have About the Orthodox Faith. 269

1. Why Are Icons and Veneration of Saints Important in Orthodox Worship?

2. What Does the Orthodox Church Teach About the Virgin Mary?

3. Why Do Orthodox Christians Pray to Saints and the Virgin Mary? Isn't that Idolatry?

4. How Does the Orthodox Church Understand the Atonement and the Role of Christ's Death on the Cross?

5. What is the Orthodox Understanding of the Pope and Papal Primacy? How Does the Orthodox Church Understand the Nature and Authority of the Church?

6. What is the Orthodox Position on Purgatory?

7. How Does the Orthodox Church View the Immaculate Conception the Virgin Mary?

8. How Does the Orthodox Church Address Doctrinal Development Over Time?

9. How Does the Orthodox Church Address the Problem of Evil and Suffering?

10. What Role Does Reason and Science Play in the Orthodox Faith?

Appendix B: Books for Inquirers. 313

**Appendix C: Websites, Blogs, and
You Tube Channels for Inquirers.** 319

Appendix D: The Nicene Creed. 325

Acknowledgements 327

Author Bio 329

Introduction

Embracing the Journey of Faith

For over two decades, I have had the privilege of guiding individuals from diverse backgrounds through an Orthodox catechism class. Many have come from other Christian traditions, seeking to understand the richness of Orthodox Christianity. Others, lifelong Orthodox faithful, have desired to deepen their knowledge and renew their commitment to the faith of their forefathers. This book is the fruit of those years of teaching, reflecting both the questions and struggles of modern seekers and the timeless truths of the Orthodox Church.

The Orthodox faith is not merely a set of doctrines or rituals—it is a living and transformative relationship with God. Rooted in the unbroken Apostolic Tradition and the teachings of the Church Fathers, Orthodoxy offers a path to Theosis, the ultimate union with God. Yet, this faith must be lived in a world that often conflicts with its truths. This book is a response to that challenge, equipping readers with a solid theological foundation while addressing the practical realities of living as an Orthodox Christian in the modern age.

The journey begins by introducing the Orthodox way of thinking, called a sacramental worldview, and how it differs from our current society's secular worldview. Next, we explore the cornerstone of the faith: Holy Tradition and Scripture. Here, we examine the Apostolic Church's history, the relationship between Holy Tradition and Scripture, the formation of the biblical canon, and a critique of Sola Scriptura. From this foundation, we move to a vibrant exploration of Living Faith, highlighting the dynamic relationship with God, the role of grace and synergy, and the sacramental life of the Church.

Understanding humanity's origins and struggles is essential, and the chapters on Creation and Ancestral Sin illuminate these topics, contrasting Orthodox teachings with Western views of original sin. From there, we delve into the heart of the Gospel message: Salvation—exploring the Incarnation, Christ's redemptive work, and the personal and communal nature of salvation as understood in Orthodoxy.

The book then addresses the critical task of Preserving Apostolic Truth, tracing the Church's defense against heresy, the impact of the Great Schism, and the challenges posed by innovations in Roman Catholicism and Protestantism. The focus then shifts to the practical aspects of the faith, with chapters on the Way of Life and the Passions, Prayer, Fasting, Worship, and Confession, offering guidance for spiritual growth and repentance.

Finally, we confront the profound mysteries of Death and the Afterlife, exploring the Orthodox understanding of the spiritual realm, paradise, hell, and the universal resurrection.

This book is not merely an academic treatise or a historical overview—it is an invitation. An invitation to discover, embrace, and live the Orthodox Way. Whether you are new to Orthodoxy, rediscovering your faith, or seeking to understand how to navigate the challenges of the modern world as a faithful Orthodox Christian, this book is for you. My prayer is that it will inspire you to dig deep, ask questions, and engage with zeal as you embark on this transformative journey.

May this book serve as a guide and companion as you seek to participate with our living God through the fullness of the Orthodox faith.

Deacon Charles Joiner, PhD
2025

Chapter 1

A Sacramental Worldview

In a world shaped by a mindset that separates the physical from the spiritual (a secular worldview), many of us have been conditioned to dismiss or misunderstand the heart of early Christian thought and practice, preserved today in the Orthodox Church. We began by examining how our understanding of reality shapes our perception of God, faith, and life itself. The secular worldview often reduces religion to a personal, subjective matter, stripping it of its universal and transformative essence.

Orthodox Christianity, by contrast, embraces a sacramental worldview—a way of seeing all of life as infused with God's presence and grace. This worldview is not merely theoretical but profoundly transformative. It offers a holistic approach to life that unites the physical and divine, the worldly and eternal, and calls for active participation in God's divine energies through His grace.

This chapter explores the core elements of the sacramental worldview, addresses common questions rooted in secular assumptions, and provides insights into how the Orthodox faith bridges the divide between the early Christian world and today's modern, often fragmented, understanding of faith and reality. Through this exploration, we are invited to begin journey to rediscover a way of living where every moment and aspect of life reflects the presence and purpose of God.

What Is A Worldview?

Definition and Importance

A worldview is the lens or filter through which we interpret reality. It influences our beliefs about God, morality, and human purpose. It involves assumptions that help our brain process all the sensory input we receive to create what we experience as reality. In every culture, worldviews are shaped by these deeply ingrained assumptions, often absorbed unconsciously.

The Secular Worldview

The modern secular worldview, shaped by materialism, rationalism, and individualism, prioritizes the material or physical over the spiritual. It is characterized by:

- **Material Focus:** Reality is confined to what is measurable and observable.

  Reality is limited by what can be proven by empirical evidence and scientific verification.

  Physical world is perceived as self-sufficient, with no inherent connection to the divine. We may believe in God as the creator but there is no longer any active involvement in our world which is now governed by what we call laws of nature. Spiritual or metaphysical experiences are dismissed as personal or irrelevant. Science or philosophic logic is called on to verify what is true.

- **Individual Autonomy:** Personal freedom and choice are prioritized over communal or divine authority. Authority figures, including religious leaders and traditions, are often questioned or dismissed as outdated. Faith becomes individualized, with statements like, "I have my beliefs and you have yours." There is no accepted universal truth.

- **Reduction of Religion:** Faith is reduced to a set of ethical rules or cultural traditions, often disconnected from transformative spiritual realities. Sacraments, where material items like bread and wine

are transformed into spiritual realities by the Holy Spirit, are seen as symbolic rather than transformative participation with God. Faith is treated as a private matter, disconnected from public or communal life.
- **Worldly Goals**: Life is oriented toward personal success, wealth, and societal progress, with little focus on eternity. Eternal realities, such as the afterlife or union with God, are ignored or de-emphasized. Religion is valued only if it contributes to worldly happiness or societal improvement. It becomes a means of worldly benefit rather than preparation for eternal life.

The Sacramental Worldview
Orthodox Christianity offers a fundamentally different perspective based on the view held by the early Christians:
- **Unity of Reality**: The physical and divine are interconnected. The material world is a means of participating in God's divine grace.
- **Communal Identity**: Faith is lived out in the community of the Church, the Body of Christ.
- **Eternal Perspective**: Life is experienced as a pilgrimage toward eternal union with God.
- **Divine Vision**: God's presence and grace permeate all of creation.

Core Elements of the Sacramental Worldview

God's Presence in Creation
Orthodoxy teaches that the material world is not separate from God but reveals His glory and presence. The natural world is a testament to God's majesty, revealing His presence, power and glory. The physical world is not separate from God but reflects His sustaining presence.
- Scriptural Basis: *The heavens declare the glory of God* (Psalm 19:1).
- *For since the creation of the world His invisible attributes are clearly seen* (Romans 1:20).
- Implications: Creation serves as a means through which believers can participate in God. Believers are called to honor all of creation.

Unity of the Physical and Spiritual
The sacraments of the Church embody this unity, using physical elements like bread, wine, water, and oil to convey divine grace.
- **Eucharist**: Bread and wine become the actual Body and Blood of Christ, uniting believers with Him (Matthew 26:26-28).
- **Baptism**: Water becomes the means of spiritual rebirth, uniting the believer with Christ's death and resurrection (Romans 6:4).
- **Chrismation**: Oil imparts the Holy Spirit through anointing with oil.
- **Implication**: The material world is a bridge to union with God, not a barrier.

The Incarnation
The sacramental worldview is rooted in the mystery of the Incarnation: *The Word became flesh and dwelt among us* (John 1:14).

- By becoming fully human, Christ sanctified the material world, making it a vehicle for divine grace. Jesus' humanity makes the invisible God visible and tangible. Through the Incarnation, Christ redeems not just humanity but the entire cosmos.
- Through baptism we too receive the Holy Spirit and our physical being is united with the divine so we can, through our life follow His teachings in union with His will, become like Him preparing for our eternal life in His kingdom.

The Church as the Body of Christ
The Church is a communal, sacramental reality where believers grow in holiness. It is the living Body of Christ, through which God's grace is mediated. It is not merely a human institution but a divine organism uniting heaven and earth. Sacraments are its lifeblood, administering the sacraments though the active participation of the Holy Spirit, to sustain spiritual life and nurture holiness. The Church connects the earthly and heavenly realms, bringing believers into participation with saints and angels.
- **Scriptural Basis**: *He put all things under His feet and gave Him as head over all things to the Church, which is His body* (Ephesians 1:22-23).

- **Role**: The Church preserves Apostolic Tradition, administers the sacraments, and provides the communal context for faith.

The Church is the means through which believers participate in God's redemptive work and grow toward union with Him preparing for eternal life.

The sacramental worldview of the Orthodox Church integrates the material and spiritual, orienting believers toward a life of participation with God through His creation, sacraments, and the Church.

Conclusion

We often come to Orthodoxy seeking a deeper faith, yet we are inevitably shaped by the culture in which we were raised. For many, this cultural worldview places great emphasis on the material world, where the physical is often seen as separate from what is spiritual. This perspective can make understanding and embracing the nature of Orthodox life challenging, as it requires examining and sometimes letting go of deeply ingrained assumptions about reality.

The Orthodox sacramental worldview does not reject scientific thinking or the benefits it brings to our worldly life. However, it reminds us that scientific methods cannot be used to verify the greater spiritual truths of heaven and the Kingdom of God. These truths are not proven through empirical evidence but are experienced through participation in God's divine energies, especially in the sacraments, prayer, and the life of the Church.

Learning about the Orthodox faith involves more than acquiring correct doctrinal knowledge rooted in Apostolic times; it also requires adopting a way of life that nurtures the soul. This includes cleansing the heart from the passions—tendencies that cloud our ability to perceive God's presence and truth.

As you progress on this journey, there will likely come a moment of realization, an "Ahhh" moment, when you recognize, "I don't have to figure this out on my own." Trusting in the teachings of the Church, participating fully in its liturgical cycle, cultivating a meaningful prayer life, and embracing the ascetic disciplines handed down from the earliest days of Christianity bring both relief and spiritual awakening. This is when you begin to experience an expanded view of reality—a reality where the physical and spiritual are deeply united, and every aspect of life becomes a means of communion with God.

Study Questions

1. What are the key differences between a secular worldview and the Orthodox sacramental worldview, particularly in their understanding of the relationship between the physical and spiritual?

2. How does the Orthodox Church's teaching on the Incarnation shape its sacramental worldview, especially regarding the sanctification of the material world?

3. What role do the sacraments, such as the Eucharist and Baptism, play in illustrating the unity of the physical and spiritual in the Orthodox faith?

4. How does the Church as the Body of Christ embody the sacramental worldview, and how does it connect the material and divine realms for believers?

5. In what ways does adopting a sacramental worldview challenge the assumptions of a modern secular mindset, and how does this transformation impact a believer's understanding of faith and reality?

Chapter 2

The Orthodox Church: Preserving the Apostolic Faith Through History

The Orthodox Church boldly asserts its identity as the one, holy, catholic, and apostolic Church established by Christ and His Apostles. This claim is grounded in its unbroken historical continuity, adherence to Apostolic teachings, and preservation of Holy Tradition. Through centuries of development, the Orthodox Church has remained steadfast in its mission to safeguard the faith, ensuring its doctrines, liturgical practices, and spiritual life reflect the fullness of the Apostolic inheritance.

This chapter explores the historical foundations of the Orthodox Church, from its establishment at Pentecost to its ongoing role as the guardian of Holy Tradition. Key moments in Church history, such as the Ecumenical Councils and the Great Schism, are examined to illustrate how the Orthodox Church has preserved its identity amidst external and internal challenges. By understanding its history, we can appreciate how the Orthodox Church's claim to Apostolic continuity is intricately linked to its theology, worship, and hierarchical structure, all of which testify to its faithfulness to the original Church of Christ and His Apostles.

Brief History:
The Orthodox Church and its Claim to Be the True Apostolic Church

Apostolic Foundations of the Orthodox Church

The Orthodox Church traces its foundation to the Apostles, whom Christ commissioned to *make disciples of all nations* (Matthew 28:19). On the day of Pentecost, the Holy Spirit descended upon the Apostles, empowering them to preach the Gospel and establish the Church (Acts 2). From Jerusalem, the Apostles spread the Christian faith throughout the Roman Empire and beyond, establishing local communities that would become the seeds of the universal Church.

Apostolic teaching and practice formed the bedrock of these communities. The Apostles handed down not only the written texts of Scripture but also oral traditions that predated the compilation of the New Testament, liturgical practices, and doctrinal teachings. These elements, safeguarded and nurtured by the Church, constitute what is known as Holy Tradition.

Timeline of Church History

Pentecost and the Establishment of the Church

While the Church has always existed in Heaven, the earthly Church's history began with Pentecost, where the Apostles, filled with the Holy Spirit, spoke in various languages, symbolizing the universal nature of the Gospel. Early Christian communities were founded in key cities such as Antioch, Alexandria, and Rome, with each developing as part of one unified body of Christ. The Apostle Paul appointed Bishops over each city and Priests to assist the work of the Bishops as the Church Grew. Deacons were also appointed as clergy to assist the bishops in their duties. This hierarchal structure is documented in the Pastoral epistles of Saint Paul (e.g. 1 Timothy and Titus).

The Development of Doctrine and Worship

As the Church grew, it developed a rich liturgical life out of the Jewish traditions including Psalmody, prayers and blessings which were adapted and fulfilled in the all important celebration of the Eucharist. This was referred to in Scripture as the *breaking of the bread* (e.g., Acts 2:42, Luke 24:30). It articulated its doctrines clarifying the nature of Jesus Christ as both fully God and fully human, in response to various challenges. By the second century, writers like Justin Martyr described the liturgical practices of the Church, including the Eucharistic celebration. These accounts show remarkable continuity with Orthodox worship today, emphasizing the Church's commitment to preserving the faith as received from the Apostles.

Ecumenical Councils and the Role in Defining Orthodoxy
The Ecumenical Councils* played a central role in safeguarding the Church's doctrinal integrity by addressing Christological controversies, such as Arianism and Nestorianism. Arianism, promoted by Arius in the 4th century, denied the full divinity of Christ, claiming that He was a created being subordinate to God the Father. Nestorianism, associated with Nestorius in the 5th century, separated Christ's divine and human natures to such an extent that it undermined the unity of His person, rejecting the title Theotokos ("God-bearer") for the Virgin Mary. Convened to address heresies and clarify essential truths, these councils, such as Nicaea (325) and Chalcedon (451), affirmed key doctrines, including the divinity of Christ, the nature of the Holy Trinity, and the hypostatic union of Christ's two natures. The decisions of these councils, guided by the Holy Spirit, reflect the practice of conciliarity—the collective discernment and decision-making of the bishops in unity with the entire Church. This practice ensured consensus in preserving Holy Tradition and safeguarding Orthodox belief and practice for future generations.

Key Historical Events: The Great Schism and Continuity
In 1054, the Great Schism divided the Church into Eastern (Orthodox) and Western (Roman Catholic) branches. While political, cultural, and theological differences contributed to the split, one of the major theological disputes was the addition of the filioque clause to the Nicene-Constantinopolitan Creed by the Western Church. Originally, the Creed declared that the Holy Spirit proceeds from the Father, in accordance with

---

*Ecumenical Council is the gathering of the whole Church represented by the Bishops and their representatives.

John 15:26 and the teachings of the early Church. The filioque clause, meaning "and the Son," was added by the Western Church to assert that the Holy Spirit proceeds from both the Father and the Son. This innovation was introduced without the consensus of an Ecumenical Council, which the Orthodox Church holds as essential for doctrinal changes. The Orthodox Church rejected this addition, emphasizing that it disrupts the balance of Trinitarian theology and undermines the Father's unique role as the sole source of the Trinity. In addition to the filioque, the doctrine of papal supremacy further deepened the divide, as the Western Church claimed universal authority for the Pope over the entire Church, which was contrary to the Orthodox understanding of conciliarity and the equality of bishops. The Orthodox Church has maintained its adherence to the faith and practices of the Apostolic era, standing in contrast to the theological and structural innovations introduced in the West.

Later in the 16th century, there was a revolt against the Western Church, known as the Catholic Church, initiated by Martin Luther. This movement, known as the Protestant Reformation, led to significant turmoil and the introduction of innovative doctrines that fundamentally altered the Western understanding of the Christian faith. Among these were "Sola Fide" (faith alone) and "Sola Scriptura" (scripture alone).

The doctrine of Sola Fide (faith alone) asserted that salvation is achieved by faith alone, apart from works, in contrast to the traditional teaching that faith must be accompanied by good works and participation in the sacraments as part of the process of salvation. Similarly, Sola Scriptura (scripture alone) claimed that Scripture alone is the sole authority for Christian doctrine, rejecting the role of Holy Tradition, which had been integral to the Church's teaching and practice since Apostolic times. This view dismissed the authority of the Church, the Ecumenical Councils, and the guidance of the Holy Spirit through the lived experience of the Christian community.

These doctrines effectively reduced the Church to a "Church of the Book," rejecting most of the Holy Traditions that had been handed down through the centuries. The Orthodox Church, being separated from the Catholic Church since the Great Schism of 1054, played no part in these events and views the innovations introduced by the Reformation as heretical. The Orthodox Church continues to affirm the inseparability of Holy Tradition and Holy Scripture, emphasizing that the fullness of the Christian faith is found only in the unity of the two, as revealed and preserved in the life of the Church.

Evidence of Apostolic Succession in Orthodoxy
The doctrine of Apostolic Succession affirms that the bishops of the Orthodox Church are direct successors of the Apostles. This unbroken chain of ordination ensures that the teachings and sacraments of the Church remain faithful to their apostolic origins. Ordination, or cheirotonia in Greek, is the sacramental act by which the grace of the Holy Spirit is conferred upon a man to enable him to serve in one of the three clerical roles established by Christ and the Apostles: bishops, priests, and deacons. This sacred act is performed through the laying on of hands by a bishop, accompanied by prayers calling upon the Holy Spirit to impart the necessary gifts and authority for the ordained ministry.

The bishop holds the highest office in the Church's hierarchy, serving as the chief teacher, shepherd, and guardian of the faith within his diocese. He is entrusted with preserving doctrinal purity, overseeing the administration of the sacraments, and providing spiritual leadership to the clergy and laity under his care. Priests, ordained by the bishop, serve as his representatives in local parishes. They celebrate the Divine Liturgy, administer most sacraments, and provide pastoral care to the faithful, ensuring that the spiritual needs of their communities are met. Deacons, also ordained, play a vital role in service, assisting bishops and priests in liturgical functions and acts of charity, embodying the ministry of service first instituted by the Apostles.

Ordination is not merely a ceremonial act but a sacrament that imparts divine grace, enabling the ordained to fulfill their sacred duties. The early Church Fathers, such as St. Irenaeus of Lyons, emphasized this unbroken chain of ordination as essential for maintaining the authenticity and unity of the Church. St. Irenaeus asserted that the true Church could be identified by its connection to the Apostles through its bishops, ensuring that the faith and practices handed down from

Christ and His Apostles remain intact. This sacred chain of ordination safeguards the Church's mission and ensures the ongoing presence of Christ's grace and authority within His Body, the Church.

The Orthodox Church's Claim to Unbroken Continuity

The Orthodox Church's use of the Septuagint, the Greek translation of the Old Testament, underscores its continuity with the Apostolic Church and highlights its theological consistency with early Christianity. The Septuagint, often abbreviated as LXX, was produced in the 3rd and 2nd centuries BC in Alexandria, Egypt, during a time when many Jews lived in the Hellenistic world and Greek was the common language. According to tradition, the translation was commissioned by Ptolemy II Philadelphus for the Library of Alexandria, and seventy-two Jewish scholars, working independently, produced identical translations of the Torah, confirming its divine inspiration.

The Septuagint quickly became the primary version of the Old Testament for the Jewish diaspora, who had become more familiar with Greek than Hebrew. By the time of Christ and the Apostles, the Septuagint was widely used and quoted in the New Testament, forming the scriptural foundation for the early Christian community. Many of the Old Testament quotations in the New Testament align with the Septuagint rather than the Masoretic Text, the Hebrew version finalized centuries later.

The Septuagint's accuracy and theological value are emphasized in the Orthodox Church because it reflects a textual tradition predating the Masoretic Text. After the destruction of the Second Temple in AD 70, rabbinical Judaism began standardizing Hebrew Scripture, culminating in the Masoretic Text (developed between the 6th and 10th centuries AD). In this process, certain passages were adjusted or reinterpreted, sometimes to downplay Christian theological claims, such as messianic prophecies fulfilled in Christ. For example, Isaiah 7:14 in the Septuagint translates the prophecy as "a virgin shall conceive," which aligns with the New Testament's account of the Virgin Birth. The Masoretic Text, however, uses the term "young woman," altering the prophecy's explicit Christological significance.

The Orthodox Church continues to hold the Septuagint as central to its worship, theology, and understanding of Holy Scripture. It is used in liturgical readings, hymns, and doctrinal formulations, reflecting its foundational role in the Apostolic Church. The Septuagint preserves the early Jewish textual tradition that informed the faith of Christ, the Apostles, and the early Christians, affirming its accuracy and authority over later textual revisions.

Early Church Fathers' Writings
The writings of the early Church Fathers, such as St. Athanasius, St. Basil the Great, and St. John Chrysostom, provide a window into the beliefs and practices of the early Church, offering a treasure trove of theological insight, pastoral guidance, and liturgical tradition. These Fathers were not only exceptional theologians and spiritual leaders but also instrumental in shaping the doctrine, worship, and life of the Church. Their writings demonstrate a consistent theology and liturgical life that align with contemporary Orthodoxy, affirming the Church's unbroken continuity with its Apostolic foundations.

- St. Athanasius of Alexandria (c. 296–373): Known as the "Father of Orthodoxy," St. Athanasius was a staunch defender of the faith during the Arian controversy, which denied the full divinity of Christ. As Bishop of Alexandria, he played a pivotal role in the First Ecumenical Council at Nicaea (325), which affirmed the consubstantiality of the Son with the Father (homoousios). His seminal work, On the Incarnation, articulates the central mystery of the Christian faith: the Word of God becoming flesh for the salvation of humanity. St. Athanasius also contributed to the recognition of the New Testament canon by listing its books in his 39th Paschal Letter.

- St. Basil the Great (c. 330–379): A key figure in the development of monasticism and theology, St. Basil was Bishop of Caesarea and a defender of the Nicene faith against Arianism. His theological writings, including On the Holy Spirit, were instrumental in clarifying the doctrine of the Trinity, particularly the divinity of the Holy Spirit. St. Basil also reformed monastic life, emphasizing community living, prayer, and works of mercy. His liturgical contributions include the Divine Liturgy of St. Basil, still celebrated in the Orthodox Church during specific liturgical seasons.

- St. John Chrysostom (c. 347–407): Renowned as one of the greatest preachers in Christian history, St. John Chrysostom, whose name means "Golden-Mouthed," was the Archbishop of Constantinople. His homilies and commentaries on Scripture reflect profound pastoral care and a deep understanding of the human condition. He is also remembered for his commitment to social justice and his courage in confronting imperial and ecclesiastical corruption. St. John's Divine Liturgy, which bears his name, is the standard Eucharistic service of the Orthodox Church and a testament to his liturgical legacy.

These Fathers, among others, are considered pillars of Orthodox Christianity, whose lives and teachings not only defended the Church against heresy but also enriched its theological depth and spiritual practice. Their writings are highly revered, studied, and quoted to this day, providing guidance and inspiration for Orthodox Christians seeking to live out the faith of the Apostles.

Preservation of Holy Tradition
Holy Tradition encompasses the totality of the Church's life, including Scripture, liturgy, iconography, the teachings of the Fathers, and the lived experience of the faithful throughout the centuries. It is the life of the Holy Spirit working in the Church, preserving the truth of the Gospel and guiding the Church in all its expressions of faith and worship. By preserving this Tradition, the Orthodox Church remains faithful to the deposit of faith entrusted to it by the Apostles, maintaining the continuity of its beliefs, practices, and spiritual life.

The preservation of Holy Tradition is evident in several key ways:

Scripture as Part of Tradition: The Orthodox Church recognizes that the Holy Scriptures were born out of the Church's Tradition, as the Apostles and their successors, inspired by the Holy Spirit, recorded the life and teachings of Christ. The Church has carefully preserved and interpreted these texts through the guidance of the Holy Spirit, ensuring they are understood within the context of the Apostolic faith.

Liturgical Life: The liturgical practices of the Orthodox Church, including the Divine Liturgy, the sacraments, and the daily cycle of prayer, are deeply rooted in Apostolic Tradition. These services, rich with Scripture and theological symbolism, have been transmitted and celebrated faithfully across centuries, uniting the Church in worship and doctrinal integrity.

Iconography: Orthodox iconography is a visible expression of Holy Tradition, conveying theological truths and the reality of the Incarnation. Icons are not merely decorative but are considered windows into the divine, aiding the faithful in prayer and contemplation. The strict adherence to traditional forms and theology in iconography ensures consistency with the Apostolic faith.

The Teachings of the Fathers: The writings and teachings of the Church Fathers have been preserved and studied, providing guidance in theology, spirituality, and pastoral care. Their consensus serves as a touchstone for understanding Scripture and combating heresies, ensuring that the Church remains faithful to its Apostolic foundation.

Councils and Dogma: The Ecumenical Councils, inspired by the Holy Spirit, articulated and safeguarded the Church's doctrine in the face of heresies. Their decisions, rooted in Holy Tradition, continue to guide the Orthodox Church, ensuring that its teachings remain consistent with the Apostolic faith.

Monasticism and Spiritual Life: Monasticism has played a vital role in preserving Holy Tradition through its emphasis on prayer, asceticism, and the pursuit of holiness. Monasteries have served as centers of theological learning, iconography, and liturgical development, helping to transmit the spiritual and theological heritage of the Church.

The Continuity of Apostolic Succession: Through the unbroken chain of ordination from the Apostles to the present-day bishops, the Church maintains its unity and fidelity to the original teachings. This succession ensures that the grace of the sacraments and the authority of the Church are preserved.

This fidelity to Holy Tradition has enabled the Orthodox Church to withstand numerous challenges, including heresies, schisms, persecutions, and cultural changes, while maintaining its identity as the original Church established by Christ and His Apostles. In this way,

Holy Tradition is not merely a static relic of the past but a living reality, continuously manifesting the presence and work of the Holy Spirit in the life of the Church.

Conclusion
The Orthodox Church's unbroken connection to the Apostolic Church underscores its identity as the original Church established by Christ and His Apostles. From its foundation at Pentecost, through the establishment of early Christian communities, and its rich development of doctrine and worship, the Orthodox Church has preserved the fullness of the faith entrusted to it by the Apostles. Its reliance on Holy Tradition, the teachings of the Fathers, and the guidance of the Holy Spirit has enabled it to withstand challenges and maintain its theological and spiritual integrity. By continuing to uphold the Apostolic teachings, practices, and hierarchical structure, the Orthodox Church remains a living witness to the transformative power of Christ's Gospel, faithfully proclaiming and embodying the Kingdom of God throughout the centuries.

Study Questions

1. How does the Orthodox Church trace its origins to the Apostles, and what role did the day of Pentecost play in the establishment of the Church?

2. What is the significance of Holy Tradition in preserving the teachings, practices, and continuity of the Orthodox Church from the Apostolic era to the present day?

3. How does the hierarchical structure of the Church, as described in the Pastoral Epistles, reflect the Apostolic foundation of Orthodox Christianity?

4. What role did the Ecumenical Councils play in addressing heresies and safeguarding the doctrinal integrity of the Church? Provide examples of specific controversies they resolved.

5. How does the Orthodox Church's use of the Septuagint and its emphasis on Apostolic Succession affirm its claim to unbroken continuity with the original Church established by Christ?

Holy Tradition and Its Relationship with Scripture

In Orthodox Christianity, Holy Tradition and Scripture form the foundation of faith, intricately connected and mutually reinforcing. Holy Tradition encompasses the Apostolic teachings, practices, the Holy Scriptures, and the lived experience of the Church. Far from being separate, Scripture is a central part of Holy Tradition, written within the life of the Church and interpreted through it. Holy Tradition is the means by which the fullness of faith has been transmitted through generations, beginning with Christ and His Apostles.

Holy Tradition encompasses the entirety of the faith handed down from Christ and His Apostles, including the Holy Scriptures, the Nicene Creed, the dogmatic and doctrinal definitions of the Ecumenical Councils, and the lived experience of the Church.

However, not all elements within this sacred inheritance hold the same level of authority. The Holy Scriptures, the Creed, and the dogmatic definitions of the Ecumenical Councils occupy a primary and unalterable place within Holy Tradition. For example, while the Nicene Creed represents an unchangeable articulation of the faith, local variations in liturgical music or minor theological expressions in patristic writings reflect the contextual application of the same faith across cultures and eras. These foundational elements are integral to the Church's identity and cannot be revised or discarded.

Other parts of Holy Tradition, such as the decrees of councils held after the Seventh Ecumenical Council (787) or the writings of later theologians, while valuable, do not hold equal rank with these primary sources. For example, the decisions of regional councils or theological opinions from Byzantine scholars do not carry the same weight as the Nicene Creed or the Gospel of St. John. This distinction is crucial to preserving the integrity of the faith while allowing for theological diversity and contextual expressions within the Church.

A further distinction must be made between Tradition and traditions. As articulated at the Council of Carthage in 257, one bishop reminded the Church that "The Lord said, 'I am Truth.' He did not say, 'I am custom.'"

This highlights the reality that not all inherited practices or ideas are of equal value or binding authority. Some traditions may be cultural adaptations, theological opinions, or even mistakes. The Church evaluates traditions by their consistency with Holy Scripture, the writings of the Church Fathers, and the Apostolic faith. This discernment is guided by the Holy Spirit, often through conciliar processes that uphold the unity and truth of the Church.

Orthodox loyalty to Tradition, therefore, is neither mechanical nor static. Tradition is not merely about preserving the past; it is a dynamic, living encounter with Christ through the Holy Spirit. As Bishop Kallistos Ware aptly states, "Tradition is not only kept by the Church; it lives in the Church. It is the life of the Holy Spirit in the Church." This living experience of Tradition is both inwardly unchanging—reflecting the unchanging nature of God—and outwardly adaptive, taking on new forms to meet the needs of each generation without compromising its essence.

Thus, Holy Tradition must be experienced from within the life of the Church, where it is constantly renewed by the Holy Spirit. While it supplements its outward forms, it does not supersede or negate its foundational truths. This dynamic interplay ensures that Holy Tradition remains both a timeless anchor and a source of life and growth for the Church, guiding the faithful toward a transformative encounter with God.

The Orthodox Church does not separate Scripture and Tradition but understands Scripture as both the product and the heart of Holy Tradition. The Church, guided by the Holy Spirit, discerned and canonized the Scriptures, preserving their intended meaning within the life of the Church. Scripture and Tradition are two facets of the same truth, both integral to the life of the Church. They are never in competition or at odds. Scripture is the supreme written witness to God's revelation, yet it is inseparable from Holy Tradition, which gave rise to it. Tradition preceded the New Testament Scriptures and provides the framework within which Scripture is interpreted and understood. Without the context of Tradition, the meaning of Scripture can become fragmented or misunderstood. Worship and liturgy, central to Orthodox practice, are expressions of this living Tradition, serving as channels for the grace and truths of the faith.

Apostolic Affirmation of Tradition
The Apostles emphasized the importance of preserving both written and oral teachings. Before the New Testament was written and canonized, the Apostles conveyed the Gospel primarily through oral Tradition, as seen in their teaching, the establishment of the Eucharist, and the governance of early Christian communities. St. Paul, for instance, urged the faithful to "stand firm and hold to the traditions" delivered by word or letter (2 Thessalonians 2:15). These exhortations highlight the Apostolic commitment to preserving the fullness of the faith. Early Church Fathers, such as St. Basil the Great, also affirmed the equal importance of written Scripture and oral Tradition, cautioning against the rejection of unwritten customs that uphold the essence of the Gospel.

How Does Tradition Influence Orthodox Worship and Practice?
The Church's liturgical life—from the Divine Liturgy to the veneration of icons—embodies the essence of Tradition, maintaining its spiritual and theological integrity through the centuries.

The Divine Liturgy, the central act of worship in the Orthodox Church, is profoundly immersed in Holy Scripture. Nearly every word, prayer, and hymn in the service either quotes directly from or alludes to biblical texts, reflecting the inseparable relationship between Scripture and Tradition. Scholars estimate that the Divine Liturgy contains over 100 references to Scripture, drawing heavily from both the Old and New Testaments. Psalms, in particular, form the backbone of the service, with numerous verses incorporated into the hymns, antiphons, and prayers.

A key part of the Divine Liturgy is the proclamation of the Word of God through the Epistle and Gospel readings. These readings are carefully selected according to a liturgical calendar that covers the entire New Testament over the course of the year, with the exception of the Book of Revelation. This ensures that the faithful hear and reflect upon the full breadth of Apostolic teaching and the life of Christ during the liturgical year. Additionally, Old Testament readings are included in certain services, particularly during Great Vespers and major feasts, enriching the liturgical experience with a holistic view of salvation history.

The reading of Scripture is not merely a didactic moment but a sacramental act, where the Word of God is made present and active among the faithful. The Gospel is read with great reverence, often accompanied by processions and incense, emphasizing its central role in the life of the Church. The Epistle and Gospel readings are surrounded by hymns and responses that further integrate the themes of Scripture into the worship experience.

The Eucharist, referred to as the *breaking of the bread* in Acts 2:42, is the culmination of the Divine Liturgy and reflects the scriptural account of the Last Supper (Luke 22:19-20). In this sacrament, the faithful partake of the Body and Blood of Christ, entering into communion with Him and with one another. This act, along with the entire liturgical structure, reveals how Scripture is not only read but lived and enacted in Orthodox worship.

The liturgical calendar and the abundance of scriptural references in the Divine Liturgy underscore the Orthodox Church's commitment to preserving the faith as handed down from the Apostles. This deep integration of Scripture into worship ensures that the faithful are constantly nourished by the Word of God, while the sacramental and liturgical acts connect them to the divine mysteries. By maintaining these practices in their original spiritual and theological integrity, the Orthodox Church preserves its identity as the Church of the Apostles, ensuring that the faith of the early Church continues to be a source of life and grace for generations to come.

Can Tradition Be Wrong?
The Orthodox Church teaches that the Holy Spirit preserves the Church from error in matters of faith and doctrine, fulfilling Christ's promise that the Holy Spirit would guide the Church *into all truth* (John 16:13). This conviction is rooted in the belief that the Church is not merely a human institution but the Body of Christ, enlivened and guided by the Holy Spirit. While individuals within the Church, including clergy, may sin or err in judgment, the collective life of the Church ensures the preservation of truth. This is not a static or automatic process but a dynamic one, rooted in the Church's commitment to prayer, humility, and the ongoing discernment of the Holy Spirit.

The Orthodox Church relies on several key mechanisms to safeguard the integrity of Tradition:

The Role of the Holy Spirit: The Church believes that the Holy Spirit is continuously active within the Church, guiding its decisions and preserving it from doctrinal error. This belief is exemplified in the Ecumenical Councils, where the bishops gathered in prayer and sought the guidance of the Holy Spirit to resolve theological disputes and clarify the faith.

The Hierarchical Structure: The Church's hierarchical structure, with its unbroken line of Apostolic Succession, ensures that teachings are passed down faithfully. Bishops, as successors of the Apostles, bear the responsibility of guarding the faith and maintaining unity. This structure provides stability and continuity, preventing fragmentation and innovation that could distort the faith.

The Conciliar Approach: Decision-making in the Orthodox Church is characterized by a conciliar approach, where bishops and other leaders deliberate together in councils. This practice reflects the model of the Apostles, who met to resolve disputes in the early Church, as recorded in Acts 15. Councils allow the collective wisdom of the Church, guided by the Holy Spirit, to discern truth and address challenges.

The Lived Experience of the Faithful: The Orthodox Church recognizes the importance of the the collective sense of the faithful. Throughout history, the laity, along with clergy and monastics, have played a crucial role in affirming true doctrine and rejecting heresy. This underscores the Church's understanding that the Holy Spirit works within the entire Body of Christ, not just its leaders.

Historical Evidence of Preservation: The Church's ability to withstand heresies, schisms, and external pressures throughout history provides tangible evidence of its divine preservation. For example, the resolution of controversies like Arianism and Nestorianism through the Ecumenical Councils highlights the Church's capacity to remain faithful to the Apostolic faith under the guidance of the Holy Spirit.

While not every aspect of Tradition is infallible—for example, certain local customs or interpretations may evolve or be corrected—the

Church discerns what is essential and unchanging through its collective, Spirit-guided life. The unbroken continuity of Apostolic teaching, the consensus of the Fathers, and the Church's liturgical and sacramental life all testify to the reliability of Tradition as a channel of divine truth.

This conviction does not deny human fallibility but places trust in the promise of Christ that *the gates of Hades will not prevail against* His Church (Matthew 16:18). It is this trust that enables the Orthodox Church to affirm that, while individuals or groups may err, the Holy Tradition of the Church—guided by the Holy Spirit—remains the sure foundation for faith and doctrine.

Conclusion: The Apostolic Church and the Continuity of Orthodox Christianity

Holy Tradition serves as the living foundation of the Orthodox Church, intricately linked with Scripture and encompassing the fullness of the faith handed down from Christ and His Apostles. It is through Holy Tradition that the Church has preserved its doctrine, worship, and spiritual life across generations, maintaining an unbroken connection to its Apostolic roots. Far from being static, Tradition is a dynamic encounter with Christ, guided by the Holy Spirit, allowing the Church to faithfully adapt its expressions without compromising its essence.

The interplay between Scripture and Tradition exemplifies this unity, with Scripture forming a central part of Holy Tradition and Tradition providing the interpretive framework for Scripture. The Church, through its hierarchical structure, conciliar decision-making, and reliance on the Holy Spirit, safeguards the integrity of Tradition, ensuring it remains a channel of divine truth. This harmonious relationship between Scripture and Tradition is not only a timeless anchor for the Church but also a source of spiritual renewal, guiding the faithful toward a transformative encounter with God.

Study Questions

1. How are Holy Tradition and Scripture interconnected in Orthodox Christianity, and why are they considered mutually reinforcing rather than separate?

2. What are the primary components of Holy Tradition, and how do they collectively preserve the fullness of the faith handed down from the Apostles?

3. What distinction does the Orthodox Church make between foundational elements of Tradition (e.g., the Nicene Creed) and other aspects of tradition (e.g., local practices or theological opinions)?

4. How does the Orthodox Church ensure the preservation of Holy Tradition and guard against error through its hierarchical structure, conciliar approach, and reliance on the Holy Spirit?

5. Why is Scripture considered both a product and a central part of Holy Tradition, and how does the Church's liturgical life embody this relationship?

The History and Canon of the New Testament

The early Church did not possess a compiled Bible resembling what we have today. Instead, it relied on the Septuagint for the Old Testament and gradually collected and recognized the writings of the New Testament. These writings were read alongside oral Apostolic teachings and liturgical practices, which formed a cohesive witness to the faith.

Many congregations possessed Greek copies of the Jewish (Old Testament) scriptures (called the Septuagint) and the four Gospels (Matthew, Mark, Luke, and John). But the exact list of epistles that should be included in the New Testament was still under discussion. The history of the Bible is a journey deeply intertwined with the life of the Church. From its earliest days, the Church has regarded the Bible as a sacred text, inspired by the Holy Spirit and integral to the life of faith. However, the Bible was never intended to stand alone but was born out of the living Tradition of the Church. Understanding its development and canonization helps illuminate how Scripture and Tradition function together as a unified whole in Orthodox Christianity.

The New Testament Canon
The New Testament, written by members of the early Church for the Church, also underwent a process of development and discernment. In the first century, Christians relied on the Septuagint and oral teachings of the Apostles. Gradually, writings such as the Gospels, the Pauline epistles, and other apostolic letters gained recognition. However, this recognition was not immediate or universal. Disputes over certain books, like Hebrews, James, and Revelation, persisted into the early centuries of the Church.

It was the rise of heretics such as Marcion that prompted the gradual process of canonizing the New Testament. Marcion's rejection of the Old Testament and selective use of Pauline letters and Luke's Gospel as his canon highlighted the need for the Church to define its own authoritative texts. This response affirmed the unity of Scripture with Holy Tradition and the continuity between the Old and New Testaments. Through the writings of several church fathers and historians (Irenaeus,

Origen, Justin Martyr, Dionysius, Eusebius, etc) we are able to see how it progressed. While there were numerous bishops, there was no central authority. Persecution kept the church underground, which further slowed coming to a consensus on a biblical canon.

The Church as a whole agreed on most writings, especially the four Gospels and letters of Paul; however, there was some dissent with a few writings: the epistles of James, Peter, John, and Jude; and the books of Hebrews and Revelation. Other popular works that did not make it into the final canon (but were included in earlier canons) included 1st Clement, Epistle of Barnabas, Epistle of Mathetes to Diognetus, the Didache, and the Shepherd of Hermas.

The early church functioned quite well without a New Testament canon through the end of the fourth century. As crazy as it sounds, the Church thrived and kept true beliefs intact without a Bible for hundreds of years.

By the 4th century, the Church sought to solidify the New Testament canon to protect the faith from heretical distortions that were causing conflicts. Lists of canonical books, such as that issued by St. Athanasius in 367 AD, largely mirror the canon recognized today.

While it's not clear whether an Ecumenical Council issued a formal decree listing the New Testament canon, the councils' consistent use of these texts and their reliance on Holy Tradition provided implicit affirmation of the canon. The Church's reliance on regional councils like Carthage, the writings of St. Athanasius, and the broader conciliar tradition all contributed to the canon's recognition within the life of the Church.

> Council of Nicaea (325 AD): Although the primary focus of the First Ecumenical Council was the Arian controversy and the formulation of the Nicene Creed, it presupposed the authority of the New Testament writings widely recognized by that time. The council's decisions and documents reflect a reliance on texts that align with the canonical New Testament.
>
> The Council of Laodicea in 363 AD – issued a canon that included all the current New Testament books except Revelation. This exclusion reflected regional hesitations about the text's apocalyptic nature but did not undermine its eventual universal acceptance..

Third Council of Carthage (397 AD): This regional council, not an Ecumenical Council but highly influential, formally listed the 27 books of the New Testament as canonical. It is significant because its canon was widely accepted in the broader Church and influenced subsequent affirmations of the canon.

Council of Chalcedon (451 AD): The Fourth Ecumenical Council referenced the decisions of earlier councils and writings consistent with the established New Testament canon. Though it did not directly address the canon, its reliance on these texts solidified their authoritative status within the Church.

The Bible is actually a product of Church tradition. Christ established the Church through the apostles who taught future leaders of the church. Those leaders passed on the teachings of the apostles, which included both written and oral sources. Neither Paul nor the writers of the Gospels thought of themselves as writing scripture, but rather utilized the written word for confirming oral traditions based on revelations already delivered in person to various Christian communities.

This process reflects the Orthodox understanding of the canon as an organic development guided by the Holy Spirit within the Church. (For detailed understanding of this refer to this article in New Advent series: https://www.newadvent.org/cathen/03274a.htm or http://orthodox-info.com/inquirers/ntcanon_emergence.aspx)

Book of Revelation in the Lexicon of the Church
The Book of Revelation, also known as the Apocalypse, was one of the most debated texts in the early Church. While it was widely attributed to St. John the Apostle, its symbolic and apocalyptic content made its interpretation challenging leading to caution in its use. Some Church Fathers and regions embraced it, while others hesitated due to its complex nature and the potential for misuse by heretical groups.

Even today, the Book of Revelation is not included in the public readings during Orthodox Divine Liturgies. This absence does not reflect a rejection of its canonical status but rather a caution stemming from its complex and symbolic nature. The Orthodox Church emphasizes Scripture that is straightforward and universally edifying for corporate worship, such as the Gospels, Epistles, and Psalms.

Despite its exclusion from liturgical readings, Revelation holds a respected place in Orthodox theology, especially in eschatological teachings and iconography. Its themes of Christ's ultimate victory and the New Jerusalem are central to the Church's understanding of salvation history. Its inclusion in the canon demonstrates its theological significance, particularly in eschatological themes of Christ's ultimate victory and the hope of the New Jerusalem.

Impact of the Printing Press
Before the invention of the printing press in the 15th century, the Bible existed in manuscript form. Variations in manuscript content and canon lists reflected regional and local differences. For example in the East, some manuscripts excluded Revelation. In the West, the Vulgate included it, following the influence of Jerome.

The printing press revolutionized the availability of books and helped standardize texts. The publication of printed Bibles, like Erasmus's Greek New Testament (1516) and later the Protestant translations, necessitated decisions about which books to include. This helped cement the uniform acceptance of the 27-book New Testament canon, including Revelation.

Protestant Influence: Protestant efforts to produce and distribute standardized Bibles further contributed to the widespread acceptance of Revelation as part of the New Testament canon.

Revelation is fully canonical within the Orthodox Church and accepted as part of the New Testament. Its exclusion from liturgical readings does not diminish its theological significance. While Revelation is not read liturgically, it is studied and revered within the Church, with figures like Andrew of Caesarea writing significant commentaries on the text.

While the printing press standardized the text of Scripture, the Orthodox Church emphasizes that the Bible must be read within the living context of Tradition. The authority of the Bible is inseparable from the Church that preserved and transmitted it.

The Role of Tradition in Safeguarding Scripture
Holy Tradition played a crucial role in both the creation and preservation of the biblical canon. The criteria for accepting books into the canon included apostolic authorship, consistency with Tradition, widespread

liturgical use, and alignment with the tenets of faith. For example, texts like the Didache and the Shepherd of Hermas, though highly regarded in the early Church, were ultimately excluded from the canon because they did not fully meet these criteria.

The Church's vigilance in safeguarding Scripture extended to combating heretical writings, such as the Gnostic gospels. For example, the Gospel of Thomas was excluded because it lacked Apostolic authorship and contradicted core Christian teachings, while Hebrews, despite initial hesitation, was eventually included due to its alignment with Apostolic theology and widespread liturgical use. Many texts, which emerged long after the Apostolic era, sought to distort the Gospel message. By rejecting these spurious writings, the Church protected the integrity of the faith.

Challenges to the Canon and Its Interpretation
The Protestant Reformation in the 16th century introduced significant challenges to the Orthodox understanding of the canon. Martin Luther, for instance, removed several books from the Old Testament, such as the Deuterocanonical books. He was influenced by his reliance on the Jewish Masoretic Text and his theological emphasis on doctrines like sola fide. This departure from Holy Tradition led to a fragmented approach to Scripture. He also questioned the status of certain New Testament books, such as Hebrews and Revelation. This departure from Tradition fragmented the Christian approach to Scripture and contributed to doctrinal divisions.

Orthodox Christianity maintains that the Bible is "the book of the Church," to be read and interpreted within the context of its living Tradition. The Church Fathers consistently viewed Scripture as a unified, Christ-centered revelation. For the Orthodox, the Bible's purpose is not merely historical or instructional but spiritual, guiding believers toward salvation and union with God.

Conclusion
The history and canonization of the Bible remind Orthodox Christians that Scripture, as part of Holy Tradition, is not merely a text to be studied but a living testament to God's revelation. It is through the Church's

liturgical, sacramental, and communal life that believers paarticipate in the fullness of the faith delivered to the saints. The Orthodox Church's commitment to this unity ensures that the Bible remains a living testament to God's revelation, faithfully guiding believers in their spiritual journey. Understanding this history enriches the appreciation of Scripture as part of the fullness of the faith delivered to the saints.

Study Questions

1. How did the early Church function and preserve the faith before the formal canonization of the New Testament, and what role did oral Tradition play during this period?

2. What challenges did the early Church face in determining the New Testament canon, and how did figures like Marcion influence the Church's response to heretical distortions of Scripture?

3. What criteria did the Church use to determine the canonicity of New Testament texts, and why were some texts, like the Shepherd of Hermas and the Didache, excluded from the final canon?

4. How did the Councils of Laodicea (363), Carthage (397), and Chalcedon (451) contribute to the recognition of the New Testament canon within the broader life of the Church?

5. Why does the Orthodox Church emphasize reading and interpreting the Bible within the context of Holy Tradition, and how does this approach safeguard the integrity and unity of Scripture?

Critique of Sola Scriptura: An Orthodox Perspective

The doctrine of Sola Scriptura, introduced during the Protestant Reformation, asserts that Scripture alone is the sole authority for Christian faith and practice. While foundational to Protestant theology, this concept represents a significant departure from the Apostolic faith and a break with the historical continuity of Christianity. Orthodox Christianity, by contrast, upholds Scripture and Holy Tradition as a unified whole, preserving the fullness of the faith transmitted by Christ and His Apostles. It is important to understand error of Sola Scriptura, its implications, and the importance of Holy Tradition in interpreting Scripture.

Origins and Definition of Sola Scriptura
The doctrine of Sola Scriptura, which emerged during Martin Luther's break with the Roman Catholic Church in the 16th century, was largely a reaction to perceived errors within the Roman Church's teachings and practices. While the Protestant Reformation rightly sought to address certain abuses within the Roman Catholic Church, it did so by rejecting not only the innovations of the Roman Church but also the Apostolic foundation of Holy Tradition. This reactionary approach inadvertently severed Christianity from its historical and sacramental roots.

At the heart of the issue was the belief that the Roman Church had deviated from Apostolic teachings by elevating non-biblical traditions and innovations to the same level of authority as Scripture. Practices such as the sale of indulgences, the assertion of papal infallibility, and doctrines like purgatory and the treasury of merits were seen by reformers as lacking clear biblical foundations. These perceived abuses and theological excesses created an environment where the authority of the Roman Church appeared to overshadow the authority of Scripture. It must be noted that the Orthodox Churches were not involved in this controversy. This is of great importance as the Church now confronts an environment where this doctrine is widely accepted.

Sola Scriptura is based on the premise that Scripture contains all necessary teachings for salvation and is sufficiently clear for individuals to interpret without the need for an external authority, such as the Church.

Protestants believed this approach allowed them to bypass what they saw as the errors and excesses of the Roman Catholic Church.

However, the Orthodox Church views this doctrine as flawed and inconsistent with the Apostolic faith. It disregards the role of Holy Tradition and the authority of the Church, the very body through which Scripture was preserved, interpreted, and canonized. The Orthodox perspective emphasizes that Christianity is not based solely on a written text but on a living relationship with God within the context of His Church.

Problems with Sola Scriptura

The Orthodox critique of Sola Scriptura highlights several key issues. First, it presupposes that Scripture is self-authenticating and self-sufficient, ignoring the fact that the Church determined the canon of Scripture over several centuries. The Bible did not drop from heaven as a complete text; it was written, preserved, and compiled within the life of the Church, guided by the Holy Spirit. The authority of Scripture is inseparable from the authority of the Church that discerned its contents.

Second, Sola Scriptura promotes individual interpretation of Scripture, leading to fragmented and contradictory understandings of the faith. The Bible is a collection of books written over centuries in various historical, cultural, and linguistic contexts. Its contents include prophetic writings, poetry, apocalyptic literature, and parables, each requiring a nuanced approach to interpretation. Without the guidance of Holy Tradition, individuals may misinterpret or distort the text, resulting in doctrinal errors and divisions. This fragmentation is evident in the proliferation of over 30,000 Protestant denominations, each claiming to base their beliefs on the Bible alone.

Finally, Sola Scriptura assumes that the Bible was intended to be an all-sufficient guide for faith and practice. However, Scripture itself points to the need for Apostolic Tradition. For instance, the New Testament provides limited details about essential practices like the Eucharist or Baptism. The Didache, an early Christian text, and the writings of Church Fathers like St. Nicholas Cabasilas preserve the detailed liturgical and sacramental practices of the Apostolic Church. The Gospel of John concludes with the acknowledgment that not all of Jesus' works and teachings were recorded in Scripture (John 21:25), further affirming the necessity of Tradition.

The divergent interpretations of baptism, the Eucharist, and even core doctrines such as the Trinity among Protestant denominations illustrate how Sola Scriptura fosters doctrinal divisions. Without a shared interpretative framework rooted in Tradition, these disagreements proliferate. This fragmentation is evident in the thousands of Protestant denominations, each claiming to base their beliefs on the Bible alone, yet often diverging significantly in their interpretations."

Apostle Paul Affirms the Importance of Tradition

In his epistles, St. Paul underscores the vital role of oral Tradition in the life of the Church, affirming its significance alongside Scripture. For instance, in 2 Thessalonians 2:15, he exhorts believers to *stand firm and hold to the traditions which you were taught by us, either by word of mouth or by letter*. This appeal demonstrates that the teachings of the Apostles were not confined to written texts but also included oral instructions, practices, and customs passed down within the community. Similarly, in 1 Corinthians 11:2, Paul praises the Corinthians for maintaining the traditions he delivered to them. These examples reveal that Tradition was an integral part of Apostolic teaching, serving as a living expression of the faith that complemented and contextualized Scripture. In the Orthodox Church, this emphasis on Tradition is foundational, as it ensures the preservation and proper interpretation of the faith in its fullness. Tradition encompasses liturgical practices, the writings of the Church Fathers, and the collective experience of the faithful, all guided by the Holy Spirit.

From the earliest days of the Church, the Apostles devoted themselves to *teaching, fellowship, the breaking of bread, and prayers* (Acts 2:42), demonstrating the oral and liturgical transmission of the faith alongside the gradual development of written Scripture.

The Meaning of Tradition from the Original Greek

The Greek word for "tradition" used in the New Testament is παράδοσις (paradosis), which literally means "that which is handed down" or "a transmission." This term appears in several places in St. Paul's epistles, such as 2 Thessalonians 2:15, where he instructs the faithful to "stand firm and hold to the traditions (παραδόσεις) you were taught, whether by word or by letter." This word encompasses both written and oral teachings that have been passed down through the Church, signifying the full scope of Apostolic teaching entrusted to the faithful.

However, in many Protestant English translations of the Bible, the word παράδοσις is often rendered inconsistently, leading to misunderstanding. For example, in passages where παράδοσις refers to Apostolic teaching (as in 2 Thessalonians 2:15), some translations, such as the King James Version (KJV), use "traditions," while others like the New International Version (NIV) opt for "teachings." This inconsistency can obscure the connection between written and oral transmission, reinforcing a bias toward written Scripture alone. Moreover, in contexts where Jesus rebukes the Pharisees for upholding human traditions over God's commandments (e.g., Mark 7:8-9), the word παράδοσις is translated as "tradition," often with a negative connotation. This dual treatment contributes to the mistaken view that all tradition is inherently suspect or opposed to God's Word.

In the Orthodox understanding, however, παράδοσις is not inherently negative; its value depends on its source. Holy Tradition, as handed down from Christ and the Apostles through the Church, is sacred and authoritative, encompassing both Scripture and the lived faith of the Church. Misinterpretation or selective translation of παράδοσις in Protestant Bibles often reflects a theological bias stemming from the doctrine of Sola Scriptura, which rejects the authority of oral Tradition. Orthodox theology views written Scripture and oral Tradition as two expressions of the same Apostolic deposit of faith. This balance is rooted in the conviction that the Holy Spirit works through both forms to safeguard and transmit the fullness of the Gospel.

The Role of Holy Tradition in Interpreting Scripture
The Orthodox Church asserts that Scripture must always be understood within the context of Holy Tradition. Tradition, guided by the Holy Spirit, provides the authoritative framework for interpreting Scripture and preserving its intended meaning. This framework includes the teachings of the Church Fathers, the decisions of Ecumenical Councils, and the Church's liturgical and sacramental life.

For example, the Nicene Creed, developed within the context of Holy Tradition, provides the interpretative key for understanding Scriptural references to the nature of Christ and the Holy Trinity. Similarly, the liturgical prayers of the Church illuminate the meaning of the Psalms and the Gospels in their Christological fulfillment.

The Church Fathers consistently interpreted Scripture through a Christ-centered lens, emphasizing its historical and symbolic dimensions. Worship and liturgy, expressions of Holy Tradition, illuminate the deeper theological truths of Scripture. Without this context, the Bible risks being reduced to a mere historical document or a tool for justifying individual interpretations.

Implications for Faith and Practice
The Orthodox view rejects the reduction of Christianity to a set of doctrines or moral principles derived from a book. Orthodox Christianity emphasizes that faith is not a matter of private interpretation or intellectual assent but a communal and sacramental way of life. This living faith is nurtured through participation in the Divine Liturgy, where Scripture and Tradition converge in the transformative encounter with Christ.

Holy Tradition, in unity with Scripture, provides the fullness of faith necessary for salvation. It ensures continuity with the Apostolic Church and protects against innovation and fragmentation.

Sola Scriptura, by severing Scripture from Tradition, undermines the very foundation of the Orthodox faith. It leads to a rejection of the Church's authority, the sacramental life, and the guidance of the Holy Spirit within the Church which can be observed in most Protestant churches today. Orthodox Christianity, in contrast, upholds the unity of Scripture and Tradition, seeing them as complementary and inseparable in conveying the fullness of God's revelation.

Conclusion
The Orthodox forceful critique of Sola Scriptura underscores the vital role of Holy Tradition in preserving and interpreting Scripture. Christianity is not merely a religion of the book; it is a living faith embodied in the life of the Church, guided by the Holy Spirit. Scripture, as part of Holy Tradition, provides a divinely inspired witness to God's

revelation, but it must be read and understood within the context of the Church's ongoing life and teaching. Together, Scripture and Tradition form the comprehensive foundation of the Orthodox faith. They are not merely sources of doctrinal knowledge but the means by which believers are guided toward Theosis—union with God—through the life of the Church. By reading Scripture within the living Tradition, Orthodox Christians encounter the fullness of God's revelation and are drawn into the mystery of His divine life.

Study Questions

1. What historical circumstances led to the development of the doctrine of Sola Scriptura, and how does the Orthodox Church view the reactionary nature of this doctrine?

2. Why does the Orthodox Church argue that Sola Scriptura is inconsistent with the Apostolic faith, particularly in its disregard for the role of Holy Tradition?

3. What are the key problems with the premise that Scripture is self-authenticating and sufficient for individual interpretation, according to the Orthodox critique?

4. How does the Orthodox understanding of the Greek word παράδοσις (paradosis) clarify the complementary relationship between Scripture and Tradition, and how has its interpretation been misrepresented in Protestant translations?

5. In what ways does Holy Tradition provide the necessary framework for interpreting Scripture, and how does this ensure continuity with the teachings of Christ and the Apostles?

Chapter 3

Faith as a Living Relationship: Embracing the Orthodox Way to Theosis

In this chapter we will explore the foundational aspects of the Orthodox Christian faith, examining how faith, grace, and the sacraments are not abstract concepts but dynamic, lived experiences that nurture participation in God's grace to move a believer toward the ultimate goal of salvation: theosis. Theosis, or deification, represents the transformation of the human person into the image and likeness of God, an ongoing process that is deeply rooted in Orthodox theological principles, Scripture, and the lived experience of the Church..

We begin by understanding that faith in Orthodox Christianity is not a mere intellectual exercise or cultural identity but a living relationship with God. This relationship is nurtured through active participation in the life of the Church, continually turning towards God through repentance, prayer, and faith. This relationship, built on trust and loyalty to God, involves experiencing God's divine presence through His energies, which are made manifest in the world, enabling believers to partake in His divine life.

The Church as the Body of Christ plays an essential role in this process, providing the communal and sacramental context within which Orthodox Christians live their faith. The sacraments, particularly baptism and the Eucharist, serve as the channels through which believers participate in God's grace though the Hoy Spirit and are united with Christ. The Church is also seen as a school of holiness, guiding its members toward the goal of theosis, which is the process of becoming more like Christ through the work of His grace and human cooperation.

As we delve deeper into the topics, we will address the key theological concepts of synergy—the cooperation between divine grace and human free will—and how they shape the Orthodox understanding of salvation. We will also examine how the Holy Spirit works within the believer to foster spiritual growth and transformation, and how the goal of salvation is ultimately eternal union with God.

Throughout this chapter, we will reflect on the practical implications of these theological principles in the life of the believer. How does one nurture a living faith? What role does the sacramental life of the Church play in this journey? How do we experience God's presence through prayer, repentance, and the Eucharist? The answers to these questions lie in the transformative process of theosis, which is the Orthodox understanding of salvation as both a personal and communal experience.

By the end, we hope you will discover a deeper understanding of living faith—an active and dynamic relationship with God that supporting a believer's spiritual growth into His likeness and prepares them for eternal life with Him in His Kingdom.

Faith is a Lived Relationship with God

Faith in Orthodox Christianity is the foundation of a dynamic, lived relationship with God. It transcends intellectual belief or cultural identity and transforms every aspect of a believer's life. Orthodox theology emphasizes faith as a deep trust in God and an active response to His grace. This includes zeal for spiritual growth, continual repentance, and an active life within the Church, all aimed at achieving theosis—union with God.

Saint Theophan the Recluse writes:
> Christian life is zeal and the strength to remain in communion with God by means of an active fulfillment of His holy will, according to our faith in our Lord Jesus Christ, and with the help of the Grace of God, to the glory of His most holy name.

More than Intellectual Understanding

In modern society, faith is often understood primarily as intellectual belief or moral behavior. While studying the Gospel and striving for a moral life are valuable, Orthodoxy emphasizes that faith must be a personal, experiential encounter and participation with the living God. Faith is not merely an intellectual understanding or belief, but a living reality rooted in a direct experience of God's presence.

The New Testament Greek word for faith, πίστις (pistis), is used over 240 times. It signifies a profound and active response involving trust and loyalty to God. It conveys the idea of loyalty or faithfulness, not just belief. Faith involves more than trusting in God; it also encompasses obeying His Word, reflecting a life of discipleship. It is an active participation in the life of God—not static but dynamic—involving continual growth in the relationship with Him.

Saint Paul describes faith as *the substance of things hoped for, the evidence of things not seen* (Hebrews 11:1). This evidence may come through an experience during prayer, reading Scripture, or even a moment of awe in nature. These experiences bring assurance that, through God's grace, believers *may be partakers of the divine nature* (2 Peter 1:3-4).

Examples of a Lived Faith

Abraham left his homeland in obedience to God's call, trusting in His promise to make him a great nation (Genesis 12:1-4). Later, he demonstrated ultimate faith by being willing to sacrifice his son Isaac, believing in God's power to fulfill His promises (Genesis 22:1-19).

Moses trusted God's promise to deliver the Israelites from slavery, even when facing Pharaoh's resistance and the Red Sea (Exodus 14:13-31). His life demonstrates steadfast faith in God's guidance and provision.

Elijah trusted God to provide for him during a drought, relying on ravens and a widow's miraculous supply of food (1 Kings 17:1-16). He also demonstrated faith by calling down fire from heaven in the face of false prophets (1 Kings 18:20-39).

Mary accepted the Archangel Gabriel's message with humility and trust, saying, *Let it be to me according to your word* (Luke 1:38). Her faith continued as she stood by Christ at the Cross.

Saint Paul, once a persecutor of Christians, encountered Christ on the road to Damascus and devoted his life to spreading the Gospel (Acts 9:1-22). His writings emphasize faith as trust in God's grace.

Each of these examples, as well as the lives of thousands of saints honored by the Church, shows individuals who experienced God and acted according to His will. Many endured severe trials and even torture without wavering in their trust in God.

Conclusion

Faith entails participation in God's divine energies, such as His glory, life, love, virtue, and power. It is not a static belief but a living reality deeply rooted in Scripture and demonstrated by the Prophets and Saints. This understanding offers those who develop this living faith a transformative pathway to spiritual growth and union with God through active cooperation with His grace.

Study Questions

1. How does the Orthodox understanding of faith differ from common modern views of faith?

2. What is the significance of the Greek word πίστις (pistis) in describing faith?

3. Why is faith described as an experiential relationship rather than an intellectual belief in Orthodoxy?

4. Which one local person best exemplifies this experiential living faith for you?

5. How can faith become a dynamic relationship with God in your own life?

God is Knowable Through His Energies

Great is the Lord, and greatly to be praised, and his greatness is unsearchable (Psalm 145:3).

Behold, these are but the outskirts of his ways, and how small a whisper do we hear of him! But the thunder of his power who can understand? (Job 26:14)

For my thoughts are not your thoughts, neither are your ways my ways, declares the Lord. For as the heavens are higher than the earth, so are my ways higher than your ways and my thoughts than your thoughts (Isaiah 55:8–9).

Oh, the depth of the riches and wisdom and knowledge of God! How unsearchable are his judgments and how inscrutable his ways! For who has known the mind of the Lord, or who has been his counselor? (Romans 11:33–34; cf. Job 42:1–6; Psalm 139:6, 17–18; 147:5; Isaiah 57:15; 1 Corinthians 2:10–11; 1 Timothy 6:13–16).

The greatness of God is both revealed and hidden. His essence is utterly transcendent, beyond the grasp of human understanding, while His energies are manifest in creation and accessible to human experience. This paradox invites us to a life of worship, awe, and participation in the divine life through His grace.

Experiencing God: His Essence and Energies
How do we obtain a living faith, a direct experience of God? To approach this mystery, we must distinguish between God's essence (ousia) and His energies (energeia).

An analogy often used in Orthodox theology is that of the sun and its rays. We feel the warmth and light of the sun through its rays, yet the sun itself remains distant and incomprehensible in its fullness. Similarly, we experience the presence and activity of God through His energies, while His essence remains utterly beyond our comprehension.

Saint Athanasius writes:
"He is outside all things according to His essence, but is in all things through His acts of power."

Both God's essence and His energies are uncreated and divine. We believe in His essence because we experience His energies. His essence reflects the transcendent, ineffable nature of God, while His energies reveal His immanence and omnipresence.

Metropolitan Kallistos Ware explains:
> "The Godhead is simple and indivisible, and has no parts. The essence signifies the whole God as He is in Himself; the energies signify the whole God as He is in action. God in His entirety is completely present in each of His divine energies."

Saint Basil the Great further clarifies:
> "His energies come down to us, but His essence remains beyond our reach."

Living Faith Through Grace

Through His energies, God is ever-present to us. While we cannot know the fullness of His being, we can experience His presence and activity. This encounter is what we often call grace—the work of the Holy Spirit in our lives. Grace is the tangible expression of God's energies, enabling us to participate in His divine life.

We are creatures, made in the image of God, yet we cannot fully comprehend the Creator. As the pot cannot know the nature of the potter, so too we cannot grasp the divine essence. However, through His energies, God reveals Himself and invites us into a direct relationship with Him.

This relationship is transformative. Like feeling the warmth of the sun's rays, we experience God's presence in ways that illuminate, comfort, and sanctify us. These encounters may come in prayer, through Scripture, in the beauty of creation, or in the sacraments of the Church.

God as Both Mystery and Revelation

God remains both a profound mystery and intimately knowable. His greatness is unsearchable, yet He draws near to us in love. As Saint Gregory Palamas emphasized, the divine energies allow us to be united with God without compromising His transcendence. This union, called theosis, is the ultimate goal of the Christian life.

By living in His grace, through continual prayer, repentance, and participation in the sacraments, we draw closer to God—not by comprehending His essence but by experiencing His uncreated energies. In this way, faith becomes a living reality, a dynamic and personal encounter with the living God.

Conclusion

In the mystery of God's essence and energies, we find both awe and intimacy. Though His essence remains unapproachable, His energies invite us into a living communion with Him. This paradox of divine transcendence and immanence is not meant to frustrate us but to draw us into deeper worship and trust. Through His grace, we experience His presence in our lives, transforming our hearts and leading us toward the ultimate goal of theosis. By participating in His energies, we come to know the unknowable God—not as an abstract idea, but as the One who loves us and works continually for our salvation. This journey is the heart of the Orthodox faith: a call to encounter the living God and to be forever changed by His uncreated light.

Study Questions

Distinguishing Essence and Energies
1. What is the difference between God's essence and His energies, and why is this distinction significant in Orthodox theology?

Experiencing God Through His Energies
2. How does the analogy of the sun and its rays help explain our experience of God's energies? Can you think of any personal experiences that reflect this concept?

The Role of Grace
3. How is the concept of grace connected to God's energies, and what role does it play in the believer's relationship with God?

The Mystery of God
4. In what ways is God both a mystery and knowable? How does this understanding shape the Orthodox view of faith and worship?

Living Faith and Theosis
5. How does participating in God's energies lead to theosis (union with God)? What practical steps can a believer take to grow in this living faith?

God Dwells in Us

A living faith based on an experience of God comes from an awareness of His inner presence within us. Scripture reveals this profound truth as Saint Paul proclaims:

You are the temple of the living God and the Spirit of God dwells in you (1 Cor 3:16). He further affirms, *Your body is the temple of the Holy Spirit who is in you, whom you have from God* (1 Corinthians 6:19).

Paul also describes this indwelling of God as Christ living in us.

It is no longer I who live, but Christ lives in me (Galatians 2:20).

Jesus confirms this when He tells His disciples:

If anyone loves Me, he will keep My word; and My Father will love him, and We will come to him and make Our home with him (John 14:23).

Paul reiterates God's promise:

I will dwell in them and walk among them.... (2 Corinthians 6:16).

These passages, among others, show us that God's indwelling is not metaphorical but a profound and transformative reality.

An Invitation to Open the Door

Jesus invites us to recognize this reality when He says:

I stand at the door and knock. If anyone hears My voice and opens the door, I will come in to him and dine with him, and he with Me. (Revelations 3:20).

This invitation reflects God's desire to restore humanity to the state of communion for which were created. He sent His only begotten Son for this purpose. Through the Incarnation when God took flesh, He transformed human nature. Christ's life on earth became the fullness of the image in which we were created, uniting human flesh with divinity. He not only taught us how to live but also made it possible for us to be transformed, establishing His Church and the sacraments as means of participating in His divine life.

Participation in Divine Life

God's presence in us is experienced through His divine energies—His grace, love, power, and life. While His essence remains unknowable, His energies allow us to partake in His divine nature, as Scripture says:

> ...*that you may be partakers of the divine nature* (2 Peter 1:4).

This process is called theosis, where we are transformed into His likeness, becoming united with God through His indwelling presence. This was revealed to the disciples during the Transfiguration, where they witnessed Christ's divine light. This same divine light is given to us through participation in the Church and sacraments.

At Baptism, the Holy Spirit comes to dwell in us, making us a new creation in Christ. Chrismation seals this gift, marking us as temples of the Holy Spirit. In the Eucharist, we receive Christ's Body and Blood, physically and spiritually uniting us with Him:

> *He who eats My flesh and drinks My blood abides in Me, and I in him* (John 6:56).

Together, as the Body of Christ, we form His living temple, experiencing His presence both individually and communally.

Practical Implications of God's Indwelling

The reality of God dwelling in us has practical implications for our daily lives:

Holiness: We are called to follow Christ, to avoid sin, and treat our bodies with reverence as temples of God.

Prayer: Prayer is a participation with the God who dwells in us. The Jesus Prayer—"Lord Jesus Christ, Son of God, have mercy on me"—helps us become more aware of His presence.

Strength and Comfort: God's indwelling assures us that we are never alone. His presence offers continual strength, guidance, and peace, even in times of difficulty.

Think of this reality as a lamp and its light. Imagine your soul as a lamp. Without electricity, it's dark and lifeless. When God dwells in you through the Holy Spirit, it's like being connected to the source of power—the lamp shines brightly and fulfills its purpose. Similarly, as breath sustains physical life, God's indwelling presence sustains spiritual life.

God's Presence in Us: Personal and Dynamic
This inner presence is deeply personal. It communicates to us through the voice of our conscience or through moments of inner warmth and love, particularly when God encourages or comforts us. God's indwelling is not static; it transforms our thoughts, actions, and desires, aligning them with His will. As Scripture says:

> *Whoever confesses that Jesus is the Son of God, God abides in him, and he in God. And we have known and believed the love that God has for us. God is love, and he who abides in love abides in God, and God in him* (1 John 4:15-16).

Recognizing God's dwelling within us goes beyond intellectual understanding. It is a living and enlivening experience. It reveals the closeness of God and confirms the truth that we are created in His image. Mental efforts to know God are valuable but serve as a means to realize His inner presence.

The Role of the Church
The Church plays a fundamental role in this transformation and awareness. Through the sacraments, we are united with Christ and nurtured in His grace. In Baptism, God begins to dwell in us. In the Eucharist, we receive Christ's Body and Blood, renewing and sustaining this union. The Church not only brings us closer to God individually but also corporately as the Body of Christ, making His living temple a shared reality.

Conclusion: A Calling and a Gift
The indwelling of God is a profound mystery and a transformative reality that touches every aspect of our being. It is both a gift of divine grace and a calling to live in constant communion with Him. Through His presence within us, we are sanctified, strengthened, and guided toward the ultimate goal of union with Him. This truth shapes how we live—calling us to holiness, deepening our prayer, and sustaining us in times of trial. As temples of the living God, we are not only vessels of His presence but also reflections of His love and light to the world. This divine indwelling is a testament to His unceasing desire to draw us into His life, making us partakers of His divine nature and participants in the mystery of His eternal love.

Study Questions

1. Scriptural Foundations
   What do the Scriptures teach about God dwelling in us? Reflect on passages such as 1 Corinthians 3:16, Galatians 2:20, and John 14:23. How do these verses describe this reality?

2. The Sacramental Role
   How do the sacraments, particularly Baptism, Chrismation, and the Eucharist, enable and sustain God's indwelling in us? Why is participation in the Church essential for this transformation?

3. Theosis and Transformation:
   What is theosis, and how does God's indwelling presence contribute to our journey toward becoming partakers of the divine nature (2 Peter 1:4)? How is this reality revealed in the Transfiguration?

4. Practical Implications:
   How should the awareness that we are temples of God influence the way we live our daily lives? Consider aspects like holiness, prayer, and the avoidance of sin.

5. Personal Experience and Relationship:
   How can we become more aware of God's inner presence in our lives? What role do prayer, love, and the voice of our conscience play in deepening this awareness and living in communion with Him?

Awakening a Living Faith

Remember the parable Jesus told about the mustard seed:

> *If you have faith as small as a mustard seed, you can say to this mountain, 'Move from here to there,' and it will move. Nothing will be impossible for you* (Matthew 17:20).

This parable highlights the power of even the smallest genuine faith when nurtured. But how do we cultivate such faith and develop a zeal for the Orthodox Christian life?

Today, many people are separated from God, living their daily lives with little or no awareness of His presence. This separation can be traced back to the fall of Adam and Eve and is reinforced by modern society, which has divided the physical from the spiritual. God has been consciously removed from many aspects of public life—our schools, workplaces, and governments—further deepening this separation.

Signs of Separation from God

Several signs may indicate a growing distance from God, including:
- Prioritizing personal success and well-being above spiritual life.
- Feeling unfulfilled despite being busy with work, activities, and pleasures.
- Experiencing persistent anxiety or a sense of emptiness.
- Seeking constant distractions, material possessions, or self-help solutions.
- Struggling with stress in relationships and daily life.

Recognizing these signs is the first step toward renewal. Just as the Prodigal Son in Christ's parable realized his spiritual destitution, we too must acknowledge our need for God. He is ever-present, calling us to return and awaken to our true state.

The Need for Spiritual Awakening

In our present condition, we need to awaken to God's constant presence in our lives. The journey toward a living faith begins with an awakening—an awareness that faith is not merely an intellectual concept or philosophy but a living, heartfelt relationship with God. We must awaken from the spiritual slumber induced by earthly comforts, pride, distractions, and the norms of modern society.

Saint Theophan the Recluse describes this awakening as:
"An act of divine grace… [where we] see our sinfulness, sense the danger of our situation, begin to fear for ourselves, and care about deliverance from our misfortune and salvation."

Awakening often comes suddenly and brings profound change. Saint Theophan further describes it as:
"An instantaneous destruction of the whole order of our willful and sinful life, and simultaneously the revelation before our consciousness of another divine order—the one true and spiritually soothing order, which partakes of the peace of Christ."

It is like living in a windowless room, unaware of the world outside. Suddenly, a window is opened, and light pours in, revealing a whole new reality.

When we experience awakening, this newfound awareness reveals the spiritual realm, filled with God's presence—a reality we were previously blind to. As our awareness of God grows, our understanding of life deepens, and a greater sense of purpose emerges. This leads to a vibrant faith, further strengthened through a deeper understanding of the Gospel, participation in the Church, and the reception of divine grace through the sacraments.

Through this process, faith comes alive—transforming our hearts and kindling a zeal for God. He becomes a real force in our daily lives, and we begin to sense that we are participating with Him in all we do.

Paths to Awakening and Nurturing Faith
There are several ways to nurture such an awakening. However, it is essential to recognize that awakening is ultimately a gift from God and not something entirely under our control.

Contemplation of Creation
For since the creation of the world His invisible attributes are clearly seen, being understood by the things that are made, even His eternal power and Godhead (Romans 1:20).

Spending time in nature with a quiet mind, reflecting on the beauty and order of creation, helps us recognize God's presence and power.

Scripture and Holy Tradition
Faith comes from what is heard, and what is heard comes by the Word of God (Romans 10:17).

Reading Scripture prayerfully—not merely as a text to be analyzed, but as a living testimony of God's presence in the world—allows His truth to penetrate our hearts. Immersion in the Holy Tradition of the Church further reveals the divine order.

Personal Experience of God
Many people come to faith through direct encounters with God's presence. These experiences often create a deep dissatisfaction with worldly pursuits and awaken a desire for something greater, drawing us closer to Him. Countless converts to Christianity describe such moments of transformation. A deep practice of prayer that focuses on a stillness of the mind can also result is such an experience. This can be seen in the lives of many of the saints.

The Church and the Holy Mysteries
Within the Church, God's grace is encountered through the sacraments—Baptism, Confession, Holy Communion, and Holy Unction—which nourish and heal the soul. The guidance of holy people within the Church can also provide support and strength in our spiritual journey.

Suffering as a Teacher
God allows suffering to awaken us to our dependence on Him. Hardships, whether through loss, illness, or struggles, can humble us and open our hearts to His grace. In these moments, we realize how small we are and how little control we have over our lives. Through suffering, God reveals Himself as our comforter and healer.

As we learn to live the Orthodox way of life we will develop greater humility and a heart purified of its sinfulness. This will create the conditions in which God's grace can work within us, leading to a deeper, living faith that transforms our lives and brings us closer to Him.

Zeal and Spiritual Discipline

Once awakened to the reality of God, zeal is the fire that fuels a believer's journey toward God. It is not mere enthusiasm but a deep desire to align one's entire life with God's will. Zeal helps believers overcome spiritual laziness, resist worldly temptations, and seek God wholeheartedly.

Zeal as a Spiritual Fire

Jesus speaks of zeal as a fire:

> *I came to send fire on the earth, and how I wish it were already kindled!* (Luke 12:49).

This fire represents the Holy Spirit, igniting within believers the passion to live according to God's commandments.

Paul also describes it as fire and as being fervent in spirit.

> *Do not put out the Spirit's fire* (1Thess 5:19).

> *not lagging in diligence, fervent in spirit, serving the Lord;* (Rom 12:11)

> *forgetting those things which are behind and reaching forward to those things which are ahead, I press toward the goal for the prize of the upward call of God in Christ Jesus* (Phil 3:13-14).

What is this goal that zeal motivates us to develop a living faith? It is a union with God Himself and being properly prepared to enter HIs Kingdom with eternal life. Since this path is long and can be difficult we need zeal to have endurance and patience to give your best effort to attain it.

Paul advises us to pursue with all our effort to obtain it.

> *Do you not know that those who run in a race all run, but one receives the prize? Run in such a way that you may obtain it* (1Cor 9:24).

Saint Theophan advises:

> "In Christian life the result of the fervor of zeal is a certain quickness and liveliness of spirit, with which people undertake God-pleasing works, trampling upon oneself and willingly offering as a sacrifice to God every kind of labor, without sparing oneself."

Saint Theophan the Recluse teaches that zeal leads to an eager willingness to undertake any effort or sacrifice for God.

Conclusion: Nurturing a Living Faith
Awakening and obtaining zeal is just the beginning. The challenge for the rest of our lives is to nurture this faith and the zeal it brings. This involves continual prayer, repentance, participation in the sacraments, and the pursuit of a life centered on Christ. As our relationship with God deepens, our faith becomes a living reality—a dynamic, transformative force leading us to theosis, union with God.

Study Questions

1. Describe the nature of spiritual awakening, and why is it essential for developing living faith.
2. What are some signs that indicate a person is spiritually separated from God? How can recognizing these signs lead to an awakening?
3. How does awakening transform a person's perspective on life and their relationship with God?
4. How do the observation of creation, Scripture, the Church's Mysteries, and suffering contribute to awakening and nurturing faith?
5. What is zeal? How does it nurture spiritual growth?

Grace, Synergy, and a Lifelong Journey of Salvation

With a living faith based on experience we turn our whole being towards God. We become united with Him and His will. We enter into a dynamic loving relationship with God knowing He is within acting through us. We become keenly aware of our sinfulness and desire His help to change. This requires a synergistic effort with the Hoy Spirit and our own free will.

Orthodox Christianity teaches that faith and grace are inseparable. God's grace—His divine energy—draws believers closer to Him but requires active cooperation, known as synergia for our salvation. This involves collaboration between divine grace and human free will. Salvation, therefore, is not a one-time event but a lifelong process of transformation.

Salvation is a Gift from God (Grace)

In Orthodox Christianity, salvation is entirely initiated by God. It is not something that humans can achieve on their own by their own efforts or works. God's grace is unmerited, meaning it is not earned, but freely given. This grace is primarily manifested in the person of Jesus Christ, through His Incarnation, Passion, Death, and Resurrection, which make salvation possible for all of humanity.

This grace is not just a theological concept but an active, life-giving presence. It is what makes our salvation possible and allows us to come into communion with God.

The Role of Human Free Will

Even though salvation is entirely a gift from God, Orthodox Christianity teaches that humans are not passive recipients of grace. We have free will, a gift from God that allows us to choose or reject His grace. This is where the doctrine of synergy becomes crucial.

God respects our free will, and He does not force Himself upon us. Instead, He invites us to respond to His grace, to choose to love Him and follow His commandments. In this way, God's grace works in harmony with human freedom—this cooperation between God and human beings is what synergy refers to.

In other words, God does not impose salvation on us, but offers it, and we must freely choose to accept it. In Orthodox thought, the idea of being "saved" is not a one-time event but a lifelong process that involves ongoing cooperation with God's grace.

Grace and Works (The Balance)
One of the critical aspects of synergy is that it avoids the extremes of both Pelagianism (the belief that humans can achieve salvation entirely by their own efforts) and hyper-Calvinism (the belief that human effort is irrelevant and that God predestines everything, including salvation). In Orthodox Christianity, we recognize that while we cannot save ourselves on our own, we must actively engage in the process of salvation.

The Apostle Paul writes in Philippians 2:12–13:

> *Work out your salvation with fear and trembling, for it is God who works in you both to will and to act according to his good purpose.*

This verse beautifully encapsulates synergy: we are to *work out our salvation, as workers together with Him....* (2 Cor 6:1), but it is God who gives us the strength and will to do so.

Faith and Works: A Key Difference
Seeing salvation as a synergy between faith and works, Orthodoxy differs from the Protestant doctrine of sola fide (faith alone). This is an errant doctrine that came from the Protestant reformation in the 16th century.

In many branches of Protestantism (especially in the Reformed and Lutheran traditions), the doctrine of faith alone teaches that salvation is attained solely through faith in Jesus Christ, apart from any works or human effort. This is based on the belief that humans are completely incapable of achieving salvation through their own actions or merits. Instead, salvation is granted by God's grace alone, and it is received by faith. The key biblical passages often cited to support this doctrine include Ephesians 2:8-9: *For by grace you have been saved through faith. And this is not your own doing; it is the gift of God, not a result of works, so that no one may boast.*

In this view, works—whether they are acts of virtue, participation in sacraments, or efforts to live a holy life—do not contribute to a person's salvation. Good works are seen as a result or evidence of faith, but they do not affect the person's status before God. Justification (being declared righteous before God) is received at the moment of faith, and there is no ongoing process of salvation beyond this moment.

This view was the basis for Martin Luther's challenge of the Roman Catholic practice of indulgences for penance, and for that reason it is called the main cause of the Protestant Reformation. Luther added the word allein ("alone" in German) to Romans 3:28 controversially so that it read: "So now we hold, that man is justified without the help of the works of the law, alone through faith." The word "allein" (alone) does not appear in the Greek manuscripts.

Orthodox Doctrine of Synergia
In contrast, the Orthodox Church teaches that salvation is not by faith alone, but involves a cooperation between faith and works. This cooperation is called synergia. Orthodox Christianity teaches that God's grace is the foundation of salvation, but it also requires the active participation of the believer. Faith is essential, but it must be accompanied by repentance, baptism, participation in the sacraments, and a lifetime of good works and virtuous living.

The Orthodox Church emphasizes that salvation is a process (often referred to as theosis or deification), which involves the transformation of the believer into the likeness of Christ, achieved gradually over time.

In the Orthodox view, works are not considered a means of earning salvation, but they are inseparable from faith. The works—such as loving your neighbor, fasting, praying, receiving the sacraments—are the means by which one cooperates with God's grace and grows in holiness. The Orthodox Church teaches that salvation is dynamic and requires an ongoing response to God's grace.

Justification vs. Theosis (Deification)
For most Protestants, justification is the central moment of salvation, where a believer is declared righteous before God by faith alone. This justification is seen as a legal or forensic declaration by God, where the

believer's sins are forgiven and they are counted as righteous because of the merits of Christ. This declaration is considered final, and no further process of salvation is required for the believer's eternal security.

In many Protestant traditions, once a person is justified by faith, they are assured of their salvation (often called the doctrine of "eternal security" or "once saved, always saved"). Though good works and a holy life are encouraged, they are seen as the natural fruits of faith, not as part of the salvation process itself.

The Orthodox Church, while affirming the importance of justification, views salvation as a process of theosis—becoming one with God, not in essence, but by grace. The goal is to be transformed into the likeness of Christ, to share in God's divine life, and to be healed from the corruption of sin. Theosis is not a one-time event, but a lifelong journey. This journey involves a continuous cooperation between the believer and God's grace.

Theosis in the Orthodox Church involves not only the forgiveness of sins but the transformation of the believer. It is about being healed and restored to the image and likeness of God, which was lost in the Fall. While justification is part of this process, it is just the beginning, not the end. Salvation in the Orthodox Church is seen as something that continues after justification and requires continual effort and grace.

Key Differences: Synergia vs. Faith Alone
The key difference between synergyia in Orthodox theology and faith alone in Protestant theology lies in the role of human effort and cooperation with God's grace. While both traditions affirm that salvation is ultimately a gift of God's grace, the Orthodox Church teaches that this grace requires an active and ongoing human response, involving faith, repentance, good works, and participation in the life of the Church. Salvation is a life-long process of transformation and deification, not just a one-time declaration of righteousness.

On the other hand, Protestantism, especially in traditions that hold to "sola fide" (faith alone), emphasizes that salvation is a one-time event that occurs through faith alone, with works seen as a natural outgrowth of faith, but not contributing to or affecting the salvation process. This results in a fundamentally different understanding of the Christian life, where faith in Jesus Christ is central, but good works do not play a role in the believer's final salvation.

The Protestant doctrine of "sola fide" (faith alone) is indeed considered a significant theological error because it does not fully align with the Orthodox understanding of salvation as a process that requires active human cooperation with God's grace. The Orthodox Church teaches that salvation is not simply a one-time declaration but an ongoing process that involves both God's grace and human effort—what we call synergia.

In Orthodox theology, salvation is viewed as the development of an intimate relationship with God and the preparation of the human being to enter the eternal Kingdom of God. This involves a continuous transformation into the likeness of Christ (the process of theosis), which requires more than just a moment of faith. Rather, it is a journey of holiness, repentance, purification, and the cultivation of virtues, all of which are accomplished through cooperation with God's grace. The Orthodox Church believes that works, virtues, and active participation in the sacraments are necessary to prepare the soul for eternal life in God's Kingdom.

From an Orthodox perspective, this view risks reducing the dynamic and transformative nature of salvation, where the soul is being prepared and purified to dwell with God forever. The Orthodox believe that salvation is a lifelong journey of becoming more like Christ, and that this transformation is not something we can neglect or treat as irrelevant to the ultimate goal of eternal union with God.

In other words, faith alone in the Protestant sense is seen as insufficient because it does not account for the full range of human participation in salvation, particularly the need for a life of continual repentance, holiness, and the pursuit of virtue through God's grace.

The Protestant view of faith alone oversimplifies salvation and neglects the necessity of a continuing relationship with God, one that is actively cultivated through both faith and works, as part of the broader process of becoming united with God in His eternal Kingdom.

Conclusion

Orthodox Church teaches that salvation is not by faith alone, but involves a cooperation between faith and works. This cooperation is called synergy. Orthodox Christianity teaches that God's grace is the foundation of salvation, but it also requires the active participation of the believer. Faith is essential, but it must be accompanied by repentance, baptism, participation in the sacraments, and a lifetime of good works and virtuous living. The Orthodox Church emphasizes that salvation is a process (often referred to as theosis or deification), which involves the transformation of the believer into the likeness of Christ, achieved gradually over time.

In the Orthodox view, works are not considered a means of earning salvation, but they are inseparable from faith. The works—such as loving your neighbor, fasting, praying, receiving the sacraments—are the means by which one cooperates with God's grace and grows in holiness. The Orthodox Church teaches that salvation is dynamic and requires an ongoing response to God's grace.

Study Questions

1. What is the role of synergy in Orthodox Christianity, and how does it differ from the concept of salvation in Protestantism, particularly with regard to faith and works?

2. Explain how Orthodox Christianity views salvation as a lifelong process rather than a one-time event. What is the significance of continuous cooperation with God's grace in the Orthodox view of salvation?

3. How does the Orthodox understanding of grace relate to human free will, and why is free will important in the process of salvation?

4. What is the Orthodox doctrine of theosis, and how does it differ from the Protestant understanding of justification?

5. Why is the Protestant doctrine of "faith alone" considered a theological error from the Orthodox perspective, and how does this doctrine fail to account for the process of becoming united with God in His eternal Kingdom?

Life in the Church and the Sacraments

In Orthodox Christianity, living faith is not a private or individualistic experience, but is always lived out by participation in the communal life of the Church. The communal nature of the Christian life is fundamental to the Orthodox understanding of faith and salvation. This communal aspect stems from several theological, sacramental, and ecclesiological principles that form the foundation of Orthodox spirituality. Here's a detailed explanation of why living faith is inseparable from the communal life of the Church.

The Church as the Body of Christ

The Church, in Orthodox theology, is understood as the Body of Christ. This is a deeply communal and mystical concept, emphasizing that every Christian is a member of the body of Christ, with Christ Himself as the head. As St. Paul teaches in 1 Corinthians 12:12-27, the Church is like a body, where each member is connected to the others, and every part plays a unique but vital role in the life of the whole body.

Just as a human body functions through the cooperation of different parts (hands, eyes, feet, etc.), the Church thrives as the Body of Christ when all its members, through their unique gifts, cooperate for the greater good. Faith is expressed, nourished, and strengthened within this community.

In this framework, salvation is never about an isolated individual journey. It is about being part of a living, functioning community that helps each person grow in faith and holiness. The body cannot function if a member is severed, just as the Christian cannot fully live their faith apart from the Church.

The Church as the "Place" of Grace

In Orthodox Christianity, the Church is not merely an institution or a gathering of people; it is the mystical presence of Christ on earth. It is within the Church that God's grace is actively at work, through the Holy Spirit, to save and transform His people.

Sacraments and Liturgy: The Orthodox Church holds that the sacraments (such as baptism, the Eucharist, confession, marriage, etc.) are not just symbolic acts, but real channels through which God's grace is imparted. These sacraments, especially the Eucharist, are celebrated in community, not individually. The Eucharist, in particular, is central to the Orthodox faith, as it is the actual participation in the Body and Blood of Christ, and it is a communal act that binds the members of the Church together as they partake of Christ's life. This emphasizes the idea that faith is meant to be lived in communion with others, united in the divine life.

The Body of Christ: Through baptism, a person becomes a member of the Church, and through the Eucharist, they receive the very life of Christ into their being. This highlights the idea that one cannot live in union with Christ without being in union with His Body, the Church. The sacraments are not just about personal spiritual experiences but are communal acts of grace that strengthen the faith of the entire Church body.

Communal Life and the Process of Salvation (Theosis)
The goal of salvation in Orthodoxy is theosis—union with God, being transformed into the likeness of Christ. However, the journey of theosis is not one that can be undertaken in isolation.

In the Orthodox Church, the faithful are called to support each other in this process. As the Apostle Paul says in 1 Thessalonians 5:11,

Therefore encourage one another and build one another up.

The communal life of the Church allows for mutual edification. Through shared prayer, teaching, and fellowship, Christians help one another grow in faith. This communal experience is essential for the Christian to stay on the path of salvation, particularly in the face of the temptations and struggles of the world.

The communal life of the Church allows Christians to witness Christ together, and to bear witness to others. Orthodox Christians believe that the whole Church is responsible for preaching the Gospel and sharing the love of Christ, not just individual believers. Faith in Christ is expressed in the love and unity of the community, and this unity is meant to be an outward sign of God's grace to the world.

The Church as a School of Holiness, a Spiritual Hospital
Orthodox Christianity understands the Church as a school of holiness. The purpose of the Church is to guide its members in the process of

healing our soul infused with sinful tendencies, to become more like Christ, to live a life of repentance, prayer, and virtue.

The Church teaches that salvation is mediated through the Holy Tradition handed down by the Apostles and preserved in the life of the Church. This Tradition is not simply a set of teachings or rules; it is a living experience of the faith that is passed on from generation to generation through the community. By living in the Church and engaging with this Tradition, believers are formed in the likeness of Christ. The wisdom of the saints, the prayers of the Church, and the liturgical life all serve to nurture the soul and draw it closer to God.

Within the Church, believers are often guided by spiritual fathers, priests, and monks who provide spiritual direction. This relationship is crucial for personal growth in holiness. The Orthodox Christian life is seen as a spiritual family, and just as a child depends on its parents for guidance, so too do Orthodox Christians rely on their spiritual family to help them grow in faith. This family is not just a metaphor but an actual experience lived out in the community of the Church.

Love and Fellowship as the Essence of Christian Life
Central to Orthodox Christianity is the call to love—love of God and love of neighbor. In fact, the very essence of the Christian life is summed up in Jesus' commandment to love one another as He has loved us (John 13:34).

Love is not a private, isolated feeling; it is expressed in community through acts of service, prayer, and sacrifice. The Church provides the context for Christian love to be lived out. The early Christians were known for their care for one another, and this is still a central characteristic of Orthodox Christian life. Through the communal life of the Church, believers practice love by caring for the poor, visiting the sick, and supporting one another in faith.

The Church is a community of people who are bound together by their shared faith in Christ. The relationship among Christians is not merely social but spiritual. Through the communal life of the Church, believers are drawn into a deeper relationship with one another and with God. This fellowship in Christ is a reflection of the perfect fellowship that exists in the Holy Trinity, and it is the ultimate goal for Christians to partake in this divine love and communion.

The Church as the Ark of Salvation

The Orthodox Church often refers to itself as the ark of salvation, an image that connects the community of believers with Noah's Ark, which saved humanity during the flood (Genesis 7).

The Church is the place where believers are protected from the storms of life, the temptations of the world, and the attacks of the enemy. It is the safeguard of salvation, offering a place of refuge and sanctuary. The faith lived in the community of the Church is meant to protect, strengthen, and nourish the soul so that it might endure in the process of salvation.

This image emphasizes that salvation is not a solitary journey. As the ark of salvation, the Church brings believers together in a communal fellowship, guiding them through the spiritual journey towards eternal life in God's Kingdom.

Conclusion: Faith Lived in the Church Community

In summary, living faith in Orthodox Christianity is inseparable from the communal life of the Church because the Church is the Body of Christ, the place of grace, and the school of holiness or a spiritual hospital. Faith is nourished, expressed, and perfected within the Church, as the believer cooperates with God's grace in a communal environment. The Church is not just a place of worship, but the mystical presence of Christ, where believers participate in the divine life together. It is in this community that the believer's faith is made alive, and through the mutual support, prayer, and guidance of the Church, they are drawn closer to Christ and prepared for eternal life in His Kingdom.

> **Study Questions**
>
> 1. How does the concept of the Church as the "Body of Christ" illustrate the communal nature of salvation in Orthodox Christianity?
> 2. In what ways does the Orthodox understanding of salvation as a lifelong process (theosis) require the active participation of the Christian within the communal life of the Church?
> 3. Explain the role of the sacraments, particularly the Eucharist, in fostering a communal experience of faith and grace in the Orthodox Church.
> 4. Why is it essential for Orthodox Christians to engage in mutual edification within the Church community, and how does this contribute to personal spiritual growth?
> 5. How does the Orthodox Church, as the "ark of salvation," provide both protection and a space for the faithful to live out their faith in communion with one another?

In Orthodox Christianity, the ultimate goal of faith is theosis, which is the process of becoming one with God, or more specifically, becoming participators in God's divine nature. Theosis is the transformative journey of a Christian being united with God, growing into the likeness of Christ, and being restored to the image of God that humanity was originally created to reflect. This process of theosis is not a mere abstract or doctrinal concept but a personal, spiritual reality that involves the entire life of the believer.

Theosis as Union with God

The Greek word theosis literally means "deification" or "divinization," which signifies a process by which a human being, by God's grace, becomes partaker of the divine nature. Theosis is the ultimate purpose of human existence and the fulfillment of God's plan for creation.

Theosis is not about becoming God in essence, but about becoming fully united with God in His energies. While humans remain distinct in their created nature, they are called to participate in God's divine energies, which are the active, life-giving forces by which God interacts with the world. This participation in God's divine life makes the believer more and more like Christ.

Jesus Christ, being both fully God and fully human, is the perfect example of theosis. He is the model for humanity's ultimate purpose—becoming united with God. In His incarnation, Christ fully assumed humanity to bring it into union with God. As the Apostle Peter writes in 2 Peter 1:4, Christians are *partakers of the divine nature.* Theosis means being transformed by God's grace into the image of Christ, the perfect image of God.

Theosis and the Restoration of the Image of God
The idea of theosis is deeply connected to the restoration of the image of God in humanity. According to the creation narrative in Genesis, God created human beings in His image and likeness (Genesis 1:26-27). However, through sin (the Fall), this image was distorted, and humanity became separated from God.

The Fall of Adam and Eve brought about spiritual death and separation from God. This disfigurement of the image of God in humanity meant that humans could no longer experience the fullness of divine life. However, God's plan for salvation through Jesus Christ seeks to restore this image by making humanity one with God again. Theosis is the process by which this restoration takes place.

Theosis is viewed as the healing of the human person, a restoration of the image of God that was originally marred by sin. Just as a wound can be healed, the human soul, through cooperation with divine grace, can be restored to its original purity, holiness, and likeness to Christ. It's about spiritual purification, healing the distortions caused by sin, and transforming the human being into the full image of God, as was originally intended.

The Role of Grace in Theosis
Theosis is not something that humans can achieve by their own power or merit. It is a gracious gift of God, facilitated by the work of the Holy Spirit.

While God's essence remains utterly beyond human comprehension and experience, God shares His divine energies with humanity. These energies are the means by which humans can experience and partake of God's presence. Theosis develops through a participation with God's divine energies, which empowers the believer to grow in holiness and to live as a true child of God.

While God's grace is essential for theosis, human cooperation is necessary. This is the doctrine of synergia—the cooperation between God's grace and human free will. The believer is called to actively engage in the process of salvation through repentance, prayer, fasting, participation in the sacraments, and the practice of virtues.

The Holy Spirit is central to the process of theosis. It is through the Holy Spirit that believers are able to grow in holiness and be conformed to the image of Christ. The Spirit dwells within the Christian, guiding, teaching, and empowering them to live a life that is increasingly aligned with God's will. The Holy Spirit is the means through which God's divine life is communicated to the believer, making theosis possible.

The Sacraments and Theosis

Yhe sacraments (or mysteries) are the primary means through which the believer participates in God's grace and undergoes the process of theosis.

Baptism: Baptism is the sacrament that initiates the believer into the life of the Church and marks the beginning of the process of theosis. Through baptism, the believer is cleansed of sin and receives the Holy Spirit. It is a new birth that sets the individual on the path toward union with God.

Eucharist (Holy Communion): The Eucharist is central to the process of theosis. Through the Eucharist, the believer partakes of the Body and Blood of Christ, which is not merely symbolic but the actual participation in Christ's divine life. This sacrament nourishes the soul and strengthens the believer's union with Christ. Regular participation in the Eucharist is essential for progress in theosis.

Other Sacraments: Sacraments such as confession, chrismation (confirmation), and marriage all play important roles in shaping the believer's life and supporting their journey toward theosis. Confession purifies the soul, chrismation seals the believer with the Holy Spirit, and marriage can become a means of mutual sanctification in love and cooperation toward God.

Theosis and the Christian Life

The process of theosis is a lifelong journey, not a single event. It involves an ongoing transformation of the entire person—body, soul, and mind—into the likeness of Christ. This transformation happens progressively as the believer grows in holiness, continually opening themselves to God's grace.

The path to theosis is a continual process of repentance—turning away from sin and turning toward God. Through repentance, the believer purifies the heart and mind, allowing more room for the Holy Spirit to dwell.

Prayer, fasting, and the cultivation of Christian virtues are necessary for theosis. These practices help to align the will with God's, to overcome sinful desires, and to strengthen the connection with God.

The ultimate goal of theosis is to become more like Christ, who embodied perfect love for God and for humanity. This love is expressed through self-sacrifice, compassion, and service to others. As the believer grows in the likeness of Christ, their love for others increases, reflecting the love of God that is poured into their hearts through the Holy Spirit.

Theosis and Eternal Life

The ultimate fulfillment of theosis is eternal life with God in His Kingdom. While the process of theosis begins in this life, it reaches its perfection in the age to come, when believers will be fully united with God. This is the hope of Orthodox Christians: that, through theosis, they will be able to enjoy unbroken communion with God for all eternity.

In the eternal state, the believer will be fully transformed into the likeness of Christ. The corruption of sin will be fully overcome, and the believer will experience the fullness of divine life in communion with God, in a way that is beyond our current understanding. This ultimate union with God is not just spiritual but encompasses the entire human person—body and soul—in the presence of God's eternal glory.

Conclusion: Theosis as the Ultimate Goal of Faith
Theosis is the ultimate goal of the Christian life in Orthodox Christianity. It is the process by which a believer is transformed into the image and likeness of God through God's grace. This transformation involves a lifelong journey of purification, repentance, prayer, and active participation in the sacraments. Theosis is about participation in God's divine life, a restoration of the image of God in the human person, and a continual journey of becoming more like Christ. Ultimately, theosis leads to eternal communion with God—the fulfillment of the Christian hope of union with God in His divine and eternal Kingdom.

Study Questions

1. What is theosis, and how does it differ from the concept of justification in other Christian traditions, such as Protestantism?

2. How does the Orthodox understanding of theosis relate to the restoration of the image of God in humanity, and what role does sin play in this process?

3. Explain the role of God's grace and human free will in the process of theosis. How do the two work together in the Orthodox understanding of salvation?

4. How do the sacraments, particularly baptism and the Eucharist, contribute to the process of theosis in the life of the believer?

5. What are the practical steps a Christian can take to participate in theosis, and how does the journey toward deification shape daily life in the Orthodox faith?

Chapter 4

Creation

The creation narrative in Genesis is foundational to understanding the Orthodox Christian worldview, offering profound insights into the nature of God, humanity, and the universe. Far from being a scientific or historical account, the Genesis creation story is a divinely inspired revelation that speaks to the spiritual realities underlying the cosmos. It invites us to contemplate not merely the mechanics of creation but its ultimate purpose—our relationship with God and our role in His divine plan.

Through the lens of Genesis, we come to see creation as an intentional and ordered act of love by a Creator who desires communion with humanity. By exploring the six days of creation, we uncover theological truths that shape our understanding of God's sovereignty, the goodness of creation, and our place within it. Drawing on the wisdom of the Church Fathers, this lesson emphasizes the spiritual significance of creation and highlights the cooperative work of the Holy Trinity in bringing the universe into existence.

This exploration will deepen your appreciation for the grandeur of God's creative work and its implications for your life. By studying Genesis through the teachings of the Church, you will discover how the story of creation reveals God's desire for humanity to live in harmony with Him and the rest of creation, offering a roadmap for spiritual growth and fulfillment.

The Six Days of Creation

The creation narrative in Genesis is central to understanding the Orthodox Christian view of the world, offering a spiritual perspective on the origin of the universe. The text of Genesis is not to be viewed solely as literal or a scientific textbook, but as a divinely inspired revelation given to Moses 3500 years ago, providing meaning and purpose to human existence through the lens of faith. Below, we explore the process of creation as described in Genesis, along with theological reflections from the Church Fathers.

Genesis uses worldly language to describe truths that transcend human comprehension, conveying the profound mysteries of God's creation in a way that is accessible to our understanding. The focus of Genesis is not on answering the "what" of creation, but on the "why"—giving deeper meaning to life and helping us understand our purpose. In interpreting Genesis, both literal and allegorical readings are considered, offering a balanced approach that acknowledges both the historical aspects of the creation story and its deeper theological and symbolic significance.

There are many commentaries from the Church Fathers to help us properly understand this part of the Bible:

- Saint John Chrysostom (347 - 407)
  Homilies on Genesis On the Creation of Life
- Saint Ephraim the Syrian (306 - 373)
  Interpretation of the Books of the Bible
- Saint Basil the Great (330 -379)
  Hexaemeron (Six Days), On the Origin of Man
- Saint Ambrose of Milan (340 - 397)
  Hexaemeron
- Saint Gregory of Nyssa (335 - 394)
  On the Making of Man
- Saint John of Damascas (676 - 749)
  On the Orthodox Faith
- Saint Symeon the New Theologian (949 - 1022)
  The Sin of Adam

How to interpret Genesis

When interpreting Genesis, it is essential to approach the text with respect, recognizing that it contains divine truth. As a work of divine inspiration, Genesis is not merely a human creation but a revelation from God. To understand it properly, we must resist the temptation to form personal interpretations without grounding them in the wisdom of the Church. It is important to familiarize ourselves with the insights of the Holy Fathers, who, despite having the scientific knowledge of their time, were primarily theologians dedicated to understanding the mysteries of faith. Care must also be taken to avoid isolating quotes from their context, as this can distort their meaning.

Humility is key in approaching Scripture, acknowledging that our understanding is limited, and we should seek to interpret it within the life of the Church, guided by the Holy Fathers and the counsel of spiritual leaders. Moreover, we must remember humbly that we are created beings, and the creation of God is beyond our full comprehension. With great gratitude, we should accept the revelation given to Moses, recognizing the limitations of our understanding and not attempting to challenge what is beyond us, as the enemies of truth once did. As St. John Chrysostom reminds us, human nature cannot fully comprehend the creation of God. Since no human witnessed creation, we must rely on God's revelation through Moses. St. Basil the Great affirms that Moses, made equal to the angels, reported to us what he heard directly from God. Thus, we must remember that when we read Genesis, it is not merely the words of Moses but the words of God Himself.

Key Doctrines
1. God Created Everything (Genesis 1:1)

In the beginning God created the heavens and the earth.

The first and most fundamental doctrine of creation is that God is the Creator of all things. The Orthodox Church affirms this truth, as stated in the Nicene Creed:

> "I believe in one God the Father Almighty, Maker of heaven and earth."

Everything that exists, both in the material and spiritual realms, originates from God's will and creative power.

Christ as the Creator

The New Testament reveals that Christ, the Word (Logos), is integral to the creation of all things. As John 1:1, 3 states,

In the beginning was the Word... all things were made through Him, and without Him was not anything made that was made.

Furthermore, Ephesians 3:9 tells us that

God created all things by Jesus Christ. Christ's role in creation is central, as He is both the means and the purpose of creation.

The Holy Spirit as the Sustainer

The Holy Spirit's role is highlighted in Genesis 1:2, where *the Spirit of God moved over the waters,* indicating that while God the Father initiates creation, it is through the cooperative action of the Trinity—the Father, Son, and Holy Spirit—that the world is both created and sustained. The Holy Spirit continues to work in the world, preserving and giving life to creation.

2. Creation Was Out of Nothing

Creation, according to Genesis 1:2, *was without form and void,* implying that God created the world ex nihilo, or out of nothing. This concept is crucial because it highlights that God is distinct from His creation. Creation is not made from pre-existing material but brought into being by God's will alone. St. Basil the Great taught that the beginning of creation marks the inception of time itself, and this moment is beyond human comprehension.

This creation was not by chance. Saint Basil writes:

The world was not conceived by chance and without reason, but for an useful end and for the great advantage of all beings, it is really the school where reasonable souls exercise themselves, the training ground where they learn to know and love God; by sight of visible and sensible things the mind is led, as by a hand, to the contemplation of invisible things.

3. Creation Was Sequential

Genesis presents creation as a structured process occurring over six days. This sequence is not random but follows a purposeful order, preparing the world for humanity, the crown of creation. Each day builds upon the previous one, moving from the inanimate to the living and then to the rational.

St. Gregory the Theologian:
> There is a certain firstness, secondness, thirdness, and so on to the seventh day of rest from works,...by these days is divided all that is created, being brought into order by unutterable laws, but not produced in an instant ...man appeared in the world last, honored by the handiwork and image of God,... like for a king, the royal dwelling had to be prepared and only then was the king to be led in, accompanied by all creatures.

St. Gregory of Nyssa observed that the creation of man comes last, symbolizing the culmination of God's work, where human beings are entrusted with dominion over all creation.

> Scripture shows the vital forces blended with the world of matter according to a gradation:
>
> first, it infused itself into insensate nature (elements);
>
> then advanced into the sentient world (life);
>
> then ascended to intelligent and rational beings....
>
> The creation of man is relegated to coming last, who took up into himself every single form of life, both that of plants and that which is seen in animals.
>
> ...what is perfect comes last, according to a certain necessary sequence in the order of things...
>
> Thus we may suppose that nature makes an ascent as it were by steps—I mean the various properties of life—from the lower to the perfect form.

4. The Six Days of Creation (Genesis 1:1-2:3)

Creation is described as a process unfolding over six days. As Genesis 2:1-2 states,

> *Thus the heavens and the earth, and all their adornment, were finished. And on the seventh day God finished the work He had done, and He rested...*

These six days occurred before the natural processes that govern our world began. As Fr. Seraphim Rose notes, God's miraculous work does not conform to the natural laws that now define our reality.

Time, as we understand it, is not a limiting factor in God's actions. As 2 Peter 3:8 reminds us,

> *With the Lord, one day is as a thousand years, and a thousand years as one day.*

The concept of "day" in the creation narrative cannot be confined to our human experience of a 24-hour period, especially considering that the sun, which marks our days, was not created until the fourth day. This leads us to question whether the "days" in Genesis refer to literal 24-hour periods or if they represent a more profound concept of time, understood in light of God's eternal nature.

Saint Basil the Great:

> "'In the beginning God created...' is not a reference to a measure of time. For the beginning of time is the same instant that time itself begins to exist. However, this beginning which is beyond all time and eternity has no reference to any time or instant."

Therefore we should avoid debates about how old the earth is.

Creation should not be viewed as a natural process but as a divine act. Don't let a secular mind try to rationalize this. The natural laws that govern our world are a result of God's creative will. Creation itself is not bound by these laws but is an act of God that precedes and transcends them.

The six days of creation unfold as follows:
- Day 1: God created light, separating it from darkness.
- Day 2: God created the sky, separating the waters above from those below.
- Day 3: God gathered the waters together, allowing dry land to appear, and He created vegetation.
- Day 4: God created the sun, moon, and stars to give light to the earth and mark times and seasons.
- Day 5: God created creatures of the sea and the sky.
- Day 6: God created land animals and humans in His image, giving them dominion over the earth.
- Day 7: God rested, sanctifying the seventh day as a day of rest.

The sequence of days is not a description of a scientific process but a theological framework that reveals the intentionality and order of God's creation. As Fr. Seraphim Rose emphasized, the natural processes we observe today do not directly correspond to the creation account, which is miraculous in nature and beyond the laws of time.

5. The Completion of Creation: *Very Good* (Genesis 1:31)
After each act of creation, God saw that it was "good," and at the completion of His work, He declared that everything He had made was "very good." This highlights the inherent goodness of creation. However, the presence of evil in the world does not contradict this goodness, as evil entered creation through the fall of humanity.

6. The Rest of God (Genesis 2:1-3)
On the seventh day, God rested from His work, sanctifying it as a day of rest. The rest of God is not due to weariness, as He is omnipotent, but serves as a model for humanity. It reflects the completion of creation and invites humanity to live in harmony with God's will, finding spiritual rest and fulfillment in communion with Him.

Conclusion

The six days of creation reveal the grandeur and purposefulness of God's work. They also provide a theological foundation for understanding our place in the world. Orthodox Christians believe that creation is not a random event but a purposeful act of a loving Creator who invites humanity to participate in His divine plan. The order and beauty of creation reflect God's wisdom and love, and humanity, made in His image, is called to care for it and grow into the likeness of God through the process of theosis.

Study Questions

1. How does the Orthodox Church interpret the creation narrative in Genesis, and why is it important to understand it as a spiritual rather than a scientific text?

2. What are the major doctrine that come from this part of genesis?

3. According to the Church Fathers, why is the sequence of creation in Genesis not random, and what does it signify about the order of creation?

4. How should we understand the concept of "days" in the Genesis creation account, especially in light of the fact that the sun was not created until the fourth day?

5. What is the significance about the creation being sequential based on some findings from modern?

6. What is the significance of God's declaration that "everything He made was very good" (Genesis 1:31), and how does this relate to the problem of evil in the world?

The Creation of Humans

In Genesis 2:7, we read that God
> formed man of the dust of the ground and breathed into his nostrils the breath of life; and man became a living soul.

The creation of humanity is central to the Christian understanding of the world, as humans are the crown of God's creation. In this lesson, we will explore the theological significance of humanity's creation and its implications for our purpose in life.

Humanity as the Crown of Creation
Mankind was created from already existing elements by God's own direct action.
> *God formed man of the dust of the earth, and breathed into his nostrils the breath of life; and man became a living soul* (Genesis 2:7).

Saint Gregory the Theologian notes:
> The soul is the breath of God, and while being heavenly, it endures being mixed with what is of the dust.

St. Gregory of Nyssa states that humanity
> "took up into himself every single form of life" and embodies the full spectrum of creation's potential.

Saint Theodorete observes:
> God created all other creatures with His word but Man He created with His own hands… He showed greater care taken for man than other creatures.

Saint Basil the Great emphasizes:
> If you consider nature alone, man is nothing and has no value; but if you regard the honor with which he has been created, man is something great…

Humanity is unique in God's creation, made in His image and likeness. According to Genesis 1:26-27, God said,
> *Let us make man in our image, after our likeness,*

and thus created humanity to reflect His divine nature. This distinction sets humanity apart from the rest of creation, as we are endowed with rationality, free will, and the capacity for communion with God. St. Gregory of Nyssa further observes that humanity encompasses all forms of life, both plant and animal, embodying the full potential of creation.

In Genesis 2:21-23, God creates woman from the rib of man, signifying the inseparable and complementary nature of man and woman. Together, they fulfill God's command to *be fruitful and multiply* (Genesis 1:28). The Orthodox Church teaches that both male and female are created in God's image and share equal dignity and value. While woman was the last to be created, she is no less important than man. In the Kingdom of Heaven, the Mother of God, a woman, holds the highest place:

> *More honorable than the cherubim, and beyond compare more glorious than the seraphim.*

Made in the Image and Likeness of God (Genesis 1:26-27)
Genesis 1:26-27 states,
> *Let us make man in our image, after our likeness; let him have dominion over... and over all the earth... So God created man in His own image, in the image of God created He him.*

The phrase "in the image and likeness of God" is central to understanding humanity's divine potential. The "image" refers to the inherent capacity of humans to reflect God's nature, especially through our rationality and free will, which allow us to align our will with God. The "likeness," on the other hand, refers to the process of moral growth and spiritual perfection, known as theosis. Through cooperation with the Holy Spirit, which we receive at Baptism, we grow in holiness and become more like God. The image of God is given to all people, but the likeness is something that must be acquired through spiritual practice and divine grace. This journey of transformation is the essence of Orthodox spirituality.

Humanity is given a Free Will
A key aspect of being made in God's image is the gift of free will. God, in His love, created humanity with the freedom to choose; He had no necessity to create, but chose to do so out of love. Free will allows humanity to

choose between good and evil, and it is through the exercise of free will that we cooperate with God's grace to become more like Him. However, free will also means that humanity has the potential to reject God, as Adam and Eve did in the Fall. St. Gregory of Nyssa teaches that humanity's free will reflects God's own freedom in creation, and it is through our choices that we grow into the likeness of God. Our purpose is to learn to use this freedom to become more like God by cooperating with the Holy Spirit, aligning our will with His out of love for Him and through His grace.

God gives us the Gift of a Soul
St. Gregory of Nyssa writes:
> "The soul is an essence created, living, and noetic, transmitting from itself to an organized and sentient body the power of living and of grasping objects of sense, as long as a natural constitution capable of this holds together."

The creation of humanity is described as a direct act of God, with man formed from the dust and animated by God's breath. The soul, as the breath of God, is eternal and immortal. It is created at conception, and as the body grows, the soul increasingly manifests its energies. The soul, in essence, is entirely different from the body and all things material.

As the Gospel of Matthew reminds us:
> *What is a man profited, if he shall gain the whole world, and lose his own soul? Or what shall a man give in exchange for his soul* (Matt 16:26)?
>
> *Fear not them which kill the body, but are not able to kill the soul* (Matt 10:28).

At death, the soul lives on but separates from the body. However, this bond is not severed forever. The soul will be reunited with the body in a new form at the Resurrection.

The Church Fathers teach that the soul is meant to govern the actions of the body according to the will of God, and the body must learn to accept this governance. The soul possesses reason, self-awareness, and free will. It is through the soul that humans can govern their actions, overcome sin, and unite their will with God's, bringing their entire being into full harmony with Him.

St. Gregory the Theologian emphasized that while the body is of the earth, the soul is of the heavens. It is through the soul that humans are capable of spiritual knowledge and communion with God. Although the body and soul are united, the soul governs the body according to God's will. After death, the soul separates from the body but will be reunited with it in the Resurrection, in a transformed and glorified state.

Our Purpose: Theosis and Union with God

The ultimate purpose of humanity is to grow in holiness and union with God through the process of theosis. Theosis is the process by which humans, through divine grace, become more like God and participate in His divine nature. This process begins in this life and is perfected in the life to come. St. Athanasius famously said, "God became man so that man might become god," emphasizing that humanity's potential for union with God is the fulfillment of our created purpose.

Conclusion

Human beings are the crown of God's creation, made in His image and likeness, and endowed with free will and a soul. The creation of humanity signifies our special relationship with God, calling us to live in communion with Him and grow in holiness. Our purpose is not simply to exist, but to fulfill our divine potential by striving to become more like God through the process of theosis. The creation of man and woman reflects the dignity and complementary nature of humanity, with both sexes called to work together in fulfilling God's plan for creation.

Study Questions

1. How does the creation of humanity in Genesis 2:7 highlight the unique nature of human beings in relation to the rest of creation, and what does this imply about our relationship with God?

2. What is the significance of being made *in the image and likeness of God* according to Genesis 1:26-27, and how does this understanding shape our spiritual potential and purpose?

3. How does free will, as a gift from God, contribute to humanity's ability to grow into the likeness of God, and what responsibility does it entail?

4. According to St. Gregory of Nyssa and other Church Fathers, what is the nature of the soul, and how does it function in relation to the body throughout life and after death?

5. What are we taught about the ultimate purpose of life? How does this process begin in this life and find its fulfillment in the life to come?

Chapter 5

Ancestral Sin

The Fall of humanity, as recounted in Genesis 3, is one of the most profound and transformative moments in Christian theology, shaping our understanding of sin, free will, and the human condition. The disobedience of Adam and Eve in the Garden of Eden not only led to their separation from God but also introduced mortality, suffering, and the inclination to sin into the human experience. Orthodox Christianity, through the concept of Ancestral Sin, emphasizes the consequences of this event rather than an inherited guilt, offering a perspective that differs significantly from Western Christian traditions.

In this chapter, we will explore the spiritual and theological implications of the Fall, drawing insights from Scripture and the writings of the Church Fathers. We will examine the nature of Paradise, the role of free will in humanity's disobedience, and the consequences that followed. Additionally, we will delve into the Orthodox doctrine of Ancestral Sin, contrasting it with the Western doctrine of original sin, to understand how each shapes the Christian view of salvation and the human journey back to God.

By understanding the Fall in its proper theological context, we can better appreciate the profound mercy of God, who continually calls humanity to repentance and offers salvation through Christ. This lesson invites us to reflect on the depth of our brokenness and the boundless love of God, who restores us through grace and the healing work of His Son.

The Fall and the Concept of Ancestral Sin

The Fall of mankind, as described in Genesis 3, is a pivotal moment in the Christian narrative. The story of Adam and Eve's disobedience is key to understanding the human condition, the nature of sin, and the need for salvation. The concept of Ancestral Sin is crucial to Orthodox theology, focusing on the consequences of the Fall rather than inherited guilt.

The story of Adam and Eve's disobedience in the Garden of Eden reveals the beginning of humanity's separation from God. Mankind was created in Paradise in full communion with God.

Saint John Chrysostom writes:
> "Before the fall men lived in Paradise like angels; they were not inflamed with lust, were not kindled by other passions either, were not burdened with bodily needs; being created entirely incorruptible and immortal, they did not even need the covering of clothing." Homilies on Genesis 13:4, 15:4

What is Paradise like?
Paradise, as described in the biblical narrative, is a beautiful and perfect place created by God. It is where humanity was made in God's image, formed from dust but with the potential for immortality. In Paradise, humans were free from bodily needs, much like the angels, and lived without suffering or the passions that would later plague them. It was a state of purity and harmony, where Adam and Eve were given both the challenge of stewardship over creation and the responsibilities that come with it. Paradise was a place of perfect communion with God, a life without pain or corruption, where the fullness of human potential was to be realized in obedience and love for the Creator.

Who is the devil?
The Devil, also known as Satan, is a fallen angel who once held a place in heaven but rebelled against God. Scripture tells us that certain angels *kept not their first estate* and left their divine habitation, choosing to defy God's will (Jude 6, II Peter 2:4). Jesus Himself said, *I saw Satan fall like lightning from heaven* (Luke 10:18), marking the moment of Satan's expulsion. Revelation 12:7-9 further describes a heavenly battle

where Michael and his angels fought against the dragon (Satan) and his followers. The dragon, also called the Devil and Satan, was defeated and cast out of heaven along with his angels, now becoming the deceiver of the world. This fallen angel's purpose is to lead humanity away from God, tempting and misleading them into sin.

The Fall
Genesis tells us:
> Now the serpent... said to the woman, *Has God indeed said, 'You shall not eat from every tree of the garden'? And the woman said... We may eat the fruit of the trees of the garden; but of the fruit of the tree which is in the middle of the garden, God said, 'You shall not eat from it, nor shall you touch it, lest you die.' Then the serpent said... You shall not die by death. For God knows in the day you eat from it your eyes will be opened, and you will be like gods, knowing good and evil. So when the woman saw that the tree was good for food, was pleasant to the eyes … she took of its fruit and ate. She also gave it to her husband with her, and he ate.*

Tempted by the serpent (Satan), Eve ate the forbidden fruit, and Adam followed her, thus violating God's command. This act of disobedience, which came from a desire for self-gratification, brought immediate consequences, including a loss of innocence, a shift from divine harmony to self-centeredness, and the beginning of suffering and death in the world.

The devil is devious, shrewd and clever. He knew that in the human heart was a desire for self-gratification and worldly things consequently with temptation they were unwilling to submit to God's will.

Consequences of the Fall
Story continues:
> *Then the eyes of both of them were opened, and they knew that they were naked; and they sewed fig leaves together and made themselves coverings* (Gen 3:7).

This nakedness shows that they lost glory of God and now only saw lower things of this earth. Their self-centeredness separated them from God. Their Souls became dominated by the body and its passions. Losing their dispassion they began a passionate earthly life. This is the Fall.

God responds:
What was God's response?
> *And they heard the sound of the Lord God walking in the garden in the cool of the day.... Then the Lord God called to Adam and said to him, 'Where are you?'*

Where are you indicates a separation from God. God is lovingly searching for them to return. This indicates that God is calling for them to repent. We see in the story three actions: Disobedience (sin), Separation, Repentance.

Adam and Eve respond:
Adam says:
> *I was afraid because I was naked; and I hid myself.*
> *The woman whom You gave to be with me, she gave me of the tree, and I ate.*

Eve Says,
> *The serpent deceived me, and I ate.*

They both responded with self-justification. Adam blamed Eve. Eve blamed the snake. They were lacking humility, remorse—both essential for repentance. They were unable to repent their disobedience.

The Fall leads to separation from God and introduces mortality, suffering, and sin into the human experience.
> *God commanded, of the tree of the knowledge of good and evil you shall not eat, for in the day that you eat of it you shall surely die* (Gen 2:15-17).

Paul says:
> *As by one man sin entered into the world, and death by sin; and so death passed upon all men, for that all have sinned* (Rom 5:12).
> *The wages of sin is death* (Rom 6:23).

As a result we inherited death and all it implies.

God acted.
> *He sent him out of the garden of Eden to till the ground from which he was taken....He placed cherubim at the east of the garden of Eden, and a flaming sword which turned every way, to guard the way to the tree of life* (Gen 3:22-24).

Having lost their original glory and becoming separated from God, the passions of the body began to dominate their soul, leading humanity into a state of brokenness that affects all of creation. This is a condition we all inherit so we can learn obedience based on humility and love and return to Paradise purified in the image of God.

The Doctrine of Ancestral Sin

In the Orthodox understanding, Ancestral Sin refers to the consequences of Adam and Eve's disobedience, not to inherited guilt. While the actions of Adam and Eve resulted in the introduction of mortality and a weakened will, Orthodox Christianity teaches that humans are born free from the guilt of original sin. Instead, we inherit a fallen nature that is prone to sin, but we are responsible for our own actions and choices.

This understanding contrasts with the Western view of original sin, which suggests that all human beings inherit the guilt of Adam's transgression.

The Need for Salvation

Humanity's fall from grace necessitates divine intervention for restoration. Although the image of God remains in humanity, along with free will, this image has been tarnished by sin. For humanity to return to Paradise, salvation is required, and it can only be achieved through the grace of God.

Paul emphasizes that death is the central issue because it is the weapon of the Devil. Eve was deceived by Satan, and through death, humanity was taken captive by the Devil. As Paul writes,

> *The last enemy to be destroyed is death* (1 Cor 15:26).
> *...the sting of death is sin* (1 Cor 15:56).

The Orthodox Church teaches that Christ's Incarnation, Crucifixion, Resurrection. sending the Holy Spirit, and establishment of the sacramental Church, are the means by which humanity is healed from the effects of the Fall, with the ultimate goal of restoring communion with a loving God who desires reunion with His creation. Our purpose is to overcome the consequences of Adam and Eve's sin, particularly death, and the tendency to sin that has become part of human nature. Salvation is not about legal guilt being removed but about healing the illness of the soul through the love of God. The idea of a broken law and a vengeful God punishing us has no place in Orthodox thinking. Christ came to heal humanity's fallen condition and defeat death, not merely to address legal guilt.

The Role of Free Will
In the Orthodox view, the Fall highlights the significance of free will. While Adam and Eve used their free will to disobey God, the restoration of humanity requires the voluntary cooperation of each person with God's grace. Free will, in the Orthodox tradition, remains intact after the Fall, allowing humans to choose either to align themselves with God or to follow their own desires.

As a result of the Fall, everyone inherits a tendency to sin, which comes from the disobedience of Adam and Eve. This tendency is passed down through generations, which is why it is called ancestral sin. We are born with knowledge of God but remain separated from Him, with souls distorted by sinfulness. Our task, as part of God's plan, is to cleanse our tarnished image and restore our souls to their original purity. Ultimately, this restoration involves uniting our will with God's will, so that we can reflect the image of Christ, who is the perfect model of humanity.

Study Questions

1. How does the story of Adam and Eve's disobedience in the Garden of Eden explain the beginning of humanity's separation from God, and the purpose of our lives?

2. What are the consequences of the Fall as described in Genesis 3, and how do these consequences affect humanity's life?

3. Explain the Orthodox understanding of Ancestral Sin.

4. What role does free will play in both the Fall and humanity's need for salvation, and how does it remain central to the process of repentance and restoration?

5. Why is salvation necessary after the Fall, and what did God arrange for our benefit? How can we benefit?

The Problem of the Western View of Original Sin and Doctrine of Guilt

In contrast to the Orthodox understanding of Ancestral Sin, Western Christian traditions, particularly those shaped by St. Augustine of Hippo (354-430), have introduced the doctrine of original sin, which asserts that all humans inherit the guilt of Adam and Eve's disobedience. This concept carries significant innovation with significant theological implications, especially for the understanding of salvation, sin, and the human condition. This led to significant differences between the Orthodox and Western views in the approach to human nature, divine justice, and the means of salvation.

The Western Innovative Doctrine of Original Sin

The innovative view of original sin unknown in the East or West was formally introduced by St. Augustine in the 5th century, and it has since become a cornerstone of Western Christian theology. Augustine's formulation of original sin, particularly his interpretation of Romans 5:12, in which Paul states, *sin entered the world through one man, and death through sin,* led him to conclude that all humans inherit the guilt of Adam and Eve's original sin.

When Paul said that *sin entered the world through one man*, Augustine took this to mean that Adam's transgression was not just an isolated event but something with cosmic consequences for all of humanity. He believed that Adam's sin affected not only his own nature but also the nature of all of his descendants. For Augustine, this meant that every person, by virtue of being a descendant of Adam, inherits this sinfulness and the guilt attached to it. The inheritance was not simply the fallen condition but also the guilt itself.

One of the critical elements in Augustine's misinterpretation was his reliance on the Latin translation of the Bible, the Vulgate. The Latin word peccatum (sin) was used to translate the Greek word hamartia (sin) in Romans 5:12, and this Latin term carried the connotation of both the condition of sin and the guilt associated with it. In the Latin context, it was easier for Augustine to interpret peccatum as something that could be transmitted in a more personal and legal sense, i.e., that the actual guilt of Adam's sin was passed down to all his descendants.

This theological framework became foundational in shaping Western Christianity's view of salvation, especially the doctrine of atonement. Augustine's view implies that humanity is born inherently corrupted and separated from God, and thus in need of divine intervention to reconcile with God. The inheritance of guilt due to original sin was seen as having lasting consequences for all of humanity, and this idea would influence later Western Christian concepts of salvation. Specifically, it gave rise to ideas like penal substitution—where Christ's death is seen as a necessary sacrifice to satisfy God's justice for humanity's inherited guilt.

However, it is important to understand Augustine's background and the context in which he formulated his views on original sin. Augustine was deeply influenced by his personal struggles and experiences, which informed his theology in significant ways. Before his conversion to Christianity, Augustine lived a life marked by worldly pursuits and sinful behavior, including a period of time when he lived in an immoral relationship. This early life of sin and his conversion experience profoundly shaped his views on human nature, sin, and the need for divine grace. He famously wrote in his Confessions, an autobiographical work, about his deep internal struggle with sin, the pleasures of the flesh, and his eventual acceptance of God's grace.

Additionally, Augustine's limitations in language and theological education also played a role in the development of his ideas. Augustine, a native Latin speaker, did not have a command of Greek, the language in which much of the New Testament was originally written. This linguistic limitation likely led to this misinterpretations of Roman 5:12 in regard to the nature of sin and the transmission of Adam's guilt.

The Western Concept of Guilt
In Western Christian thought, original sin is typically understood through the lens of a legal framework. The idea is that the guilt of Adam and Eve's sin is transmitted to all their descendants, meaning that every human being, from the moment of conception, is born guilty of sin. Theologians beginning with Augustine emphasized that because all humans inherit this guilt. This inherited guilt cannot be avoided or escaped through human effort; it requires divine intervention to be cleansed.

In this legal understanding, sin is framed as a breach of divine law. The transgression of God's command by Adam and Eve is not merely a disobedient act but a legal violation that has consequences for every human being. As a result, every person is seen as born condemned, necessitating a process of redemption. The most significant consequence of original sin in the Western view is that it leaves humanity in a state of alienation from God. This contrasts to the Orthodox view of Ancestral sin which implies that we only receive the consequences of sin death and mortality and the tendency to sin. The Orthodox place the emphasis on the need for healing instead of atonement of any guilt.

The West's Implied Need for Atonement and Payment
Since in this Augustinian view original sin is seen as a legal debt, it logically follows that this debt requires some form of atonement or payment. This is where the concept of penal substitution comes into play, especially in Protestant theology. Penal substitution theory holds that Christ's death on the cross served as a necessary sacrifice to satisfy God's justice. In this view, the wrath of God was poured out on Christ, who bore the punishment that humanity deserved for their inherited guilt.

The doctrine of atonement in the Western context thus focuses heavily on God's justice and the necessity of satisfying that justice through Christ's sacrifice. The atonement is understood as a means of paying for the sin that humans have inherited from Adam. Christ's death is viewed as the legal payment for the debt incurred by original sin, allowing humanity to be pardoned and reconciled to God. This emphasis on legal retribution is central to the Western view of salvation and presents sin as something that needs to be forgiven or remitted through a process of restitution.

The Orthodox Rejection of Guilt Inheritance
In contrast, the Orthodox Church rejects the Western concept of inherited guilt and instead teaches the doctrine of Ancestral Sin. According to Orthodox theology, Ancestral Sin refers to the consequences of Adam and Eve's disobedience, rather than the inheritance of their guilt. While the Fall introduced death, suffering, and a weakened will into

the human condition, it did not result in a legal inheritance of guilt passed down to all descendants. Orthodox Christianity affirms that each person is responsible for their own actions and choices and is not condemned for the actions of Adam and Eve.

The consequences of Ancestral Sin are the introduction of mortality, suffering, and a tendency toward sin, but these consequences do not imply that every human being is born guilty. In Orthodox thought, sin is not a legal debt but a brokenness or illness that needs healing. Humanity's need for salvation is not because of a legal penalty that must be paid, but because of the spiritual and existential effects of the Fall. Humans are born with free will, and while they inherit a weakened nature, they are still responsible for their own choices.

Christ's Role in Overcoming Death, Not Just Guilt
In the Orthodox view, the focus of Christ's work of salvation is not primarily about satisfying divine justice for inherited guilt but about healing the brokenness caused by sin and defeating death. In this understanding, sin is not a legal transaction to be corrected through payment, but an illness to be cured by Christ's healing grace. Christ's Incarnation, death, and resurrection were the means by which He overcame death and restored humanity's ability to commune with God.

For the Orthodox Church, Christ's ultimate victory was over death and the devil, not over a legal debt. Christ's life and resurrection offer new life and restoration for all who cooperate with God's grace. Salvation, therefore, is not simply the legal removal of guilt but the transformation of human nature, allowing humanity to be restored to the divine image and likeness. Theosis, or the process of becoming one with God, is the ultimate goal of salvation in the Orthodox faith.

Conclusion
The Western and Orthodox views of sin and salvation differ significantly in their understanding of original sin and guilt. The Western view, especially as developed by St. Augustine, emphasizes inherited guilt, which requires legal atonement through Christ's sacrifice. This has led to the development of doctrines such as penal substitution and a focus on satisfying divine justice. In contrast, the Orthodox Church teaches

that while humans inherit the consequences of the Fall—mortality, suffering, and a tendency to sin—they are not born guilty of Adam's sin. Instead, salvation is seen as the healing of human nature and the defeat of death, with Christ's role centered on restoring humanity to its original state through divine grace, not through a legal transaction. This difference in understanding shapes the way salvation is conceived, as the Orthodox view focuses on transformation, healing, and communion with God, rather than legal absolution.

Study Questions

1. Compare and contrast the Western doctrine of original sin and the Orthodox understanding of Ancestral Sin. How do each view the consequences of Adam and Eve's disobedience and the role of human responsibility?

2. Explain how the concept of guilt in the Western Christian tradition, particularly in light of Augustine's teachings, differs from the Orthodox perspective on sin and the need for salvation?

3. How does the Orthodox view of salvation, focusing on healing, differ from the Western emphasis on legal atonement and the satisfaction of divine justice?

Chapter 6

The Path to Salvation

This chapter offers a comprehensive exploration of God's divine plan for the salvation of humanity, beginning with the preparation for Christ's coming and culminating in the Church's role as the vessel of this salvation.

The chapter begins detailing how God's providence guided humanity through key events and figures in the Old Testament foreshadowed the coming of the Messiah and the ultimate fulfillment of God's promise of redemption.

In second section, the focus shifts to the mystery of the Incarnation, where the Son of God took on human flesh. The Incarnation is explored as the cornerstone of God's plan, revealing Christ's dual nature as fully God and fully man.

The third section delves into the Orthodox understanding of salvation. It presents Christ's death and Resurrection not as a transactional payment but as a victory over sin and death.

The fourth section examines the universal and personal dimensions of salvation. This section emphasizes the dynamic interplay of divine grace and human free will in the ongoing journey of salvation.

Finally, the last section discusses the Church's role as the Body of Christ as the guardian of the apostolic faith.

God Prepares the Way

The Need for Salvation
After the Fall of Adam and Eve, all of humanity inherits the consequences of their disobedience, primarily the inevitability of physical death and a tendency to sin. The Fall introduced a fundamental rupture in humanity's relationship with God, and as a result, death entered the world. This physical death is not merely the end of life but a manifestation of spiritual death—separation from God, the Source of life.

The tendency to sin, often referred to as the "passions," arises from this fallen nature. Humanity, now subject to the consequences of Adam and Eve's sin, is inclined toward selfishness, pride, and desires that lead them away from God. As a result, every human being is born into a state where their will is weakened and prone to disorder, though they retain the freedom to choose between good and evil.

Thus, the Fall's consequences are both spiritual (alienation from God) and physical (death and suffering), and they lead to a tendency within human nature to sin, which requires divine healing and restoration through Christ. This healing is what we call salvation.

In the Orthodox faith, salvation involves our perfection and reunion with God, a process called Theosis. Through this union with God, we gain victory over death, just as Christ did. We become prepared to enter His Kingdom with eternal life. However, we must be careful not to intellectualize this process, as it involves a deep, personal transformation that only those who are spiritually advanced can fully understand. Don't let a secular worldview destroy this mystery of great depth and spiritual significance.

How the Events of the Old Testament Prepared the Way for the Coming of Christ
The Old Testament is rich with events, figures, and prophecies that laid the groundwork for the coming of Jesus Christ, the Savior. Through key moments in history, God gradually revealed His plan for humanity's salvation. These events not only shaped Israel's identity but also pointed forward to the ultimate fulfillment of God's promises through Jesus Christ. Below, we explore how these Old Testament events prepared the way for Christ's redemptive work.

Noah's Ark: God's Promise of Salvation

Adam and Eve after being expelled from Paradise lived a mortal life, suffering a life of trials and tribulations of a normal mortal life They had two children: Cain a farmer, and Abel a Shepherd. The envy of Cain resulted in him killing Abel. As time progressed Man had continual difficulty in maintaining a respect for their Creator and living a life based on His love.

As humanity's wickedness grew, God chose Noah, a righteous man, to preserve life through the flood. God instructed Noah who lived an honest and hard-working life, to destroy all things on the earth. He told Noah to build an ark to save his family and the animals, ensuring that life would continue after the destruction of the earth by the flood. This story of salvation through God's intervention prefigures Christ, who would ultimately offer salvation to all people. The ark became a symbol of God's protection and deliverance, with Noah serving as a model of faithful obedience. After the flood, God promises:

> *never again to curse the works of the earth because of man's works… nor will I destroy every living thing as I have done* (Genesis 8:21).

Abraham: The Father of Faith and a Foretaste of Christ's Sacrifice

The narrative of Abraham begins the direct line of salvation. God made a covenant with Abraham, promising that all nations would be blessed through his descendants.

> Now the Lord said to Abram, *Go from your country and kindred and your father's house to the land that I will show you.*
> *And I will make you a great nation, and make your name great, so that you will be a blessing … and in you all families of the earth shall be blessed* (Gen 12:1-3, See also 17:1-8, 22:1-18).

This promise is fulfilled in Jesus Christ, who, as the descendant of Abraham, brings salvation to all nations. Abraham's faith and obedience were key in understanding the nature of salvation, and his willingness to sacrifice his son Isaac at God's command is a powerful prefiguration of God's own sacrifice of His Son for the redemption of mankind. When Abraham obeyed God and was willing to offer Isaac, God stopped him and provided a ram as a substitute, demonstrating His ultimate provision of Christ, the true Lamb of God, renewing His promise.

Abraham's faith is also highlighted in the New Testament as the model of faith by which believers are justified..

> *Was not Abraham our father justified by works, when he offered his son Isaac upon the altar? You see that faith was active along with his works, and faith was completed by works, and the scripture was fulfilled,* (Romans 4:3)
>
> *Abraham believed God, and it was reckoned to him as righteousness; and he was called the friend of God. You see that a man is justified by works and not by faith alone* (James 2:21-24).

His faith, expressed through works, prefigures the dynamic faith that believers in Christ must have for salvation. Abraham's life serves as a type of the Christian faith, which must be alive, active, and willing to follow God's commands, even in the most difficult circumstances.

Abraham introduces the world to the Holy Trinity. In an event known as the Hospitality of Abraham we see the revelation of the Trinitarian nature of God.

> And the Lord appeared to him by the oaks of Mamre, as he sat at the door of his tent in the heat of the day. He lifted up his eyes and looked, and behold, three men stood in front of him.
>
> When he saw them, he ran from the tent door to meet them, and bowed himself to the earth, and said, *My lord, if I have found favor in your sight, do not pass by your servant.* (Gen. 18:1-5).

Abraham addresses the three angels as one, calling them Lord. They eat in his presence and foretell the birth of Isaac from Sarah in her old age. In this visitation of God to Abraham, we see prefiguration of full revelation of Holy Trinity in New Testament.

The Passover and Exodus: Deliverance from Slavery

The Passover and Exodus are central events in the Old Testament that point directly to Christ's mission. The Israelites, under Moses' leadership, were liberated from slavery in Egypt, marking a key moment in salvation history. God instituted the Passover as a way for the Israelites to be spared from the plague of death that struck Egypt. They were instructed to sacrifice a lamb and spread its blood on their doorposts, and those who obeyed were saved from death. This event foreshadows the sacrifice of Jesus Christ, the true Passover Lamb, whose blood would protect believers from eternal death (John 1:29).

The Exodus itself is a powerful symbol of salvation. Just as Moses led the Israelites out of slavery in Egypt, Christ would later lead humanity out of the slavery of sin and death. The crossing of the Red Sea is particularly symbolic of baptism, as the Israelites passed through the waters to freedom, prefiguring the new birth into eternal life through Christ's baptism. Christ's death and resurrection would become the ultimate Exodus, leading humanity from the captivity of sin into the promised land of eternal life.

In the desert, God provided the Israelites with manna, the *bread from heaven*, to sustain them. This points to Christ as the true Bread of Life, who would sustain His people spiritually, offering Himself as the bread of life to all who believe in Him (John 6:31-35).

Moses and the Law: Preparing for the New Covenant
Moses' role in delivering the Israelites from Egypt and receiving God's law on Mount Sinai was another preparation for the coming of Christ. The Ten Commandments were given to Israel to guide them in moral and religious life, but these laws ultimately highlighted humanity's inability to perfectly fulfill God's commands, demonstrating the need for a Savior. Christ would fulfill the law, not by abolishing it, but by bringing a new covenant based on grace rather than works of the law.

The law, which once demanded external obedience, would be fulfilled in the heart through the Holy Spirit. The Sermon on the Mount, where Jesus delivered the Beatitudes, marks the internalization of the law, where Christ reveals that God's commandments must be written on the heart, a transformation that could only be achieved through the Holy Spirit.

The Kings and Prophets: Foretelling the Messiah
Throughout the Old Testament, the kings and prophets foretold the coming of a Messiah who would rule with justice, peace, and righteousness. King David, though an imperfect ruler, was seen as the model for the Messiah, who would come from his line and establish an everlasting

kingdom. The prophets, such as Isaiah, spoke of a coming Redeemer who would be a suffering servant, bearing the sins of the people (Isaiah 53). These prophecies pointed to the coming of Jesus, who would fulfill the role of the Messiah by bringing salvation not through political power, but through His death and resurrection.

The prophets also spoke of a new covenant that would be established by God, one that would bring true peace and healing to humanity. Christ would be the fulfillment of these promises, inaugurating the Kingdom of God through His ministry and sacrifice.

The Time Was Right: A Prepared World

By the time of Christ's birth, the world was prepared in various ways. The Roman Empire, with its extensive roads and peaceful administration, allowed for the spread of the Gospel throughout the known world. The common language of Greek facilitated communication, and the Jewish people, scattered throughout the empire, were expecting the Messiah. The influence of Hellenistic philosophy also prepared minds to understand the Logos—the divine Word—who would be revealed in Christ.

The Fulfillment of God's Plan in Christ

All the events, figures, and prophecies of the Old Testament pointed to the coming of Christ, the true Savior. Jesus, as the fulfillment of the promises made to Abraham, Moses, and the prophets, came to offer salvation through His life, death, and resurrection. He is the true Passover Lamb, whose sacrifice delivers humanity from the power of sin and death. His Resurrection brings victory over death, offering eternal life to all who believe in Him.

Conclusion

In conclusion, the Old Testament is filled with types, figures, and prophecies that prepared the way for Christ's coming. Each step in salvation history—from the fall of Adam and Eve, to Noah's ark, to Abraham's faith, to the Exodus, to the giving of the law—points to the ultimate fulfillment of God's promise in Jesus Christ. Through His life and work, Christ accomplishes what the Old Testament only prefigured: the redemption of humanity from sin and death, and the restoration of the relationship between God and His people.

Study Questions

1. How does the story of Noah's Ark prefigure Christ's redemptive work, and what was the significance of God's promise after the flood?

2. Explain the role of Abraham in preparing the way for Christ. How does Abraham's faith and willingness to sacrifice Isaac prefigure God's ultimate sacrifice in Christ?

3. How do the events of the Exodus, including the Passover, crossing the Red Sea, and the provision of manna, foreshadow Christ's mission of salvation? How is Christ the fulfillment of these Old Testament symbols?

4. How does the story of Moses receiving the law on Mount Sinai prepare the way for the coming of Christ and the New Covenant?

5. In what ways do the kings and prophets of the Old Testament foreshadow the coming of Christ, particularly in relation to His role as the Messiah and the fulfillment of God's promises?

6. What was significant about the the role of the Roman Empire?

Coming of Our Savior—The Incarnation of God

The Significance of the Incarnation

The Incarnation is one of the most profound and central doctrines in Christianity, representing God's ultimate act of love and His plan for the salvation of humanity. Through the Incarnation, the Second Person of the Trinity, the Son of God, took on human flesh from the Virgin Mary and became fully human while remaining fully divine. He came to transform humankind, enabling them to become like Him.

In the Incarnation God Himself entered into human history, uniting His divine nature with human flesh in the person of Jesus Christ. Jesus was fully God and fully human—two natures united without confusion. He became like us in everything except sin (Hebrews 4:15). This union of divine and human nature is essential because it allows Christ to transform humanity and lead them to salvation. As both God and man, Christ bridges the gap created by the Fall, restoring the union of love that was lost in the Garden of Eden.

Through the Incarnation, He demonstrated what it means to live as God intended, showing us the way to live in communion with God and fulfilling the Image in which God created humanity. Jesus' life serves as the perfect example of human life in its intended form—free from sin and perfectly aligned with God's will. We are commanded to become like Him so that we may return to Paradise and live eternally in His Kingdom.

Rebirth Through Baptism

When Jesus was baptized, He sanctified the waters of Baptism, making it a means by which human beings are reborn in Him. Baptism marks the beginning of this renewal, where we receive the Holy Spirit and are united with Christ, becoming members of His Body, the Church. Through Baptism, we share in Christ's death and resurrection, and we are empowered to live a new life, following Christ's example.

In Baptism, the Holy Spirit is given to believers, transforming them into the temple of God (1 Cor. 3:16–17). Through the indwelling of the Holy Spirit, God dwells within us (1 Cor.3:16; 6:19; Eph. 2:22), and we become

His adopted children (John 1:12). This enables us to grow in the likeness of Christ. As we are united with Christ's flesh and divinity, we begin the process of becoming like Him, fulfilling our original purpose of being in communion with God. This transformation shifts the focus from an external observance of the law, as seen in the Old Testament, to an internal disposition of the soul, emphasized in the New Testament. The grace and power of the Holy Spirit, given to us in Baptism, empowers us to fulfill this potential and to continue growing in the likeness of Christ, fulfilling our original purpose and returning to the Paradise that God intended for us.

Transfiguration of Christ
The union of divinity and humanity in Christ is powerfully demonstrated in the Transfiguration (Matthew 17). On Mount Tabor, His beloved Apostles Peter, James, and John witnessed the divine light emanating from Christ, revealing His full divinity. This divine revelation points to the reality that, through Christ, we too can share in His divine nature. In our rebirth through Him, we are invited to partake in the divine light that was revealed to the Apostles, becoming sharers in His divine life.

The Example Christ Shows Us
Christ's life not only demonstrated the power to live without sin but also revealed the way to live in union with God. He lived a fully human life, preserving free will while directing it toward love for God. He showed us that it is possible to live in full alignment with God's will, free from the control of the passions or desires of the body. Christ's life is the perfect example of how humans were intended to live—completely in harmony with God's divine will.

His obedience to the Father, even in the most difficult circumstances, serves as the model for all who follow Him. He empowers us to live lives of obedience, teaching us that true freedom is found in surrendering to God's will. Through the Incarnation, Christ reveals how human nature can be perfected, showing us the way to restore the image of God within us and our union with Him.

The Crucifixion and Resurrection
While the Incarnation was a significant step in God's plan of salvation, the Crucifixion and Resurrection of Christ showed us the path we too can follow, the ultimate act of redemption came through Christ's Resurrection. Through His death, Christ showed us that the way to eternal life is through sacrifice. By His Resurrection, He conquered death showing that we have nothing to fear in our future death if we follow Him.

As St. Paul writes in 2 Corinthians 5:15, Christ died for all so that we may no longer live for ourselves, but for Him who died and was raised for our sake. Through His death and resurrection, Christ offers us the possibility of eternal life. The Resurrection demonstrates that by following Christ, we too can conquer death and live forever.

The Ascension: Christ Opens the Gates of Paradise
After His Resurrection, Christ ascended into heaven, where He sits at the right hand of the Father. His Ascension opened the gates of Paradise that had been closed at the time of the Fall of Adam and Eve. This restored humanity's access to eternal life in Paradise. Through His Ascension, Christ not only returned to His rightful place in glory but also paved the way for us to share in that same glory. The Ascension marks the culmination of Christ's earthly mission, showing that humanity, in Christ, has been restored to its original dignity.

Pentecost: The Empowering of the Church
After His Ascension, Christ promised His disciples that He would send the Holy Spirit to empower them for the mission ahead. On Pentecost, the Holy Spirit descended upon the Apostles, transforming them into bold witnesses of the Gospel. The Holy Spirit transformed them, empowering them to spread the Good News of the Gospel in a hostile environment and establish Christ's Church on earth as a "spiritual hospital" for the healing of souls. The Holy Spirit continues to guide the Church today, leading believers into all truth and enabling them to live out the new life that Christ has made possible.

Filled with the Holy Spirit, the Apostles spread the message of salvation to the ends of the earth. Their work laid the foundation for the Church, which remains the body of Christ on earth, offering the grace of the sacraments, teaching the Word of God, and guiding people toward salvation.

Conclusion: The Salvation Christ Offers

Through the Incarnation, Crucifixion, Resurrection, Ascension, and Pentecost, Christ has completed the work necessary for our salvation. He has made it possible for humanity to be reborn, transformed, and restored to fulfill the image of God. The power to live in union with God is now within us, and through the sacraments of His Church, especially Baptism and the Eucharist, we are continually empowered to grow in Christ's likeness.

The Church, as the Body of Christ, exists to continue this work, offering healing and salvation to all who seek it. Through Christ, we have the hope of eternal life and the power to live in harmony with God, as He intended. As we follow Him, we are empowered by the Holy Spirit to become like Him, perfectly united with His divinity and humanity, drawing closer to our final return to Paradise.

Study Questions

1. Why is the Incarnation considered a central doctrine in Christianity, and how does it demonstrate God's ultimate act of love?

2. How does the union of Christ's divine and human natures enable the salvation of humanity, and why is this union essential for restoring the relationship between God and humankind?

3. In what ways does Christ's life serve as the perfect example of how humans are intended to live, and how does His obedience to the Father guide us in our spiritual journey?

4. How does the Holy Spirit, received in Baptism, empower believers to live in union with God and grow in the likeness of Christ?

5. How do the Incarnation, Crucifixion, Resurrection, Ascension, and Pentecost together form the complete framework for humanity's salvation and the restoration of access to Paradise?

How Christ Saves Us

Nature of Salvation
Salvation is the process God has established to perfect humanity, renew us, and restore the divine image imprinted upon us at creation. It is a journey of healing and transformation, lifting us from the fallen condition inherited from Adam and Eve and guiding us toward union with God. This process requires our cooperation with God's grace through faith, works, and spiritual disciplines.

Salvation as Liberation
Through the Incarnation, Jesus Christ united His divinity with human flesh, transforming the nature of humanity. His purpose was to liberate humanity from the bondage of sin, death, and the fear that accompanies it. Christ's Resurrection is proclaimed as a victory over death, offering humanity the hope of new life and eternal communion with God.

Orthodox theology does not view salvation as a transactional payment for sins, as is sometimes taught in other Christian traditions. Rather than interpreting Christ's death as a ransom paid to the devil or a means to appease God's anger, the Orthodox Church emphasizes that Christ's Resurrection liberated (ransomed) humanity from the powers of sin, death, and the devil. His self-offering was a voluntary act of love, freely given to restore humanity to union with God.

The word ransom (Greek: lytrosis) signifies liberation or deliverance, not a financial transaction. Christ's Crucifixion is understood as a means of rescuing humanity from the enslaving power of sin and death, a deliverance affirmed and completed in His Resurrection. The Orthodox Church rejects the notion that God needed to "pay" a debt to the devil or Himself. Instead, Christ freely offered Himself out of love to liberate humanity from the consequences of sin.

An analogy often used is that of a parent who jumps into the water to save a child. The parent does not pay someone else to perform the rescue but acts out of pure love, risking their own safety to deliver the child from danger. Similarly, Christ's death was not a payment to a third party but a voluntary, loving sacrifice made to free humanity from the grip of sin and death.

Christ did not die to satisfy divine wrath or to fulfill a transactional debt but to overcome the forces of evil that enslaved humanity. His sacrificial act was motivated entirely by love, demonstrating His desire to restore humanity to union with God. In His self-offering, Christ defeated death, redeemed humanity, and opened the way for eternal life in communion with God.

The Resurrection is a Victory

Christ's Resurrection is the foundation of Christian hope, showing that eternal life is available to all who are united with Him. Christ though His life, death, and resurrection has given humanity the hope of being restored to humanities original glory and gaining entrance into Paradise to live eternally in union with God. As Paul writes about our life to come,

> *We will see God face to face and will shine like the sun illuminated by the light of divine glory.* (1 Cor 13:12, Matt 13:43).

St. Symeon the New Theologian beautifully affirms this,

> "O wonder, like angels and like sons of the most high shall they be after death, gods united to God, by adoption they are made like Him who is God by nature."

Salvation as Theosis

The ultimate goal of redemption and salvation is union with God. This union is the fullness of salvation, which Orthodox Christianity calls Theosis where believers are progressively made more like Christ, becoming partakers of the divine nature (2 Peter 1:4). The ultimate goal is to achieve union with God, which is the fullness of salvation. This union is not just a spiritual state, but an intimate relationship with God that continues into eternity.

Through Christ's work of redemption, believers are offered the hope of eternal life where theosis is fulfilled. This eternal life is not merely unending existence but is a life in perfect union with God, filled with love, joy, and peace.

Salvation Begins with Baptism and Chrismation

The Orthodox Church teaches that our participation in Christ's redemptive work begins with Baptism and Chrismation. In Baptism, we are spiritually reborn, united to Christ's death and Resurrection, cleansed of sin, and empowered to live as children of God. Salvation is not only about being forgiven but involves spiritual rebirth and transformation, gradually becoming more like Christ. Through Chrismation, we receive the Holy Spirit, who strengthens us to live according to God's will.

After Baptism, the believer is not immediately free from the tendency to sin. The process of salvation involves continual spiritual growth and purification. This requires ongoing effort to align our will with God's, cooperating with His grace.

Key Takeaways
Salvation in Orthodox Christianity is not about paying a debt to the devil or appeasing God's wrath but is centered on Christ's voluntary self-offering, which liberates humanity from sin, death, and the devil.

Christ's work of salvation is accomplished through His Crucifixion and Resurrection, which defeated death and offers humanity the possibility of eternal life.

Baptism and Chrismation are essential first steps in participating in Christ's redemptive work, initiating believers into the life of grace and empowering them to live as children of God.

Salvation is a process that begins with Baptism, but involves ongoing purification and transformation, which the Orthodox Church calls Theosis—becoming more like Christ. The role of the Church is to nurture this process.

Study Questions

1. What does "ransom" mean in Orthodox theology, and how does it differ from the understanding of ransom in some other Christian traditions?

2. How does Christ's self-offering, motivated by love, change our understanding of His death and resurrection?

3. In what ways does the concept of salvation as Theosis challenge the idea of salvation as a one-time event? How does this affect our Christian life?

4. Why is Baptism and Chrismation so central to the Orthodox process of salvation, and what do they signify in terms of our relationship with God?

5. How can we actively participate in this process of salvation, and what practices can help us on this journey?

6. How does Christ's Resurrection inspire hope in your daily life?

General vs. Personal Salvation

It is important to distinguish between general and personal salvation. General salvation refers to the universal gift of salvation made available to all through Christ's Incarnation, Crucifixion and Resurrection. In contrast, personal salvation depends on each individual's response to and cooperation with God's grace. While Christ's redemptive work is offered to all, salvation requires personal participation to be fully realized.

General Salvation

Through Christ's Incarnation, Crucifixion and Resurrection, all of humanity is offered the possibility of reconciliation with God. The acts of Christ open the door to eternal life for all people. It makes salvation available to every person, regardless of their individual actions or beliefs. All of humanity is called to be saved. As John the Baptist proclaimed,

> *Behold the Lamb of God, Who takes away the sin of the world* (John 1:29).

and St. John the Apostle emphasized,

> *He is the propitiation for our sins, and not for ours only, but also for the sins of the whole world* (1 John 2:2).

This universal act of salvation is offered freely to all, but each person must respond to it.

Personal Salvation

For personal salvation each individual must actively cooperate with God's grace through repentance, faith, and participation in the sacraments in the Church. Personal salvation is not a one-time event but a lifelong journey of transformation, where believers align their will with God's. As St. Paul writes,

> *Work out your salvation with fear and trembling* (Philippians 2:12).

This process calls for a conscious choice to follow Christ, to obey His commandments, and to reject sin. This demands ongoing effort and continual cooperation with God's grace. It is a dynamic journey of spiritual growth in which the believer's heart and actions are progressively transformed to reflect the likeness of Christ.

Role of Synergia and Cooperation with Grace—the Holy Spirit
The first step is to embrace the truth of Christ's gift—the possibility of salvation. From this foundation, we must then act with the cooperation of our human free will in harmony with His divine grace, a process known as synergia.

Synergia (Greek for "co-working"), means that while God freely offers His grace through the Holy Spirit, we must respond by participating in that grace through faith, works, and spiritual disciplines.

Synergia emphasizes the essential role of human free will in the process of salvation. While God provides all the necessary grace for salvation, humans are called to actively respond and participate in this grace. This cooperation is expressed through a willingness to follow God's commandments, engage in the sacraments, engage in the recommended spiritual disciplines and continually purify ourselves from sin. Through this dynamic partnership, we align our will with God's and are transformed into the likeness of Christ.

Faith and Works
Faith alone is not sufficient; it must be accompanied by works—acts of love, mercy, and obedience to God's will. As St. James writes, *Faith without works is dead.* (James 2:17). These works are the natural fruit of genuine faith and a life transformed by God's grace.

Saint Gregory Palamas teaches that salvation is not limited to those who achieve perfection in this life. Even those who struggle to purify their souls are on the path of salvation, provided they persevere in their efforts. This continual struggle against sin and commitment to growth in holiness are essential aspects of the spiritual journey toward union with God.

Purification: Overcoming the Passions
In our fallen condition, humanity is marred by what the Orthodox tradition calls the passions—the distorted desires and tendencies that incline us toward sin. Purification is a critical part of the salvation process, helping believers overcome these passions and live in accordance with God's will. As Scripture teaches,

Nothing unclean can enter the Kingdom of God
(Eph 5:5, Rev 21:27).

Salvation, therefore, involves not only forgiveness for sins but also the purification of the soul to overcome the tendency to sin.

Purification is achieved through a life lived in accordance with God's commandments, aided by His grace. The sacraments and ascetic practices offered by the Church help tame the passions and purify the soul. This process is not about achieving moral perfection but about striving to live in harmony with God's will, continually seeking His help through prayer, repentance, and sacramental participation.

Ascetic Practices: Aids for Spiritual Growth

It is necessary for believers to engage in ascetic practices to cleanse the heart and mind. Practices such as prayer, fasting, and almsgiving are not meant to "earn" salvation but to foster humility, discipline, and self-control. These spiritual disciplines help believers struggle against the passions and desires that separate them from God, creating space in their lives for God's grace to work.

- Prayer: A vital connection to God that fosters a spirit of humility and dependence on His grace.
- Fasting: A tool for self-discipline and detachment from worldly desires, helping believers focus on their spiritual growth.
- Almsgiving: An act of love and mercy that reflects God's generosity and strengthens our communion with others.

The Role of the Sacraments

The sacraments are central to the believer's spiritual life and play a crucial role in the process of salvation. Each sacrament is a means of participating with God's grace and being strengthened for the journey toward union with Him:

- Baptism: Marks the beginning of the believer's spiritual rebirth, cleansing them from sin and uniting them with Christ's death and Resurrection.
- Chrismation: The anointing with the Holy Spirit that empowers the believer to live as a child of God.

- The Eucharist: The Body and Blood of Christ, which nourishes the soul and strengthens the believer to live according to God's will.

These sacred acts are not merely symbolic but are real encounters with God's grace. They provide the spiritual sustenance needed for purification, growth in holiness, and the ongoing process of salvation.

The Transformative Role of the Holy Spirit in Salvation

The Holy Spirit plays a vital and transformative role in our salvation. It is through the Holy Spirit that we participate in the sacraments of the Church and are empowered to grow in holiness, overcoming sin and weakness. This divine cooperation, where the Holy Spirit works with our free will, is essential for salvation. Without the Spirit's active presence, our human efforts would fall short of attaining the fullness of salvation. Through continual cooperation with the Holy Spirit, we are gradually purified and transformed, seeking union with God and eternal life in His Kingdom.

The Holy Spirit After Christ's Ascension

After His Ascension, Christ sent the Holy Spirit to empower His disciples to become more like Him, to heal, and to establish the Church as the vehicle for proclaiming the Good News. This same Spirit, given to all believers in Baptism and Chrismation, is indispensable for cooperating with God's will. The Holy Spirit enables us to walk faithfully according to God's commandments and to grow in virtue. As St. Paul exhorts, we must learn to walk in the Spirit, not according to the flesh or worldly desires, allowing the Spirit to direct our lives in ways that reflect Christ's love and holiness (Galatians 5:16).

St. Paul explains this dynamic role of the Holy Spirit:

For the law of the Spirit of life in Christ Jesus has made me free from the law of sin and death. For what the law could not do in that it was weak through the flesh, God did by sending His own Son in the likeness of sinful flesh, on account of sin: He condemned sin in the flesh, that the righteous requirement of the law might be fulfilled in us who do not walk according to the flesh but according to the Spirit (Romans 8:2-4).

For to be carnally minded is death, but to be spiritually minded is life and peace (Romans 8:6).

These verses emphasize the crucial difference between living according to the flesh and living according to the Spirit, underscoring the Spirit's role in leading believers into holiness and newness of life.

Cultivating an Awareness of the Holy Spirit — Spiritual warfare

To live a Spirit-filled life, we must actively cultivate an awareness of the Holy Spirit within us, inviting Him to guide us toward virtue, holiness, and goodness. This requires the purification of the heart, as Christ promises in Matthew 5:8:

> *Blessed are the pure in heart, for they shall see God.*

This purification, often referred to as spiritual warfare, is central to our salvation. It is an ongoing process that demands our cooperation with the Holy Spirit. This cooperation involves both resisting sin and positively cultivating virtues through practices such as prayer, fasting, and participation in the sacraments. Through these spiritual disciplines, we align our will with God's and grow in holiness.

Spiritual warfare is not merely about avoiding sin but about being actively conformed to the likeness of Christ. The Holy Spirit empowers us in this struggle, providing strength and grace to persevere. By relying on the Spirit's guidance, we are gradually transformed, growing in faith and love, and being prepared for eternal communion with God.

The Kinds of Works Required for Salvation

Orthodox Christianity teaches that works, especially those that reflect God's love, are necessary for salvation. These works provide visible evidence of a transformed life, showing that faith is alive and active.

Works that Reflect God's Love:

In the Sermon on the Mount (Matthew 5–7), Jesus emphasizes that the works accepted by God must flow from genuine love and humility. These include:

- Acts of Kindness, Mercy, and Forgiveness: Demonstrating love for one's neighbor and embodying God's compassion.
- Selflessness and Meekness: Living in humility and placing others' needs above one's own.

- Ascetic Efforts: Practices such as prayer and fasting, which purify the soul, discipline the will, and draw the believer closer to God.

These works not only reflect God's love but also help the believer overcome sinful tendencies and grow in virtue.

Faith and Works in Harmony
Faith provides the foundation and vision for a life oriented toward God, while works provide the tangible pathway for living out that vision. Together, faith and works enable believers to grow in holiness, align their will with God's, and move closer to union with Him.

Orthodox Christianity emphasizes that true faith is not passive but must be expressed through action. As St. James teaches, *Faith without works is dead* (James 2:17). By combining faith with works, believers cooperate with God's grace, manifest the love of Christ in their lives, and progress toward the ultimate goal of salvation: union with God.

Conclusion: The Lifelong Journey of Salvation
In Orthodox Christianity, salvation is not a one-time event but a lifelong journey. While Christ has already accomplished the work of redemption, each believer must cooperate with God's grace through faith, works, and participation in the life of the Church. The Church, as the Body of Christ, nurtures believers through the sacraments, prayer, and ascetic practices, helping them grow in holiness and move closer to union with God. This ongoing process gradually transforms believers into the image of Christ, preparing them for eternal life with God in His Kingdom.

Study Questions

1. What does synergia mean in the context of salvation, and how does it influence the way we live out our faith?

2. How do ascetic practices like prayer, fasting, and almsgiving contribute to the purification of the soul in Orthodox theology?

3. What is the difference between general salvation and personal salvation in the Orthodox Church, and why is the personal response essential?

4. How does the Holy Spirit help believers in their journey of salvation, and what role does the Spirit play in the process of Theosis?

5. In what ways do faith and works work together to bring about salvation, and how can we ensure that our actions reflect a transformed life in Christ?

The Church and the Nicene Creed: Doctrine on the Nature of Christ and the Holy Trinity

The Church

Christ established the Church as a means to provide us with the necessary help of the Holy Spirit to overcome our sinful tendencies and receive spiritual healing. Through the Church, the Holy Spirit works within us, guiding and empowering us to live in accordance with God's will. This healing and transformation are only accessible through the Church—the Holy, Universal, and Apostolic Church, which preserves and administers the means of salvation. Our rebirth begins with Baptism, which initiates us into the life of the Church, and is nurtured through the sacraments and spiritual disciplines that the Church offers. The ultimate goal of the Church is to perfect us in cooperation with God, enabling us to live with love and in union with Him. The Church is thus our Spiritual Hospital, where we are continually healed, strengthened, and prepared for eternal life with God.

The Nicene Creed

The Church, as the Body of Christ, holds to the foundational truths of the Christian faith as expressed in the Nicene Creed (page 130), which defines the nature of Christ and the Holy Trinity. The Creed serves as a concise summary of the essential doctrines of the faith, passed down from the Apostles through the Church's Tradition, and it is recited in every Divine Liturgy to reaffirm our belief in the one true God and the salvific work of Christ.

The authority and creation of the Nicene Creed stem from the early Church's need to define and safeguard the core doctrines of the Christian faith, particularly in response to various heresies that arose in the first few centuries. In 325 AD, the First Ecumenical Council of Nicaea, convened by Emperor Constantine, sought to address the Arian controversy, which denied the full divinity of Christ. The resulting Creed was a clear and authoritative statement affirming the divinity of Christ, His equality with the Father, and the doctrine of the Holy Trinity. The Nicene Creed was further refined at the Council of Constantinople in 381 AD, solidifying the Church's teaching on the Holy Spirit and affirming the unity of the Father, Son, and Holy Spirit as one God in three Persons. The Creed, as a result, became the standard declaration of Christian faith, uniting all Orthodox believers in the essential truths of the gospel. It holds ultimate authority as a reflection of the apostolic faith and remains a central part of Christian worship, recited in liturgies worldwide as a testament to the Church's commitment to the truth revealed by God.

The Holy Trinity
The doctrine of the Holy Trinity teaches that God is one in essence but exists in three distinct Persons: the Father, the Son, and the Holy Spirit. This means that while God is one, He exists in perfect communion and unity as three persons, coequal and coeternal. The Father is the source of all life, the Son is begotten of the Father, and the Holy Spirit proceeds from the Father, working in perfect unity with the Father and the Son.

The Nicene Creed opens with the declaration of belief in the one true God, the Father Almighty, the Creator of heaven and earth. It then affirms the divinity of Jesus Christ, the Son of God, and the work of the Holy Spirit, which proceeds from the Father. The Creed's formulation of the Trinity underscores the eternal relationship and unity of the three Persons while maintaining the distinctiveness of each.

The Nature of Christ
The central focus of the Creed is the belief in the nature of Christ—His divinity and His humanity, united in the person of Jesus Christ. The Creed affirms that Jesus Christ is "the only-begotten Son of God, begotten of the Father before all worlds." This means that Christ is eternal, having existed with the Father from the beginning and sharing fully in the divine nature.

The Creed also affirms the Incarnation: "Who, for us men and for our salvation, came down from heaven, and was incarnate by the Holy Spirit of the Virgin Mary, and was made man." This statement encapsulates the central mystery of the Christian faith—that God became man in the person of Jesus Christ, remaining fully divine while becoming fully human. Christ's divinity and humanity are united without confusion, so that He is both fully God and fully man, allowing Him to reconcile humanity to God through His life, death, and resurrection.

The Creed further affirms Christ's redemptive work: "And was crucified also for us under Pontius Pilate; He suffered and was buried." His crucifixion, death, and burial were essential to the salvation of humanity, as through His sacrifice, Christ took on the consequences of sin and death, offering humanity the possibility of eternal life. "And the third day He rose again, according to the Scriptures." The resurrection of Christ is the triumph over death, confirming His divine nature and sealing the victory over sin and death that He won for humanity.

Finally, the Creed confesses Christ's exaltation: "And He ascended into heaven, and sits on the right hand of the Father." Christ's ascension marks the completion of His earthly mission and the beginning of His reign in glory, where He intercedes for humanity before the Father, preparing a place for all who follow Him.

The Role of the Holy Spirit

The Holy Spirit, the third Person of the Holy Trinity, plays a crucial role in the life of the Church and in the sanctification of believers. The Creed states: "And I believe in the Holy Spirit, the Lord, the Giver of Life, who proceeds from the Father, who with the Father and the Son together is worshiped and glorified." The Holy Spirit is the life-giver, the one who empowers believers to live according to God's will and who sanctifies them, making them partakers of God's divine nature.

The Spirit works through the Church, guiding believers into all truth, and through the sacraments, especially through Baptism and the Eucharist, He unites the faithful with Christ and empowers them to live as children of God. The Holy Spirit is also present in the life of the Church, sustaining it through His gifts and guiding it toward the fulfillment of God's Kingdom.

Conclusion

The Nicene Creed provides a clear and concise summary of the Church's doctrine on the nature of Christ and the Holy Trinity. It affirms the divinity and humanity of Christ, the eternal relationship of the Father, Son, and Holy Spirit, and the redemptive work of Christ through His life, death, resurrection, and ascension. The Creed encapsulates the faith that has been handed down through the centuries, forming the foundation of Christian belief and guiding the life of the Church. By confessing this faith, Christians affirm their belief in the triune God and the saving work of Christ for the redemption of humanity.

The Nicene Creed

I believe in one God, Father Almighty, Creator of heaven and earth, and of all things visible and invisible.

And in one Lord Jesus Christ, the only-begotten Son of God, begotten of the Father before all ages; Light of Light, true God of true God, begotten, not created, of one essence with the Father through Whom all things were made. Who for us men and for our salvation came down from heaven and was incarnate of the Holy Spirit and the Virgin Mary and became man. He was crucified for us under Pontius Pilate, and suffered and was buried; And He rose on the third day, according to the Scriptures. He ascended into heaven and is seated at the right hand of the Father; And He will come again with glory to judge the living and dead. His kingdom shall have no end.

And in the Holy Spirit, the Lord, the Creator of life, Who proceeds from the Father, Who together with the Father and the Son is worshipped and glorified, Who spoke through the prophets.

In one, holy, catholic, and apostolic Church.

I confess one baptism for the forgiveness of sins.

I look for the resurrection of the dead, and the life of the age to come.

Amen

Study Questions

1. Why did Christ establish the Church, and what role does the Church play in the spiritual healing and transformation of believers?

2. How does the Nicene Creed define the relationship between the Father, Son, and Holy Spirit, and what is the significance of this doctrine for understanding the Holy Trinity?

3. What does the Nicene Creed teach about the nature of Christ, and how does it affirm both His divinity and His humanity?

4. What is the role of the Holy Spirit in the Church, and how does the Spirit work in the lives of believers according to the Nicene Creed?

5. How does the Nicene Creed summarize Christ's redemptive work, including His crucifixion, resurrection, and ascension? Why are these events central to Christian faith?

Chapter 7

Preservation of Apostolic Doctrine in the Orthodox Church

The Orthodox Church holds that it has faithfully preserved the doctrine of the Apostles unchanged throughout its history. This fidelity to Apostolic teaching is a hallmark of Orthodoxy, rooted in the belief that the Church is the Body of Christ and guided by the Holy Spirit. This chapter explores how the Orthodox Church has maintained doctrinal continuity through its structure, practices, and reliance on Holy Tradition.

First we discuss the Apostolic Foundation. This includes Apostolic succession and the Holy Tradition of the Church. Second, we address the important role of the Ecumenical Councils to defend the faith from Heresy. Third is a review of the schism and divisions that were dealt with. Fourth, innovations introduced by the Catholic Church after the split, and fifth, innovations introduced by Protestants in the Reformation and other factors like monasticism.

Apostolic Foundations

The Apostolic Mission
The Church was founded by Jesus Christ, who commissioned His Apostles to preach the Gospel to all nations, saying:
> *Go therefore and make disciples of all nations, baptizing them in the name of the Father and of the Son and of the Holy Spirit, teaching them to observe all that I have commanded you* (Matthew 28:19–20).

Empowered by the Holy Spirit at Pentecost (Acts 2), the Apostles began spreading the faith, establishing communities of believers, and teaching them the doctrines of Christ. Their mission was not only to proclaim the Good News but to ensure the preservation of the Truth as they had witnessed and been taught by Christ. As the Apostle Peter writes:
> *I have written briefly, exhorting and testifying that this is the true grace of God in which you stand* (1 Peter 5:12).

This commitment to preserving the true teaching is why the Church is called the Orthodox Church. The term "Orthodox" comes from the Greek words orthos (straight or right) and doxa (glory or opinion), meaning "right opinion" or "true glory." Throughout history, the Church has encountered numerous attempts to distort the Apostolic teachings, but guided by the Holy Spirit, it has consistently proclaimed the Truth handed down by the Apostles.

Apostolic Succession
One of the primary ways the Orthodox Church has preserved Apostolic doctrine is through Apostolic Succession. This is the unbroken line of bishops descending directly from the Apostles, who were given their authority by Christ Himself. Through Apostolic Succession, the Church ensures the continuity of teaching and leadership, as each bishop receives the authority to preserve and transmit the faith entrusted to the Apostles.

St. Paul instructed his disciple Timothy:
> *Guard what was committed to your trust* (1 Timothy 6:20).

This charge reflects the sacred duty of the Church to safeguard the Apostolic teaching. Through the ordination of clergy—bishops, priests, and deacons—the Orthodox Church continues to uphold the faith and doctrine passed down from the Apostles, ensuring the integrity of the Gospel message throughout the generations.

Holy Tradition: The Life of the Church

Scripture and Tradition

The Orthodox Church teaches that Holy Tradition encompasses the entire life of the Church, serving as the context in which the Scriptures were written, compiled, and interpreted. Holy Tradition is not separate from Scripture but includes it as an integral part. Tradition also consists of the oral teachings of the Apostles, the writings of the Church Fathers, the liturgical practices of the Church, the decisions of Ecumenical Councils, and the lives and witness of the saints. This holistic understanding ensures that the faith remains consistent with the Apostolic teaching across generations, preserving the truth in its fullness.

The Role of the Church Fathers

In early Christian writings, there is frequent mention of maintaining "the rule of faith" and "the rule of truth," emphasizing the Church's responsibility to guard the Apostolic teaching. The Church Fathers played a vital role in this endeavor, expounding on Scripture, addressing heresies, and articulating doctrine to safeguard the faith. Figures such as St. Athanasius, St. Basil the Great, and St. John Chrysostom are exemplary in their efforts to preserve and transmit the Apostolic doctrine. Their works remain foundational to Orthodox theology, offering clarity and depth while addressing the challenges of their time.

For instance, St. Athanasius defended the divinity of Christ against Arianism, St. Basil the Great expounded on the Holy Spirit's role in the Trinity, and St. John Chrysostom illuminated Scripture with his profound homilies. Together, the Church Fathers form a unified voice of theological clarity, continually guiding the Church in faithfulness to the Apostolic tradition.

Liturgical Life

The liturgical life of the Orthodox Church is not only a form of worship but also a means of preserving and transmitting doctrine. The prayers, hymns, and structure of the Divine Liturgy are imbued with theology, reflecting and affirming the Apostolic teaching.

For example, the Nicene Creed, recited during every Divine Liturgy, is a concise and definitive summary of the Orthodox faith, established by the first two Ecumenical Councils. The liturgy serves as a living expression of Holy Tradition, teaching the faithful about the nature of God, the Incarnation, the Resurrection, and the hope of eternal life. In this way, worship becomes both an act of glorification and a means of theological instruction, uniting the faithful in truth and love.

Study Questions

1. What is the significance of the Apostolic Mission in the establishment of the Church, and how does it relate to the Orthodox Church's commitment to preserving the truth?

2. How does Apostolic Succession ensure the continuity of Apostolic teaching and leadership in the Orthodox Church? Reflect on the role of bishops in this process.

3. Explain the relationship between Scripture and Holy Tradition in the Orthodox Church. How does Holy Tradition contribute to the preservation and interpretation of the Christian faith?

4. What role did the Church Fathers play in safeguarding Apostolic doctrine, and how do their writings continue to shape Orthodox theology today?

Defending the Faith from Heresy

Conciliar Nature of the Church
The conciliar nature of the Orthodox Church is fundamental to its understanding of governance and decision-making. In Orthodoxy, the Church is not governed by a single individual or centralized authority but operates through a system of councils (synods) where decisions are made collectively by the bishops, in communion with the clergy and laity, under the guidance of the Holy Spirit. This conciliarity reflects the belief that the Church, as the Body of Christ, is a living community where the faithful, guided by the Holy Spirit, discern and safeguard the truth of the Gospel. Ecumenical Councils, such as those that defined key doctrines of the faith, and local synods, which address regional matters, are vital expressions of this conciliarity. The process ensures that the Church's teachings remain faithful to the Apostolic Tradition, maintaining unity and continuity across time. The conciliar nature of the Church thus emphasizes both the collegiality of the bishops and the participation of the entire Body of Christ in the preservation and transmission of the faith.

The first recorded conciliar action in the early Church, as described in Scripture, occurred during the Jerusalem Council in Acts 15. The issue at hand was whether Gentile converts to Christianity needed to be circumcised and follow the Mosaic Law in order to be saved. This controversy arose as some Jewish Christians insisted that circumcision was necessary for salvation, while others, particularly the Apostles Paul and Barnabas, argued that Gentiles should not be burdened with the requirements of the Law. The council, convened in Jerusalem by the Apostles and elders, deliberated the issue, prayerfully seeking the guidance of the Holy Spirit. After careful discussion, the council issued a decree stating that Gentile converts were not required to be circumcised but should abstain from certain practices that were particularly offensive to Jewish believers. This decision, recorded in Acts 15:28-29, marked a pivotal moment in the early Church, affirming that salvation comes through grace, not through adherence to the Law, and that the unity of the Church was to be preserved despite cultural and ethnic differences. This first conciliar action set a precedent for the Church's practice of gathering in council to address theological disputes and to guide the faithful in preserving the purity of the Apostolic faith.

Ecumenical Councils

The Ecumenical Councils were gatherings of all the Bishops of the Church. They serve as a vital means by which the Orthodox Church preserves and protects the truth of the Apostolic faith across time. These councils were convened to address specific theological controversies and heresies that arose in the early centuries of Christianity, ensuring that the Church's doctrine remained true to the teachings of Christ and the Apostles. Rather than introducing new ideas or doctrines, the councils clarified and defined the core truths of the Christian faith that had already been handed down. Each council's decisions were not seen as innovations, but as faithful expressions of the truth, reaffirming the Church's commitment to maintaining the unbroken transmission of the Apostolic faith.

Major Councils and Their Contributions

First Ecumenical Council (Nicea, 325)

The First Ecumenical Council was convened to address Arianism, a heresy that claimed that Christ was a created being and not fully divine. The council declared that Christ is "of one essence with the Father" (homoousios), affirming the full divinity of Christ. This declaration was foundational for Christian theology and safeguarded the orthodox understanding of the nature of Christ. The council also formulated the Nicene Creed, which serves as a succinct summary of the Apostolic faith and is used in Orthodox liturgy to this day.

Second Ecumenical Council (Constantinople, 381)

The Second Ecumenical Council addressed Macedonianism, a heresy that denied the divinity of the Holy Spirit. It reaffirmed the teaching that the Holy Spirit is co-equal and co-eternal with the Father and the Son, completing the revelation of the Holy Trinity. The Nicene Creed was expanded to include a more detailed confession of faith regarding the Holy Spirit, making it the Nicene-Constantinopolitan Creed. This council emphasized that the Creed should remain unaltered and upheld the unity and co-equality of the three persons of the Trinity.

Third Ecumenical Council (Ephesus, 431)

This council addressed Nestorianism, a heresy that sought to separate the divine and human natures of Christ, and that denied Mary the title of Theotokos (Mother of God). The council declared that Mary is indeed Theotokos, because she gave birth to the person of Jesus Christ, who is both fully God and fully man. By affirming the unity of Christ's person and the inseparable nature of His two natures, this council defended the Orthodox understanding of the Incarnation and the role of the Virgin Mary in salvation.

Fourth Ecumenical Council (Chalcedon, 451)

The Fourth Ecumenical Council responded to the heresy of Monophysitism, which overemphasized the divine nature of Christ to the point of denying His true humanity. The council defined the doctrine of the two natures of Christ—divine and human—as existing "without confusion, without change, without division, and without separation." This Chalcedonian definition is essential to Orthodox Christology, affirming that Christ is fully God and fully man, a doctrine that protects the integrity of both His divine and human natures in the mystery of the Incarnation.

Fifth Ecumenical Council (Constantinople II, 553)

The Fifth Ecumenical Council dealt with lingering Christological controversies and reaffirmed the decisions made at the Council of Chalcedon. It sought to reconcile factions within the Church and clarify misunderstandings related to certain writings and individuals who were perceived to support Nestorianism, even implicitly. This council reinforced the unity of Christ's divine and human natures and emphasized that any teachings that undermine this unity should be rejected.

Sixth Ecumenical Council (Constantinople III, 680-681)

This council addressed Monothelitism, which claimed that Christ had only one will—the divine will—and denied the reality of His human will. The council affirmed that Christ has two wills, divine and human, and that these wills work in perfect harmony. This doctrine, known as Dyothelitism, is crucial because it teaches that Christ's human will was fully active in His obedience to the Father, thus providing a model for human cooperation with divine grace.

Seventh Ecumenical Council (Nicea, 787)
The Seventh Ecumenical Council addressed the heresy of Iconoclasm, which sought to abolish the veneration of icons, mistakenly viewing it as idolatry. The council reaffirmed the use of icons in the Church, emphasizing that the veneration of icons is not worship directed at the image itself, but an honor given to the person depicted—especially Christ and the saints. Icons, as windows to the divine, are seen as a reflection of the truth of the Incarnation, in which the invisible God became visible in Christ.

Defending the Apostolic Faith
The Ecumenical Councils were not moments of theological innovation, but were rather a faithful response to challenges that arose within the Church. They ensured that the teachings of the Apostles remained unaltered and that the Christian faith would not be distorted by heresies. The Orthodox Church sees these councils as the collective voice of the Church, guided by the Holy Spirit to safeguard the truth of the Gospel. The decisions made at these councils have been upheld throughout history and remain binding for Orthodox Christians today.

The Orthodox Church holds that the decisions of the Ecumenical Councils are expressions of the Church's "mind" or phronema, the collective understanding of the faith, which is preserved by the Holy Spirit. This understanding ensures that the faith is transmitted without distortion from generation to generation. The councils, by clarifying and codifying the truth, have preserved the unity of the Church and its witness to the Gospel, ensuring that the faith remains consistent across time and space. Through the Ecumenical Councils, the Church continues to uphold the truth of the Apostolic faith, defending it against false teachings and heresies.

Study Questions

1. How does the conciliar nature of the Orthodox Church ensure the preservation of the Apostolic faith and unity across time?

2. What was the central issue addressed at the Jerusalem Council in Acts 15, and how did it set a precedent for future conciliar actions in the Church?

3. In what ways did the First Ecumenical Council (Nicea, 325) address Arianism, and how did it contribute to the formulation of the Nicene Creed?

4. What was the key contribution of the Second Ecumenical Council (Constantinople, 381) in defining the doctrine of the Holy Trinity?

5. How did the Third Ecumenical Council (Ephesus, 431) defend the title of Theotokos for the Virgin Mary, and why is this significant for Orthodox Christology?

6. What was the heresy addressed by the Fourth Ecumenical Council (Chalcedon, 451), and how did the Chalcedonian Definition protect the integrity of Christ's divine and human natures?

7. How do the Ecumenical Councils, particularly the Seventh (Nicea, 787), defend key Orthodox teachings, such as the veneration of icons and the preservation of Apostolic Tradition?

Schisms and Divisions

The Great Schism (1054)
The Great Schism, also known as the East-West Schism, marks the formal division between the Eastern Orthodox Church and the Roman Catholic Church. It was the culmination of centuries of theological, liturgical, cultural, and political differences that had slowly developed between the Latin-speaking West and the Greek-speaking East. While there were tensions between the two branches of Christianity for many years, the events of 1054 made the division official. The Schism was not a single event but rather a series of disagreements that had built up over time. These disagreements were not solely theological but were also shaped by political power struggles, cultural differences, and ecclesiastical authority, leading to a deep rift that persists to this day.

Theological Disagreements
One of the central theological issues that contributed to the Schism was the Filioque controversy. The Latin Church, during the 6th century, added the phrase "and the Son" (Filioque) to the Nicene-Constantinopolitan Creed, which was originally established at the First and Second Ecumenical Councils. The phrase in the original creed stated that the Holy Spirit proceeds from the Father (John 15:26). However, the Latin Church altered this to say that the Holy Spirit proceeds from the Father and the Son. This change was made unilaterally by the Western Church and was never authorized by an Ecumenical Council, making it highly contentious.

The Eastern Orthodox Church rejected the Filioque addition, arguing that it was a theological and doctrinal distortion that undermined the unique role of the Father in the Holy Trinity. The Orthodox Church maintained that the original formulation of the Creed, as set forth by the Councils of Nicaea and Constantinople, should remain unaltered. According to Orthodox teaching, the Father is the sole source of the Holy Trinity, and any modification that implied a shared causality with the Son disrupted the perfect unity and distinctiveness of the persons of the Trinity.

This disagreement over the Filioque clause became a symbol of deeper theological tensions between the East and West, and the Western insistence on its inclusion became a significant point of contention in the growing rift between the two Churches.

Papal Authority
Another major point of disagreement that contributed to the Schism was the issue of papal authority. The Roman Catholic Church, based in the West, claimed that the Pope, as the Bishop of Rome, held supreme authority over the entire Christian Church, including the Eastern Churches. The Pope's claim to universal jurisdiction was grounded in the belief that Peter, the chief Apostle, was the first Pope and that his successors inherited this divine authority.

On the other hand, the Eastern Orthodox Church rejected the idea of papal supremacy. While the Orthodox Church acknowledged the honor and importance of the Bishop of Rome, it maintained that all bishops were equal and that authority in the Church should be shared among the bishops, with the Ecumenical Patriarch of Constantinople as "first among equals." The Orthodox Church also emphasized conciliar governance, in which decisions on matters of faith and practice were made by councils of bishops rather than by one central authority figure.

This difference in understanding of ecclesiastical authority led to significant tension between the two Churches. The Roman Catholic insistence on papal primacy was a central factor that divided the Eastern and Western branches of Christianity. The Orthodox Church viewed the papacy as a power grab that undermined the conciliar and collegial structure of the Church, while the Western Church saw the Pope's authority as divinely ordained and necessary for maintaining unity.

Liturgical and Cultural Differences
In addition to theological and ecclesiastical disagreements, there were also significant liturgical and cultural differences that contributed to the Schism. These differences reflected the diverse histories and traditions that had developed in the Eastern and Western parts of the Roman Empire.

> **Liturgical Practices:** The Eastern Orthodox Church and the Roman Catholic Church had different liturgical practices, including

variations in the celebration of the Divine Liturgy and the Mass. The Orthodox Church retained the ancient Christian tradition of using leavened bread in the Eucharist, while the Roman Catholic Church used unleavened bread. Additionally, the Orthodox Church maintained a more elaborate form of liturgical chant, while the Western Church developed its own style of liturgical music.

Clerical Celibacy: The Roman Catholic Church required celibacy for all clergy, including bishops and priests, while the Eastern Orthodox Church allowed married men to become priests (although bishops were required to be celibate). This difference in clerical practice further highlighted the cultural and theological divides between the two branches of the Church.

Cultural Differences: The cultural differences between the Greek-speaking East and the Latin-speaking West were also significant. Over time, these linguistic and cultural barriers became more pronounced. The Eastern Church was heavily influenced by Greek philosophy and theology, while the Western Church was shaped by Latin traditions and the rise of the Holy Roman Empire. These differences in language, philosophy, and political structure further deepened the divide between the two Churches.

The Final Break: 1054
In 1054, the conflict between the Eastern and Western Churches reached its climax. The Pope, Leo IX, sent a delegation to Constantinople, led by Cardinal Humbert, to assert papal authority over the Eastern Church. The Patriarch of Constantinople at the time, Michael I Cerularius, was strongly opposed to papal claims and had already taken steps to distance the Eastern Church from Rome. When the papal legates arrived in Constantinople, tensions were high, and after several confrontations, Cardinal Humbert excommunicated Patriarch Michael. In response, Patriarch Michael excommunicated the papal legates, thus formalizing the split between the Eastern and Western Churches.

While the excommunications of 1054 were not immediately recognized by all members of the Church, they symbolized the growing divide between the East and West. Over time, the Schism deepened, and the political and theological differences between the two Churches hardened. The mutual excommunications were not formally lifted until 1965, during the Second Vatican Council, when Pope Paul VI and Patriarch Athenagoras I mutually removed the excommunications, though full communion between the Churches has not been restored.

Lasting Effects
The Great Schism of 1054 had a lasting impact on the Christian world. The division between the Roman Catholic Church and the Eastern Orthodox Church continues to this day, with each Church maintaining its distinct theological, liturgical, and ecclesiastical practices. Despite efforts at dialogue and reconciliation, the Schism remains a powerful reminder of the challenges of maintaining unity within the Body of Christ.

The Schism also had profound effects on the history of Europe and the wider world. It helped shape the political and cultural development of the Byzantine Empire in the East and the rise of the Holy Roman Empire in the West. It also contributed to the development of different Christian theological traditions, with the Eastern Orthodox Church emphasizing the importance of Tradition, conciliar governance, and the mystery of the Incarnation, while the Roman Catholic Church developed its doctrines of papal supremacy and the role of the Church in salvation.

Conclusion
The Great Schism of 1054 was not the result of a single event but rather a series of theological, liturgical, political, and cultural disagreements that had been developing over centuries. At the heart of the Schism were the Filioque controversy, the issue of papal authority, and differences in liturgical practices. While both the Eastern Orthodox Church and the Roman Catholic Church share a common Christian heritage, the division that occurred in 1054 continues to affect the relationship between the two Churches. The Orthodox Church maintains the Tradition as established by the Apostles while the Roman Church has introduced additional innovation in addition to the issue involved in the Great schism. Despite the divisions, efforts for dialogue and ecumenical understanding continue, with the hope of eventual reconciliation and the restoration of unity in the Church.

Study Questions

1. What were the theological, political, and cultural factors that contributed to the Great Schism of 1054 between the Eastern Orthodox and Roman Catholic Churches?

2. Explain the Filioque controversy and its role in the division between the Eastern and Western Churches. How did the Orthodox Church respond to the addition of "and the Son" in the Nicene Creed?

3. How did the issue of papal authority contribute to the Great Schism? What was the Orthodox Church's stance on papal supremacy, and how did it differ from the Roman Catholic understanding of the Pope's authority?

4. In what ways did liturgical and cultural differences between the East and West influence the division between the two Churches? Provide examples of these differences in practice.

Other Innovations Introduced in the Roman Catholic Church since the Great Schism.

Since the Great Schism of 1054, the Roman Catholic Church has introduced several innovations that the Orthodox Church views as departures from Apostolic Tradition. These innovations have contributed to the theological and liturgical differences between the two Churches. Below is a list of some of the key innovations:

In addition to the filioque clause and papal infallibility discussed in a previous section, the Catholic Church in more recent times has introduced additional changes.

The Immaculate Conception of the Virgin Mary:
The Roman Catholic Church proclaimed the dogma of the Immaculate Conception in 1854, teaching that the Virgin Mary was conceived without original sin. The Orthodox Church venerates the Virgin Mary as "All-Holy" (Panagia), but it does not accept the dogma of the Immaculate Conception, believing that all humans, including Mary, are born with a tendency to sin (ancesttral sin) and that Mary's holiness comes through her cooperation with God's grace.

Transubstantiation:
The Catholic doctrine of transubstantiation, formally defined at the Fourth Lateran Council (1215), teaches that during the celebration of the Eucharist, the substance of bread and wine is transformed into the actual body and blood of Christ, while retaining the appearance of bread and wine. The Orthodox Church believes in the real presence of Christ in the Eucharist but rejects the specific philosophical explanation of transubstantiation, maintaining that the mystery of the Eucharist cannot be fully explained in human terms.

The Use of Unleavened Bread in the Eucharist:
The Catholic Church uses unleavened bread (azymes) in the celebration of the Eucharist, while the Orthodox Church uses leavened bread. The Orthodox Church sees the use of leavened bread as symbolizing the risen Christ, while the use of unleavened bread in the Catholic Church is seen as a symbol of the Passover meal.

The Doctrine of Purgatory:
The Catholic Church teaches the existence of purgatory, a temporary state where souls are purified before entering heaven. While the Orthodox Church acknowledges the reality of post-mortem purification, it does not hold to the specific doctrine of purgatory as defined by the Catholic Church, nor does it emphasize it to the same extent.

The Assumption of the Virgin Mary:
In 1950, the Catholic Church declared the dogma of the Assumption, which teaches that the Virgin Mary was taken bodily into heaven at the end of her earthly life. While the Orthodox Church honors the Dormition of the Theotokos (the death and falling asleep of the Virgin Mary), it does not accept the dogma of her Assumption, viewing it as an innovation beyond the teachings of the early Church. Orthodox theologians believe that Mary's deification was not a transformation from humanity to divinity, but rather her falling asleep and being raised up by her Son. Orthodox churches are wary to seeing Mary as being similar to Christ. They say that she was a human being just like you and me but one who was able to live a sinless life.

The Development of the Rosary:
The Rosary, as a form of prayer and devotion to the Virgin Mary, became a widespread Catholic practice during the Middle Ages. The prominence of the rosary is linked to alleged Marian apparitions, which the Orthodox Church does not accept. While the Orthodox Church also venerates the Virgin Mary and uses prayer ropes for personal devotion with a focus on the Name of Jesus. The Rosary is not a part of Orthodox spiritual practice.

The Use of Latin in the Liturgy:
The Catholic Church, particularly after the 12th century, adopted Latin as the official liturgical language, even in places where the local language was different. The Orthodox Church, on the other hand, has always used the vernacular or local languages in its liturgical services, maintaining a closer connection to the original languages of the Bible and the early Church.

These innovations, while central to the Roman Catholic Church, are viewed by the Orthodox Church as deviations from the practices and teachings of the early Church. The Orthodox Church believes that it has preserved the Apostolic Tradition without adding these later doctrines and practices that were introduced in the West after the Great Schism.

Study Questions

1. How does the Orthodox Church view the development of papal supremacy and papal infallibility in the Roman Catholic Church, and how does this differ from the Orthodox understanding of ecclesiastical authority?

2. What is the Orthodox Church's response to the Filioque clause added to the Nicene Creed by the Roman Catholic Church, and why does the Orthodox Church maintain the original wording of the Creed?

3. How does the Orthodox Church's understanding of the Assumption of the Virgin Mary differ from the Catholic dogma, and why does the Orthodox Church emphasize the Dormition instead?

4. What is the Orthodox Church's stance on the doctrine of purgatory, and how does it differ from the Catholic understanding of post-mortem purification?

Innovations Introduced by the Protestants in the Reformation

The Protestant Reformation introduced several theological and ecclesiastical innovations that significantly diverged from the Apostolic doctrine preserved by the Orthodox Church. The Orthodox Church maintains that it has remained faithful to the original teachings of Christ and the Apostles, as transmitted through the Church's Sacred Tradition. In contrast, the Reformation introduced new ideas that the Orthodox Church views as departures from this Tradition. Here is a list of key innovations introduced by the Reformers, highlighting how they differ from the Apostolic doctrine of the Orthodox Church:

Sola Scriptura (Scripture Alone)
Innovation: The principle of Sola Scriptura asserts that the Bible alone is the ultimate authority in matters of faith and practice, rejecting the authority of Sacred Tradition and the Church's magisterium.

The Orthodox Church teaches that both Scripture and Holy Tradition are essential to understanding the fullness of the Christian faith. Scripture emerged from the Church's Tradition, and it cannot be separated from the lived experience of the Church, including the teachings of the Fathers, the Ecumenical Councils, and liturgical practices. The Orthodox Church rejects the idea that Scripture alone is sufficient for salvation and doctrine. This is considered a very serious error.

Sola Fide (Faith Alone)
Innovation: The doctrine of Sola Fide asserts that salvation is achieved through faith alone, apart from any works or sacraments.

The Orthodox Church teaches that salvation involves both faith and works, rooted in the transformative grace of God. Orthodox theology emphasizes synergy—the cooperation between God's grace and human free will. This means that works (such as participation in the sacraments, acts of charity, and obedience to God's commandments) are seen as necessary responses to God's grace, not as the means of earning salvation but as expressions of living faith. Often this leads to a passive view of salvation and a rejection of the ascetic practices taught by the Orthodox Church.

Sola Gratia (Grace Alone)

Innovation: Sola Gratia teaches that salvation is by grace alone, not by any merit or human effort.

While the Orthodox Church agrees that salvation is a gift of God's grace, it teaches that this grace works in cooperation with human will, enabling believers to live in accordance with God's commandments. The Orthodox Church does not view salvation as something entirely outside of human participation. Synergy between divine grace and human freedom is a core Orthodox teaching.

The Priesthood of All Believers

Innovation: The Reformation emphasized the priesthood of all believers, meaning that all Christians have direct access to God and do not need a priest to mediate between them and God.

The Orthodox Church maintains the necessity of the sacramental priesthood, which it believes was instituted by Christ and handed down through the Apostles. Priests are seen as essential mediators in the sacramental life of the Church, administering the mysteries (sacraments) of salvation such as Baptism, Eucharist, and Confession. While all baptized Christians share in the priesthood of Christ in a broader sense, the Orthodox Church upholds the distinctive role of ordained clergy.

Rejection of Papal Authority

Innovation: The Protestant Reformers rejected the papal authority of the Roman Catholic Church, which claimed universal jurisdiction over the Church and its teachings.

The Orthodox Church also rejects papal supremacy but affirms the role of the bishop of Rome as the "first among equals" in the collegial leadership of the Church. The Orthodox Church is governed by a conciliar system, where authority resides in the collective body of bishops (Ecumenical Councils), not in any one bishop, even if he is the Patriarch of Rome. The Orthodox Church has maintained a decentralized ecclesiastical structure with shared authority among bishops, with no single bishop having absolute control over the whole Church.

The Eucharist — Holy Communion
Many Protestants view the sacrament of Holy Communion as symbolic. They do not accept the Orthodox understand for the practice of the early Church that the bread and wine offered as a bloodless sacrifice is the actual Body and Blood of Christ. For Orthodox this is the main focus of their worship.

Reduction of the Sacraments
Innovation: The Protestant Reformers reduced the number of sacraments from seven to two (or three, depending on the tradition), retaining only Baptism and Eucharist as essential.

The Orthodox Church teaches that there are seven major sacraments (Baptism, Chrismation, Eucharist, Confession, Matrimony, Unction, and Priesthood), all of which are essential means of divine grace. The Orthodox Church believes that the sacraments are not mere symbols but real channels of God's grace, which work in the life of the believer to transform and sanctify them. Most Protestants today view the sacraments as ordinances and only symbolic.

Veneration of Saints and the Virgin Mary
Innovation: Many Protestant denominations rejected the veneration of saints and the Virgin Mary, viewing these practices as unbiblical.

The Orthodox Church affirms the veneration (not worship) of saints and the Virgin Mary as an integral part of its faith and practice. Orthodox Christians honor the saints as models of holiness and intercessors before God. The Orthodox Church teaches that the saints, and especially the Virgin Mary, play a vital role in the life of the Church, and their intercessions are seen as a source of grace and support for the faithful.

Rejection of the Use of Icons
Innovation: The Reformers, particularly the Calvinists, rejected the use of icons in worship, seeing them as idolatrous.

The Orthodox Church maintains the use of icons as vital expressions of faith. Icons are seen not as objects of worship but as windows to the divine, helping the faithful connect with the heavenly realities. The veneration of icons, which has been a part of Christian tradition since the early Church, is considered a means of honoring the person depicted, particularly Christ, the Virgin Mary, and the saints. This view was clarified in the Seventh Ecumenical Council.

The Doctrine of Predestination (Calvinism)

Innovation: The doctrine of predestination, particularly in its Calvinist form, teaches that God has already chosen who will be saved and who will be damned, independent of any actions or decisions by human beings.

The Orthodox Church teaches that while God's grace is given freely, human beings have free will to accept or reject it. The Orthodox Church rejects the fatalistic view of predestination that undermines human free will, emphasizing instead the synergy between divine grace and human choice in salvation.

The Rejection of the Sacrament of Confession

Innovation: The Reformation led many Protestant denominations to reject the Sacrament of Confession (also known as Penance or Reconciliation), believing that direct repentance to God through prayer was sufficient.

The Orthodox Church maintains Confession as a central sacrament, through which believers receive forgiveness of sins and healing from God. The sacrament is understood as a means of spiritual renewal and reconciliation with God and the Church, emphasizing the importance of both the divine grace and the personal act of repentance.

Conclusion

The Protestant Reformation introduced many innovations that departed from the Apostolic Tradition preserved by the Orthodox Church. While the Reformers sought to reform what they perceived as excesses or errors within the Catholic Church, their teachings, such as Sola Scriptura, Sola Fide, and the rejection of the sacraments, represent significant theological shifts that the Orthodox Church views as inconsistent with the teachings and practices handed down by the Apostles. The Orthodox Church believes that it has faithfully preserved the whole counsel of God as it was entrusted to the Church by Christ and the Apostles, and continues to reject these innovations that diverge from the early Church's understanding of Christian doctrine and life.

Study Questions

1. How does the Orthodox Church's understanding of Sola Scriptura differ from the Orthodox Church's belief in the relationship between Scripture and Holy Tradition?

2. What is the Orthodox Church's response to the Protestant doctrine of Sola Fide (faith alone), and how does the Orthodox Church view the role of works in salvation?

3. How does the Orthodox Church's teaching on the sacraments, particularly the Eucharist and Confession, differ from the innovations introduced by the Protestant Reformation?

Other Factors in Preserving the Truth

The Role of Monasticism
Preserving and Living the Faith
Monasticism has played a critical role in preserving and embodying the Apostolic doctrine throughout the history of the Orthodox Church. Monasteries have served as centers of prayer, theological study, and spiritual renewal. The monastic tradition is deeply rooted in the Apostolic teaching, emphasizing asceticism, devotion to prayer, and the pursuit of holiness. Through their way of life, monks and nuns live as witnesses to the transformative power of the Gospel, often standing as defenders of the faith in times of trial.

Monastics have been instrumental in maintaining the Church's integrity during periods of heresy, persecution, and schism. By committing themselves to a life of prayer and sacrifice, they have ensured that the truths of the faith were preserved and passed on to future generations. When the Church faced external oppression or internal disputes, monks often served as its guardians, refusing to compromise on the teachings of Christ and His Apostles.

Monastic Saints and Theologians
In times of dispute and efforts to eradicate the Church, monastics stood firm in their faith, often paying the ultimate price for their steadfastness. Many monks became martyrs, laying down their lives as witnesses to the truth of the Apostolic doctrine. Their unwavering commitment inspired the faithful and strengthened the Church during its darkest hours.

Notable monastic figures have contributed significantly to the preservation and articulation of Orthodox theology:

> St. Anthony the Great: Known as the father of monasticism, St. Anthony's life of asceticism and prayer set the standard for monastic practice. His example inspired countless others to pursue holiness through a life of simplicity and devotion.

> St. Maximus the Confessor: A staunch defender of Orthodox Christology, St. Maximus opposed the heresy of Monothelitism, which denied Christ's two wills (divine and human). Despite persecution, his theological insights clarified and safeguarded the Apostolic faith.

St. Gregory Palamas: A champion of Hesychasm, St. Gregory defended the experiential knowledge of God through prayer and asceticism. His teachings on the uncreated energies of God and theosis remain foundational to Orthodox spirituality and theology.

Monasticism continues to be a vital force in the life of the Church. Through their prayers, writings, and example, monastics serve as living witnesses to the enduring truth of the Apostolic faith, inspiring all believers to seek deeper communion with God. This unwavering commitment to holiness and truth has ensured that the faith remains intact, even amidst persecution and adversity.

The Continuity of Worship
The Orthodox Church's liturgical practices have remained remarkably consistent over the centuries, offering a tangible connection to the worship of the early Christian Church. The Divine Liturgy of St. John Chrysostom and the Liturgy of St. Basil the Great, celebrated today, are rooted in ancient Christian worship and reflect the Church's commitment to preserving the Apostolic faith. These liturgies are more than rituals; they are expressions of Orthodox theology, incorporating prayers, hymns, and Scripture that embody and transmit the Apostolic teaching.

The liturgical texts, many of which were composed by the Church Fathers, are carefully preserved and convey the unchanging truths of the faith. The consistent structure of worship underscores the Orthodox Church's role as the guardian of Apostolic Tradition, ensuring that every generation of believers participates in the same faith and theology as the early Church.

Icons and Sacred Art
Icons, as a visible expression of the Apostolic faith, hold a central place in Orthodox worship and theology. These sacred images are not merely decorative but serve as theological affirmations of Christ's Incarnation and the sanctity of creation. By depicting Christ, the Theotokos (Virgin Mary), and the saints, icons bear witness to the reality of God's presence in the world and the transformation of humanity through Christ.

The veneration of icons, affirmed by the Seventh Ecumenical Council, links modern Orthodox Christians with the Apostolic era. Icons act as "windows to heaven," inviting believers to contemplate the divine mysteries and participate in the life of the Church. Far from being idolatrous, the veneration of icons acknowledges the Incarnation of Christ, who took on visible human form, sanctifying matter itself.

Sacred art in Orthodoxy extends beyond icons, encompassing architecture, music, and other expressions that reflect the glory of God. The continuity of these artistic traditions demonstrates the Church's enduring commitment to preserving the Apostolic faith not only through words but also through visual and sensory experience.

Through its liturgical consistency and the veneration of icons, the Orthodox Church maintains an unbroken link to the worship of the Apostles. These practices embody the Apostolic faith, guiding believers into deeper communion with God and preserving the Church's teachings across generations.

The Role of the Holy Spirit
Guiding the Church
The Orthodox Church teaches that the Holy Spirit is the divine guide who leads the Church into all truth, as Christ promised:

> *When the Spirit of truth comes, He will guide you into all truth"*
> (John 16:13).

This guidance ensures that the Apostolic doctrine remains unaltered and faithfully transmitted across generations. The Holy Spirit works through the Church's hierarchy, councils, liturgical life, and the collective witness of the faithful to safeguard the truth of the Gospel.

The presence of the Holy Spirit is evident in the decisions of the Ecumenical Councils, the writings of the Church Fathers, and the lives of the saints. It is the Holy Spirit who inspires the Church to confront heresies, affirm doctrinal clarity, and preserve the unity of faith. This divine guidance is not limited to a single moment but is an ongoing process that sustains the Church's mission in every era.

The Church as the Pillar of Truth

St. Paul's declaration that the Church is the *pillar and ground of the truth* (1 Timothy 3:15) underscores the Orthodox understanding of the Church as the guardian and proclaimer of Apostolic teaching. This role requires unwavering faithfulness to the truths revealed by Christ and handed down through the Apostles.

The Church's responsibility as the "pillar of truth" is carried out through:

- Holy Tradition: Preserving the teachings of the Apostles in Scripture, liturgy, and oral tradition.
- Conciliar Decisions: Resolving theological disputes in harmony with the guidance of the Holy Spirit.
- Liturgical Worship: Embodying and transmitting the faith through the prayers, hymns, and sacraments of the Church.

The Orthodox Church does not compromise on the Apostolic faith, recognizing that it has been entrusted with guarding the truth for the salvation of all humanity. Through the active presence of the Holy Spirit, the Church continues to fulfill this sacred calling, providing a firm foundation for believers to grow in faith and holiness.

Conclusion

The Orthodox Church has faithfully preserved the doctrine of the Apostles through its reliance on Holy Tradition, the guidance of the Holy Spirit, and the collective witness of the Church throughout history. From Apostolic Succession and the writings of the Church Fathers to the decisions of Ecumenical Councils and the continuity of liturgical worship, Orthodoxy remains steadfast in its commitment to the faith *once delivered to the saints* (Jude 1:3).

This unwavering dedication ensures that the Orthodox Church continues to proclaim the Gospel and guide believers on the path of salvation, standing as a living testament to the enduring truth of Apostolic teaching.

The truths preserved by the Church are referred to as dogmas or doctrines. These are not innovations but careful reflections of the original teachings of Christ and the Apostles, safeguarded against distortions.

Throughout the ages, the holy people of the Church have addressed contemporary controversies by faithfully maintaining the Apostolic faith, avoiding the introduction of innovations like those seen in the Roman Catholic Church after the Great Schism or in Protestantism during the Reformation. It is crucial to remember that dogma "does not inspire faith, but presupposes that faith already exists in the heart."

As Fr. Michael Pomazansky explains in Orthodox Dogmatic Theology:

> "Faith, and more precisely faith in the Son of God Who has come into the world, is the cornerstone of Sacred Scripture; it is the cornerstone of one's personal salvation; and it is the cornerstone of theology. But these are written, that ye might believe that Jesus is the Christ, the Son of God; and that believing ye might have life through His name (John 20:31), writes the Apostle John at the end of his Gospel, and he repeats the same thought many times in his epistles; and these words of his express the chief idea of all of the writings of the Holy Apostles: I believe."

Orthodoxy is founded on a living faith—a faith that fosters a personal relationship with God. This faith seeks union with Him and strives for transformation into the likeness of Christ. Through this living relationship, Orthodox Christians are safeguarded against heresies and are continually prepared for eternal life in His Kingdom. This dynamic and transformative faith is the heart of Orthodox life, keeping the Apostolic doctrine alive and relevant for every generation.

Study Questions

1. How has monasticism contributed to the preservation and embodiment of Apostolic doctrine throughout the history of the Orthodox Church?

2. In what ways does the Orthodox Church's liturgical consistency, including the Divine Liturgy and the veneration of icons, preserve and transmit the Apostolic faith across generations?

3. What role does the Holy Spirit play in guiding the Orthodox Church to preserve the truth of the Gospel, and how does this divine guidance manifest in the Church's decisions, writings, and teachings?

4. How do you view the efforts of the Orthodox Church to preserve the original teachings of the Apostles?

Chapter 8

Orthodox Way of Life: A Life of Repentance

While doctrine is important, Orthodoxy is normall described as a way of life. To be a Christian we strive to live like Christ, following all He taught His disciples. It is participating in this way of life in the context of His Church that we are purified to becone like Him and united with His divinity.

This chapter explores the essential elements of the Orthodox Christian way of life, guiding believers toward healing, transformation, and union with God. It begins with repentance (metanoia), the foundational act of turning away from sin and reorienting one's heart and mind toward God.

Next it examines the soul, created for communion with God, highlighting its faculties—the mind (nous), intellect, and heart (kardia)—and their role in perceiving divine truth and aligning with God's will. It is the soul that needs healing.

The cause of the disease of the soul are the passions, disordered desires that hinder spiritual growth, offering practical ways to tame and transform them.

Finally, it explains important spiritual disciplines like prayer, fasting, confession, and the sacraments, which serve as tools for overcoming the passions and healing the soul. Together, these elements provide a practical framework for the lifelong journey of becoming like Christ and a union with God.

Repentance (Metanoia): The Foundation of the Orthodox Christian Life

Repentance, or metanoia, is central to Orthodox Christian life. It involves a "change of heart and mind," representing a continual reorientation of our desires, thoughts, and actions toward God. Repentance is more than remorse; it is a commitment to change, seeking His mercy and grace for healing. This turning away from sin and returning to God initiates the journey of healing and transformation at the heart of Orthodox Christianity. Repentance is not like pleading guilty to breaking a law in expectation of punishment, it is a commitment to become like Christ and to seek God's loving help for the healing of the soul.

Jesus began His ministry with this call: *Repent, for the kingdom of heaven is at hand* (Matthew 4:17). His call to repentance is a call to enter God's Kingdom. It opens the way for healing and communion with God, helping us overcome sinful tendencies and preparing us for His kingdom.

"Repentance is the renewal of baptism." — St. John Climacus

Understanding Our Fallen Condition
The Orthodox path begins with an awareness of humanity's fallen condition, inherited from Adam and Eve, as described in Genesis. This condition is marked by self-centeredness, fear of death, and attachment to worldly desires, which create separation from God. Modern distractions like social media, entertainment, and materialism reinforce these tendencies, diverting our focus from spiritual growth. Recognizing our fallen state and the temptations in modern culture reveals our need for God's grace and the transformative practices of the Orthodox Church.

Orthodoxy rejects doctrines like "faith alone," which imply that salvation requires only belief in Christ. Instead, Orthodox teaching emphasizes a life of active faith, seeking perfection and purification. St. Paul warns, "See to it that no one takes you captive through philosophy and empty deception, according to the tradition of men… rather than according to Christ" (Colossians 2:8). In earlier times, Orthodox life was naturally integrated into daily life, with churches, monasteries, and community values supporting spiritual growth. Today, with secular influences and fragmented communities, living an Orthodox life requires greater vigilance and intention.

Recognizing our fallen condition and the need for active repentance brings us to the importance of cooperation with God, a key element of Orthodox salvation.

Synergia: Cooperation with God
Orthodox Christianity teaches that salvation is a cooperative effort, or synergia, between human effort and divine grace. St. Paul instructs believers to *work out your own salvation with fear and trembling; for it is God who works in you both to will and to do for His good pleasure* (Philippians 2:12-13). This cooperative dynamic combines our commitment with God's grace, helping us grow in faith and virtue. While God grants the grace for salvation, we must actively participate through prayer, humility, and the pursuit of holiness. While given that faith is necessary, synergia is not about "earning" salvation but responding to God's grace through action—*Thy will be done.*

During the Protestant Reformation, this concept was rejected in favor of "faith alone." This separation of faith from works, unheard of in early Christianity, can lead to spiritual complacency. Orthodox Christianity calls believers to a life of continual effort, transformation, and union with Christ, known as theosis. This journey involves spiritual warfare against our passions, discipline through the sacraments, and a deep commitment to Christ's teachings.

Faith without works is dead (James 2:26).

Paul says, *Work out your own salvation with fear and trembling; for it is God who works in you …* (Phil 2:12-13).

Next we will outline the nature of our spiritual being to help better understand our spiritual task.

Study Questions

1. How does the Orthodox understanding of repentance (metanoia) differ from a mere feeling of remorse or guilt, and what role does it play in the believer's transformation?

2. Why is it important for Orthodox Christians to recognize their fallen condition, and how does this awareness shape their spiritual practices and relationship with God?

3. What is the concept of synergia in Orthodox Christianity, and how does it emphasize the cooperation between human effort and divine grace in the process of salvation?

4. How does the Orthodox Church's teaching on faith and works challenge the doctrine of "faith alone" introduced during the Protestant Reformation?

5. In what ways does the Orthodox concept of salvation, which involves active participation and spiritual warfare, help believers grow in holiness and prepare for union with Christ (theosis)?

Nature of Our Spiritual Being

The Soul: Created for Communion with God

Human beings experience the world through their five senses, processed by the brain, which operates with assumptions and habits formed through experience and inheritance. The brain, a physical organ, governs our bodily functions and triggers automatic responses as well as the results of reason. It is the part of the soul called mind which allows us to reason, make choices, and connect spiritually with God.

The Orthodox understanding of the soul is that it animates the body through conscious, willful actions. St. John of Damascus describes the soul as "a living substance, simple and incorporeal… using the body as an organ and giving it life." The soul, created in God's image, is designed for eternal communion with Him and possesses the ability to know and love God. Sin clouds this capacity, weakening the soul's connection to God.

Within the soul is the nous, a spiritual faculty enabling direct perception of divine truths. The nous serves as a guiding light, directing the soul toward God, and requires healing to restore its capacity for divine perception. It is often referred to as the "eye of the soul."

The Heart: The Spiritual Center of Being

In Orthodox thought, the heart (kardia) is the innermost part of the person, the center of our spiritual being, the seat of divine knowledge where God reveals Himself. Jesus emphasizes this, saying, *Blessed are the pure in heart, for they shall see God* (Matthew 5:8). Purity of heart is essential for experiencing God's presence, and the Orthodox way cultivates this purity through spiritual disciplines. These practices help clear the obstacles, our sinful tendencies, that cloud our spiritual vision, allowing the heart to become a place where God's presence is known and experienced.

Renewing the Mind and Reprogramming our Brain

The mind (dianoia) is the rational, intellectual part of the soul, enabling logic and reasoning. It makes thinkable what the nous spiritually experiences. It works in harmony with the nous and the heart guiding the soul on its spiritual journey. The mind works through the brain effecting actions of good and evil.

The brain, however, is the physical organ through which the mind operates. It allows that body to adapt and interact with its environment. It regulates our bodily function like breathing, the beating of our heart and other bodily functions without the action of the mind. Its focus is on the body, its needs and desires. It takes inputs from all the senses and causes actions in the body based on the way its cells have been interconnected or "programmed." In this way it can act quickly based on the assumptions making for shortcuts based on the continual stream of information from the senses.

It is an incredibly complex set of neural networks formed by repeated actions, including passions that lead to sin. Over time, these neural pathways can become engrained, reinforcing good and well as negative behaviors.

Orthodox practices help "reprogram" the brain's pathways by replacing sinful habits with virtuous ones. Through spiritual disciplines like prayer, meditation, and attentiveness, we use the mind to train the brain to override and change automatic responses to align our lives with God's will.

St. Paul calls believers to this renewal: *Be transformed by the renewing of your mind* (Romans 12:2), encouraging us to shape our thoughts and actions to seek communion with God.

Mind vs. Brain: An Analogy
Think of the brain as a field and the mind as the gardener. Our repeated thoughts and actions are like seeds planted in this field, which grow into habits over time. Through attentiveness, the mind can "weed out" harmful thoughts and cultivate virtues, helping the brain adapt toward spiritual growth.

With this background let's examine the nature of the passions we must learn to control.

Why does it seem so difficult to act like Christ?
Considering the core spiritual elements of our being along with the brain and the mind, we are psychosomatic beings. It would seem with these wonderful faculties God has gifted us with, it should not be difficult to do what He has commanded us to do. So why does it seem like a struggle?

Listen to Saint Paul and how the great Apostle relates his difficulty in this regard.

> *For I know that in me (that is, in my flesh) nothing good dwells; for to will is present with me, but how to perform what is good I do not find. For the good that I will to do, I do not do; but the evil I will not to do, that I practice. Now if I do what I will not to do, it is no longer I who do it, but sin that dwells in me. I find then a law, that evil is present with me, the one who wills to do good. For I delight in the law of God according to the inward man. But I see another law in my members, warring against the law of my mind, and bringing me into captivity to the law of sin which is in my members?* (Rom 7:18-23)

The focus for this problem is centered in what are called passions. These we examine next.

Study Questions

1. How does the Orthodox understanding of repentance (metanoia) differ from a mere feeling of remorse or guilt, and what role does it play in the believer's transformation?

2. Why is it important for Orthodox Christians to recognize their fallen condition, and how does this awareness shape their spiritual practices and relationship with God?

3. What is the concept of synergia in Orthodox Christianity, and how does it emphasize the cooperation between human effort and divine grace in the process of salvation?

4. How does the Orthodox Church's teaching on faith and works challenge the doctrine of "faith alone" introduced during the Protestant Reformation?

5. In what ways does the Orthodox concept of salvation, which involves active participation and spiritual warfare, help believers grow in holiness and prepare for union with Christ (theosis)?

The Nature of Passions that Cause Sin

In Orthodox Christianity, passions (πάθος) are disordered desires and attachments that lead to sin. They drive us to seek temporary satisfaction, blocking us from eternal communion with God. These passions include excessive attachment to food, anger, material goods, pride, and self-centeredness. Jesus says, *From within, out of the heart of man, come evil thoughts... All these things... defile a man* (Mark 7:21-23). They result from the way our brains are organized for quick responses to our environment.

Passions fall into two types: natural and unnatural. Natural passions, such as hunger and the need for rest, are essential for survival but become sinful when excessive. Unnatural passions, like greed and lust, distort spiritual desires, leading us to seek fulfillment in worldly pleasures we gain through the senses. Through prayer, fasting, and other disciplines, the Orthodox way aims to tame these passions, bringing them under control, and align our bodily actions with God's will.

"The natural passions become good in those who struggle when... they use them to gain heavenly things." — St. Maximus the Confessor

Main passions:

>Gluttony: Excessive attachment to food or drink.

>Lust: Disordered desire for sensual or sexual pleasure.

>Avarice (Greed): Excessive desire for wealth or material possessions.

>Anger: Uncontrolled wrath or resentment that disrupts inner peace and love.

>Sadness (Despair or Sloth): Spiritual despondency, often a lack of hope or zeal for God.

>Vainglory: Desire for attention, admiration, and validation from others.

>Pride: Self-centeredness and an inflated sense of one's importance, leading to separation from God.

Knowing these passions that we must control, let's consider the ways that we can better control them. One of those is what is termed watchfulness.

Watchfulness and Overcoming Bad Habits

Watchfulness, or nepsis, is key to Orthodox spiritual practice, helping believers guard their minds and hearts. By recognizing harmful impulses early, believers can redirect them before they act and form sinful habits. This practice of vigilance enables believers to "reprogram" automatic responses, forming good habits that align with Christ's values.

Emotions can also be an indication of passions; though natural, they can lead to sin if they become excessive and uncontrolled. Emotions arise quickly, often triggering automatic responses. The brain has an automatic response to these that can trigger emotions. When this happens the brain sends signals through the blood stream and then through neural networks throughout the body resulting in a global change in our being. Anger is one we can relate to. When we become angry our whole nature changes. We are no longer our normal self. To avoid such actions that are sinful, the Fathers teach that we must act at the moment of stimulus to guard the heart and redirect emotions before they trigger such emotions that result in sinful behavior. Watchfulness is the key to this inner work, helping us maintain Christ-centered love and peace. Later we will explore spiritual disciplines that help us develop this capability.

Repetition, Focus, and Attentiveness: Tools for Reprogramming the Mind

Modern science confirms that the brain can change, and habits can be transformed. The Orthodox way emphasizes this transformation through spiritual disciplines like prayer, such as the Jesus Prayer ("Lord Jesus Christ, Son of God, have mercy on me, a sinner"). A practice of repeated prayers will gradually reshape the brain with new habits, leading to a Christ-centered life. This same repetiveness is found in our way worship as well. Regular participation in it along with the sacraments also help in this reorientation of the brain.

> Jesus says, *Blessed are those who hunger and thirst for righteousness, for they shall be filled* (Matthew 5:6).

Attentiveness (prosoche) and regular participation in the Divine Liturgy help keep the mind focused on God. This continual focus on Christ, continual prayer, overcomes worldly distractions, gradually purifying the soul the soul leading to ever-increasing grace to support our desire to become like Christ.

Spiritual Warfare: The Battle Against Sin
Spiritual warfare is an essential concept we learn from Saint Paul, teaching that Christian life is a struggle against passions and temptations that separate us from God. This battle takes place within the heart, where divine grace competes with sinful inclinations. St. Paul describes this struggle, *For we do not wrestle against flesh and blood, but against principalities, against powers… of this age* (Ephesians 6:12). Engaging in spiritual warfare requires vigilance, faith, and the "armor of God," including truth, righteousness, faith, and the Word of God, to resist the forces that attempt to lead us astray.

Engaging in spiritual warfare involves practicing the disciplines taught by the Church. Orthodox teachings emphasize that spiritual warfare is not about eliminating all desires but controlling and transforming them to serve God's purposes. As believers resist temptations, they develop spiritual resilience, a strong will to serve God drawing closer to Him to refine their souls and prepare them for His kingdom.

This spiritual war that we are engaged in is the battle that Christ established His Church to help us win. He is love and wants us to win this battle. His Church provides many ways to do this.

Study Questions

1. What is a passion? What are the differences between natural and unnatural passions in Orthodox Christianity, and how can natural passions be transformed into virtues?

2. How does the practice of watchfulness (nepsis) help Orthodox Christians control their emotions and passions, and why is it critical in overcoming sinful behavior?

3. In what ways can spiritual disciplines like prayer, fasting, and attentiveness help "reprogram" the brain and form good habits that align with God's will?

4. What does spiritual warfare mean in the context of Orthodox Christianity, and how does it relate to the struggle against passions and temptations in daily life?

Spiritual Disciplines: Tools for Transformation and Growth

Orthodox Christianity provides a set of spiritual disciplines that serve as essential tools for healing, purification, and growth. These disciplines include prayer, fasting, confession, almsgiving, participation in the sacraments, and study of Scripture. Each of these practices has a unique role in helping believers cooperate with God's grace and cultivate inner virtues.

Prayer: Prayer fosters a relationship with God, attuning the heart to His presence. Through regular prayer, especially the Jesus Prayer, believers continually turn their hearts toward God, inviting His grace into daily life.

Fasting: Fasting disciplines the body and helps weaken the passions, teaching self-control and detachment from material desires.

Confession: Confession allows believers to examine their lives, acknowledge their sins, and seek forgiveness, renewing their commitment to live in harmony with God's will.

Almsgiving: Almsgiving teaches generosity, humility, and love for others, reflecting God's care for humanity.

Participation in the Sacraments: The sacraments, especially the Eucharist, bring believers into intimate communion with Christ, providing spiritual nourishment and healing.

Study of Scripture: Scripture grounds believers in the teachings of Christ and provides wisdom, comfort, and guidance for the spiritual journey.

These disciplines are not ends in themselves but means to open the soul to God's transformative power. Practiced regularly, they help tame the passions, purify the heart, and reshape the mind, drawing the believer closer to union with God.

Conclusion: The Path to Union with God

The Orthodox way of life is a path of purification, healing, and transformation, preparing the soul for eternal communion with God. Through repentance, cooperation with God's grace, the disciplined efforts made to reprogram our brain cultivate in it responses of virtue, Orthodox Christians actively participate in their salvation, allowing the Holy Spirit to restore them to the image of God. This journey requires both inner vigilance and outward discipline—a commitment to let go of sinful habits, reorient emotional responses, and refocus the brain so the mind can direct action based on Christ's teaching. In this lifelong journey, the believer gradually becomes like Christ, purified and ready to enter His kingdom, where they will dwell in eternal communion with God.

By embracing the Orthodox way of life, we open ourselves to a transformative journey of growth, guided by faith, humility, and love. This journey prepares us to answer Christ's call to *be perfect, as your Father in heaven is perfect* (Matthew 5:48), and through God's grace, we move steadily closer to Him, striving to embody His love and holiness in all that we do.

Study Questions

1. How do the spiritual disciplines of prayer, fasting, and confession work together to help Orthodox Christians purify their hearts and cultivate virtues?

2. In what ways does participation in the sacraments, particularly the Eucharist, nourish and strengthen the believer's relationship with Christ and their spiritual growth?

3. Why is the study of Scripture considered an essential discipline in Orthodox Christianity, and how does it provide wisdom and guidance for the spiritual journey?

Chapter 9

Orthodox Prayer: A Journey Toward Communion with God

"He who is able to pray correctly, even if he is the poorest of all people, is essentially the richest. And he who does not have proper prayer, is the poorest of all, even if he sits on a royal throne.

—St John Chrysostom

Prayer is at the heart of Orthodox Christian life, serving as the primary means of communion with God. Through prayer, we enter into a sacred relationship with our Creator, seeking to align ourselves with His will and to experience His transformative grace. In the Orthodox tradition, prayer is not merely an obligation but a vital pathway to deepen our connection with God, encounter His presence, and purify our hearts. Daily prayer is essential to a healthy Orthodox Christian life—it is not optional.

In this chapter, we briefly explore the nature of prayer and the challenges it presents. We then outline the stages of prayer, from oral prayer to noetic prayer, followed by an explanation of the practice of the Jesus Prayer.

Finally, we offer practical guidance on cultivating a life of prayer, addressing key aspects such as when and where to pray, how to prepare for prayer, and the proper approach to prayer itself. Additionally, we suggest a daily prayer rule to help establish a consistent and meaningful prayer life.

What is Orthodox Prayer?

In its essence, Orthodox prayer is a mystery, an opportunity to enter into the life of God through the Holy Spirit. It is not merely about the act of speaking words; it's about encountering God and being transformed in the process. Prayer is central to the Orthodox Christian faith, as it is in prayer that we receive God's wisdom, guidance, and grace to resist sin and grow spiritually. St. Theophan the Recluse describes prayer as the raising of the mind and heart to God, both in praise and thanksgiving, for our spiritual and physical needs.

Prayer in the Orthodox tradition is deeply relational, centered on the idea of communion—not simply asking for things, but experiencing God's presence. As in the story of the Prodigal Son (Luke 15), prayer is about returning to God, asking for His mercy, and experiencing His mercy, and experiencing His embrace. In this way, prayer is a return to the Father, deepening our relationship with Him and fulfilling the image of God that He instilled in us from the beginning.

Why do We Pray?
Christ asks us to pray. He tells us in the Gospel of Luke, *How much more will the heavenly Father give the Holy Spirit to those who ask him* (Luke 11:13). We pray so that God can help us to become more like Him in our actions.

>For renewal and the growth of our soul.
>To give thanks to God for all he provides for us.
>To seek forgiveness for our sinfulness as humility
>   is a prerequisite for prayer.

We can also pray to seek help for others as well as ourselves. But we must not forget to pray for His help in our own spiritual growth. This is not selfish, but essential for us to better love and serve others and carry out God's commandments. We can ask also for His help in supporting us in the various ascetic practices we choose to undertake.

The Centrality of Prayer in Orthodox Life

Prayer is considered the most direct way to connect with God. It is through constant prayer that Orthodox Christians align their hearts and minds with God's will. Through prayer, the believer is purified, as prayer cleanses the heart and draws the individual closer to God's holiness. The Orthodox Church teaches that prayer is transformative—it is a means of spiritual healing and growth, purifying the soul and overcoming temptations.

One of the most important aspects of Orthodox prayer is its communal nature. When Orthodox Christians pray, they are not isolated in their prayer, but are united with the entire Body of Christ—the faithful, the saints, angels, and even Christ Himself. This connection to the Church throughout time and space helps strengthen the believer's prayer life, making it a living, dynamic part of the tradition.

The Challenges of Prayer: Why It Isn't Easy

One of the primary challenges in prayer is the distraction of the mind. The world and our own sinful tendencies often pull our attention away from God. The body, too, resists prayer, as it seeks comfort or indulgence, making it difficult to maintain the focus necessary for true prayer. Prayer in the Orthodox faith is a discipline that requires time, humility, intentionality, and concentration.

In times of difficulty or trial, it may feel like God's presence is hidden, and prayer becomes a struggle. This spiritual dryness is a common experience for many, but it should not discourage the believer. Orthodox prayer encourages perseverance, even when the mind wanders or the heart feels distant. Prayer is about returning to God each time we falter, and over time, through discipline and humility, we develop a more focused, deeper prayer life.

Study Questions

1. How does Orthodox prayer differ from simply speaking words, and what is the deeper purpose of prayer in the Orthodox Christian tradition?

2. Why is prayer considered a central and transformative practice in Orthodox Christian life, and how does it purify the soul and help overcome temptations?

3. What is the communal aspect of Orthodox prayer, and how does it connect believers to the wider Body of Christ, including the saints and angels?

4. What are some common challenges in prayer, and how does the Orthodox tradition encourage perseverance and humility in the face of spiritual dryness or distraction?

Stages of Prayer: From Oral to Noetic Prayer

Orthodox prayer can be categorized into several stages, each representing a deeper level of engagement with God.

Oral Prayer: This is the starting point, where the believer engages in prayers read aloud or recited from memory. Oral prayer is essential, especially in the beginning, as it helps the believer establish a rhythm of prayer and learn to direct their mind and heart toward God. For many, oral prayer is the entry into the deeper stages of prayer. It is important that the mind and heart are engaged in oral prayer, otherwise, it risks becoming mere repetition without purpose. Establishing concentration during oral prayer is essential to moving toward a more intimate relationship with God.

Mental Prayer: As the believer progresses, prayer becomes more internal. Mental prayer involves the thoughts and meditations on God's presence and truths. The mind is still engaged, but the heart also begins to join in the prayer. This is a time for deeper reflection, allowing the mind to absorb the meaning of the words and meditate on Scripture or other prayers. Mental prayer helps prepare the heart for the next stage, as the believer becomes increasingly focused on God's presence.

Noetic or Inner Prayer: The final stage of prayer is often described as noetic or inner prayer—the prayer of the heart. In this stage, the believer experiences God's grace more deeply, and prayer becomes a living encounter with God. This is where the mind and heart are fully united with God. Inner prayer leads to stillness (hesychia), a state where the soul is at peace and able to experience God's presence fully. It is in this inner stillness that true communion with God occurs.

The Power of Concentration in Prayer

One of the primary challenges in moving from oral prayer to noetic prayer is the ability to concentrate. Distractions in the mind, temptations, and even the body's natural desires can pull attention away from God. But concentration is key—prayer is not just about speaking words, but about focusing the mind and heart on God. Through focus, the believer begins to enter into deeper communion with God. Even if concentration is difficult, persistence in prayer helps build this spiritual muscle.

In times when concentration is lacking, Orthodox prayer encourages the believer to return to God. St. Theophan the Recluse writes that concentration in prayer is essential to moving from the oral to the inner stages of prayer. He emphasizes that the struggle against distraction is itself part of the spiritual journey, and that every effort to remain focused is pleasing to God.

Study Questions

1. What is the significance of oral prayer in the Orthodox tradition, and how does it serve as the foundation for progressing to deeper stages of prayer?

2. How does mental prayer differ from oral prayer, and what role does meditation on God's presence and Scripture play in preparing the heart for noetic prayer?

3. What is noetic prayer, and how does the experience of inner stillness (hesychia) lead to a deeper communion with God? How can concentration and focus be developed in prayer to reach this stage?

Jesus Prayer

The Jesus Prayer, also known as the Prayer of the Heart, is one of the most revered and powerful prayers in the Orthodox Christian tradition. It is a simple, repetitive prayer that expresses profound humility and the desire for God's mercy. The Jesus Prayer is used for personal prayer, contemplation, and spiritual healing, and it plays a key role in the ascetic practices of the Church.

The Jesus Prayer, says Metropolitan Anthony Bloom, "more than any other," helps us to be able to "stand in God's presence." This means that the Jesus Prayer helps us to focus our mind exclusively on God with "no other thought" occupying our mind but the thought of God. At this moment when our mind is totally concentrated on God, we discover a very personal and direct relationship with Him.

Meaning and Significance
The Jesus Prayer is simple in its wording, yet deep in its spiritual meaning. It is traditionally phrased as:

> **"Lord Jesus Christ, Son of God, have mercy on me, a sinner."**

This prayer consists of three key elements:

> "Lord Jesus Christ"—This addresses Jesus Christ as Lord, affirming His divinity, authority, and role as the Savior.

> "Son of God"—This acknowledges the divine nature of Christ, affirming the Orthodox belief in His full divinity and full humanity.

> "Have mercy on me, a sinner"—This is a humble plea for God's mercy, recognizing our sinfulness and need for forgiveness. It reflects a spirit of repentance and the desire for God's grace to heal and transform us.

The Jesus Prayer embodies the core of Orthodox spirituality, which centers on humility, repentance, and communion with God. It expresses our total dependence on God's mercy and invites us to seek His presence continually in our lives.

The History of the Jesus Prayer
The Jesus Prayer has its roots in early Christian monasticism. The prayer became a cornerstone of the spiritual practices of the Desert Fathers,

who lived in solitude in the Egyptian desert in the 4th and 5th centuries. The practice of the Jesus Prayer was closely connected with the practice of hesychasm, a form of prayer that emphasizes inner stillness, quiet, and focusing the mind on God.

Hesychasm comes from the Greek word hesychia, meaning "stillness" or "silence." The aim of hesychastic prayer is to quiet the mind and heart, making them receptive to God's presence. The Jesus Prayer, repeated continuously, helps the practitioner achieve this stillness and focus.

The Philokalia, a collection of writings by the early Church Fathers on spiritual practices, is one of the main sources that preserves the teachings and practices related to the Jesus Prayer. Notably, St. Gregory Palamas, a key figure in Orthodox spirituality, strongly emphasized the practice of the Jesus Prayer as a means to experience the uncreated energies of God and deepen one's union with Him.

The Practice of the Jesus Prayer

The Jesus Prayer can be practiced in various ways, and its effectiveness lies in the consistency and sincerity with which it is said. Here are some practical guidelines for practicing the Jesus Prayer:

Quiet, Focused Prayer

The Jesus Prayer is best practiced in a quiet place, free from distractions. The goal is to focus the mind and heart on God, making space for His presence. As you begin, take a few deep breaths to center yourself and prepare your heart for prayer.

Repetition and Rhythm

The power of the Jesus Prayer lies in its repetition. Repeating the prayer allows the mind to become focused and the heart to become more attuned to God's presence. It can be helpful to say the prayer aloud or silently, with a steady rhythm. You may choose to pray for a set amount of time (e.g., 15–30 minutes) or repeat the prayer for as long as you feel led, allowing it to become a natural rhythm of your day.

Use of the Prayer Rope

The prayer rope, or komboskini, is a tool often used to help keep count of the prayers during the practice of the Jesus Prayer. Each knot on the rope corresponds to one repetition of the prayer. The prayer rope serves as a physical reminder to remain focused and committed to prayer, helping to keep distractions at bay.

Practicing in Daily Life
The beauty of the Jesus Prayer is that it can be integrated into daily life. You can pray it while walking, working, or doing other routine activities. The goal is to create a continuous awareness of God's presence, making prayer a constant part of your day. Even in moments of stress or distraction, returning to the Jesus Prayer helps redirect the heart toward God.

The Transformative Power of the Jesus Prayer

The purpose of the Jesus Prayer is not merely to recite words, but to invite a deep encounter with God. The more we pray the Jesus Prayer, the more it transforms us from within. Some of the benefits and transformative effects of the Jesus Prayer include:

Humility and Repentance: The prayer centers on recognizing our sinfulness and asking for God's mercy. This cultivates humility and repentance, as we acknowledge our need for God's grace.

Inner Peace and Stillness: By calming the mind and focusing on God, the Jesus Prayer helps bring inner peace and stillness. It quiets the noise of the world and opens our hearts to God's presence.

Union with God: The Jesus Prayer is not only about speaking words; it is an invitation to experience God in the depths of our hearts. Over time, this prayer leads to greater intimacy with God, drawing us closer to His love and mercy.

Freedom from the Passions: The Jesus Prayer helps combat the passions (such as anger, pride, and lust) that separate us from God. As we focus on God's mercy and love, we are more easily able to resist these temptations.

The Role of the Jesus Prayer in the Life of the Church

In the Orthodox Church, the Jesus Prayer is not only an individual practice but is also deeply connected to the communal life of the Church. It is often used in conjunction with the Divine Liturgy and other prayers, particularly during the seasons of Great Lent and during times of personal prayer and spiritual struggle.

In monastic communities, the Jesus Prayer is central to daily life. Monks and nuns use it as part of their daily rhythm of prayer, seeking to cultivate a continual conversation with God.

Conclusion
The Jesus Prayer is a powerful tool for spiritual transformation, drawing us closer to God through humility, repentance, and the continuous awareness of His presence. By incorporating the Jesus Prayer into our daily lives, we open our hearts to God's mercy, deepen our relationship with Him, and grow in holiness. It is a prayer of the heart that leads to healing, peace, and union with the divine. Let us, like the early Christian monks, strive to pray the Jesus Prayer with sincerity and faith, seeking God's grace and mercy in every moment of our lives.

Study Questions

1. What are the key elements of the Jesus Prayer, and how do they reflect the core beliefs of Orthodox Christianity?
2. How does the practice of the Jesus Prayer contribute to achieving inner stillness and focusing the mind on God, according to the teachings of hesychasm?
3. What practical methods are suggested for practicing the Jesus Prayer, and how can they help incorporate prayer into daily life?
4. In what ways does the Jesus Prayer promote spiritual transformation, and how does it aid in cultivating humility and repentance?
5. How has the Jesus Prayer been historically linked to Orthodox monasticism, and what role does it play in the life of the Church today?
6. What are the benefits of using tools such as the prayer rope and integrating breathing techniques in the practice of the Jesus Prayer?

When Do We Pray?

First, you need to establish a regular time for prayer. As a minimum, you should set aside specific times in the morning and the evening for prayer. With our busy lives, this requires making conscious changes to prioritize prayer. Choose a time that you know you can consistently maintain, no matter what. Strict discipline is essential. The duration of your prayer should be determined in consultation with your spiritual father, but it should not be less than ten minutes in the morning and another ten in the evening. Your time in prayer will naturally grow as your relationship with God deepens.

Initially, maintaining this seemingly simple discipline may be challenging, as negative forces will try to distract you from regular prayer. However, there will come a time when you eagerly anticipate your prayer sessions. Expect an initial struggle to adhere to a strict schedule. As the popular saying goes, "Just do it!" Consider how you routinely prioritize other aspects of your life, such as getting to work or school on time, or personal hygiene routines like brushing your teeth. Surely, you can also make prayer a fixed routine.

Making Time for Prayer
For many, finding time for prayer is one of the biggest hurdles in establishing it as a cornerstone of life. Our schedules are overloaded with activities. Children are highly programmed with school, sports, music, dance, and other commitments, and parents are equally affected by their busy routines. We are constantly tethered to our cell phones and the internet, which competes with television for our time. So when is there time to pray?

The key is to wake up earlier in the morning, which in turn requires going to bed earlier. Creating quiet time in the morning is crucial because our minds are at their quietest and most receptive to prayer. Beginning the day with prayer provides strength to face the day's temptations.

Consider setting your alarm clock thirty minutes earlier. This will allow you time for prayer and preparation for the day in an unhurried manner. After prayer and personal hygiene, allocate time for other responsibilities, such as preparing the children for school. A leisurely breakfast should also be part of your routine; do not rush and eat in the car. Helping your household start the day peacefully fosters a calm environment. Remember, calm people create calm people, and if your day starts with tranquility, the rest of the day is more likely to follow suit. Take time to enjoy God's creation in the morning by observing the sunrise, the morning dew, and the birdsong. All of this depends on making sufficient time for these activities.

The next step is to adjust your evening routine by going to bed earlier. A conscious change in your daily routine is essential; otherwise, new time for prayer will not be created.

Evaluate the activities that consume your evenings. Television and social media are often the biggest culprits. Eliminating just one program and one app can free up an extra hour for prayer. Media consumption places a huge burden on our lives. Recent surveys show that the average person spends over 2 hours per day on social media and over 3 hours a day watching TV. This presents an opportunity to reallocate time to prayer, spending time with loved ones, and participating in worship services.

Today's technology allows for recording shows and keeping up with news throughout the day, eliminating the need to stay up late. Carve out a sacred space in your daily schedule, ensuring time in the morning and evening to be with God.

Bringing work home can also consume precious time and negatively impact your spiritual life. Consider work like a jacket you wear when you leave and remove when you return home. Put away work-related distractions such as briefcases and cell phones upon returning home. Focus on your family, listen to their joys and struggles, and support them. Sharing a meal together is crucial; do not let meals become solitary events where family members eat separately. Just as we come together as a Christian community for the Divine Liturgy, families should unite in love and gratitude at mealtimes. Offer prayers of thanksgiving for the food, the joy of family, forgiveness for the day's shortcomings, and blessings for the nourishment of both body and soul.

Once you have made time for prayer, commit to it. Treat prayer time as an appointment with God, which includes a specific time and place. This discipline is not easy, and your to-do list will always feel overwhelming. However, it is essential to let go of distractions and protect this sacred space.

Now is the time to stop making excuses. It is dangerous to think that God understands when we cut corners in prayer due to our busy lifestyles. God expects us to prioritize Him above all else. While He is compassionate and understands our struggles, we must make an effort to seek Him with humility and dedication.

Study Questions

1. Why is it important to establish a regular time for prayer, and what are the key factors to consider when setting a prayer schedule?
2. What practical steps can you take to make time for prayer amidst your busy schedule, and what are the common obstacles that might hinder this effort?
3. How can adjusting your morning and evening routines contribute to a more disciplined and fulfilling prayer life?
4. What role does technology and media consumption play in hindering prayer time, and how can you consciously reallocate their time to prioritize spiritual growth?

Where Do We Pray: Create A Quiet Place

The first thing an Orthodox Christian should do when moving into a new apartment or house is to determine a place for prayer. Some suggest that this should be a conspicuous place where everyone can see it, while others believe it should be in a corner. What is most important is that it provides a place where you can be in private for personal prayer.

Determining this place may require some creativity depending on your living situation. In a large home, you can designate a spare room. In a smaller home, you can create a space in a closet. In a small apartment, a corner in the bedroom or the living room may be the best option. In a dorm room, you will likely need to use your desk. In some cases, you may need to locate a quiet space outside of your living area, such as a nearby chapel. A self-standing screen can be used to create privacy, and a bookcase can also help to form a secluded nook. Thoughtful consideration is required, as this space will become a sacred place within your home.

Once you have determined the space, you can create a home altar or icon stand, as it is often called. It is best to have a small table to hold a cross, prayer books, a hand censer, and blessed items such as palms from Palm Sunday, a flower from the Epitaphio on Holy Friday, holy water from Theophany, and other religious items.

Icons can be placed on the wall above the altar table, or if this is not possible, they can be placed on stands on the table. Traditionally, the icon stand or prayer corner should face east, as we do in church. East is preferred because it is the direction of sunrise, which serves as an "icon in nature" of the resurrection. Additionally, it is believed that Christ will return from the east at the Second Coming. However, if the best space for prayer does not face east, do not worry; the important thing is to have a space conducive to prayer.

Regarding the placement of icons, there is no strict rule, but you can follow the general order seen on the church iconostasis (Christ to the immediate right, the Theotokos to the immediate left, and other saints in decreasing rank). If you have only one icon, it is natural to place Christ or the Cross in the center. Take care in arranging the icons thoughtfully. A poorly arranged assemblage can evoke a sense of dissatisfaction. Keep in mind the principle of hierarchy—do not place an icon of a locally venerated saint above that of the Holy Trinity, the Savior, the Mother of God, or the Apostles.

It is beneficial to have an oil lamp on your prayer table, which you light during your prayers. There are different types of utensils for burning oil, with a common option being the wick-float. This device uses cork to keep the wick and flame floating on the oil. When using an oil lamp, consider the following key elements:

- The Glass: Any low, wide-mouthed glass may be used. Clear glass is commonly used in Greece, but red, blue, or milk-colored glass is also suitable. It is recommended to add a small amount of water at the bottom of the glass to prevent cracking from heat.
- The Oil: The tradition of using olive oil for lamps dates back to the time of Moses. Olive oil burns best when left open to age or even become slightly rancid.
- The Wick: A cotton string is ideal; avoid coated or waxed strings. A six-ply cotton string is thick enough for consistent burning. For a brighter and cleaner flame, soak the wick in vinegar and allow it to dry thoroughly before use.

In addition to an oil lamp, it is also beneficial to have a small hand censer for burning incense. Small hand censers are available in various styles, often modeled after church censers. It is recommended to use incense made by Orthodox monasteries, which comes in a variety of fragrances. Light the charcoal and place the incense on it, allowing the sweet aroma to fill your space as a reminder that your prayers rise to heaven like incense.

All these elements—light, fragrance, and space—contribute to making prayer a participatory activity that engages the whole body and soul.

Creating and maintaining a dedicated place for prayer is an essential step in cultivating a consistent prayer life. Whether your space is large or small, setting aside an area exclusively for prayer fosters a deeper connection with God.

Study Questions

1. Why is it important to establish a dedicated space for prayer in one's home, and what factors should be considered when selecting this space?
2. What are the key elements that should be included in your home prayer space, and what is their spiritual significance in Orthodox tradition?
3. Why is it traditional to pray facing east, and how should one approach the orientation of their prayer space if facing east is not possible?
4. What is the significance of burning olive oil before icons, and what practical steps should be taken to maintain the lamp properly while ensuring safety?

How Do We Prepare for Prayer?

Before beginning any prayer, the Orthodox tradition emphasizes the importance of preparation. This involves physically quieting the body and mentally preparing to enter into the presence of God. St. Theophan the Recluse recommends taking a few moments to calm the mind, consider who you are about to address, and cultivate a sense of humility. This preparation helps the soul enter into prayer more fully, making it a true dialogue with God.

To pray, we must draw inward in such a way that both our heart and mind are absorbed in the content of the prayer. This requires becoming very attentive to the actual words of the prayer and setting aside all other thoughts.

St. Theophan uses the analogy of sitting down to write a note, article, or term paper. One does not simply sit down and begin writing; first, thoughts must be gathered, and the mind must be prepared for the task. This kind of preparation is even more necessary when approaching prayer.

He writes: "Morning or evening, immediately before you begin to repeat your prayers, first stand for a while, sit for a while, or walk a little. Try to steady your mind, then turn it away from all worldly activities and objects."

He asks us to set aside thoughts of daily concerns, whether they be problems, upcoming tasks, or past conflicts with family or friends. We must pull our minds away from worldly cares so that they may be uplifted in prayer to the heavenly realm, where we encounter God.

St. Theophan continues: "After this, think of who He is, Him to whom you turn in prayer. Next, recollect who you are; who it is who is about to start this invocation to Him in prayer."

God is no less than our Creator, and even more, as He created all that is visible and invisible. He is all-powerful and has infinite love and patience for all His creation. He desires union with us and that we love Him as He loves us. As we prepare for prayer, we should consider how we would prepare to meet an important person whose help we need. We would focus on their needs and approach them with respect. Similarly, in prayer, we must focus on who God is and approach Him with reverence. St. Theophan reminds us to be mindful that God is not merely a familiar figure but the Almighty Creator.

He further instructs: "Do this in such a way as to waken in your heart a feeling of humility and reverent awe because you are standing in the presence of God."

Reflecting on what it means to stand in God's presence is crucial. This is precisely what happens in prayer.

St. Theophan explains: "When the heart is conscious and feels the need for prayer, then the attentive heart itself will not let your thoughts slide to other matters. It will force you to cry out to the Lord in your prayers. Most of all, be aware of your own helplessness: were it not for God, you would be lost. If someone who is doomed to disaster were to stand before the one person who, with a glance, could save him, would he look here and there for his salvation? No, he would fall down before him and beg mercy. So it will be, when you approach Him in prayer with an awareness of all-encompassing peril and the knowledge that only God can save you."

Too often, we enter prayer without proper preparation. We may rush through it as if it were just another routine obligation. St. Theophan warns against this: "Without preparation, how can there be a gathering of thought and feeling in prayer? Without preparation, prayer proceeds shakily instead of firmly... Such a careless attitude toward prayer is a crime, a serious one— a capital one. Consider prayer the central labor of your life and hold it in the center of your heart. Address it in its rightful role, not as a secondary function!"

Always remember that God is our helper. Be diligent in fulfilling your prayer rule, and you will experience great benefit when you properly prepare yourself for prayer. Work diligently, for you will encounter many forces that seek to discourage you.

St. Theophan encourages us: "Once experienced, pure prayer will draw you on and enliven your spiritual life, bringing you to more attentive, more difficult, and ever-deepening prayer."

Study Questions

1. Why is preparation important before beginning prayer, and what steps does St. Theophan recommend to properly prepare for prayer?

2. How does St. Theophan's analogy of writing a note or paper relate to preparing for prayer, and what lessons can we draw from this comparison?

3. What role does humility and reverent awe play in prayer, and how does reflecting on God's greatness help us enter into prayer more fully?

4. According to St. Theophan, what are the consequences of neglecting proper preparation for prayer, and how can we develop a more diligent and focused approach to our prayer life?

How Do We Pray?

St. Isaac the Syrian provides additional guidance on how to approach prayer:

- Pray with attention—so that we can have a true encounter with God.
- Pray with humility—because this sort of prayer goes straight to God's ear.
- Pray with affection and tears—with joy and thanksgiving, but also with true repentance and purity.
- Pray with patience and ardor—to deny oneself is courageously to persevere in prayer.
- Pray from the depths of the heart—even if we pray using 'the words of another,' they should be uttered as if they are our own. St. Isaac says this is especially true of the Psalms.
- Pray with faith and absolute trust in God—because He knows our life.

Follow a Prayer Rule and Use Written Prayers
You should have a specific prayer rule for both morning and evening. Avoid improvising; developing a discipline goes beyond what you feel like doing. Prayer is not a relaxation exercise but a path to communion with God. Have a set of guidelines to follow each time, with no excuses for shortcuts. Incorporate standing, prostrations, kneeling, making the sign of the cross, reading, and singing when appropriate. Use Orthodox prayer books, which contain prayers well-tested over centuries. Prayer does not need to be creative, but it must be sincere. Keep your awareness in your heart and concentrate on the words. Once you establish a rule, always keep it, and work with your spiritual father to refine it.

Focus on Each Word – Don't Rush Your Prayer
As you begin to pray, enter into every word with full attention. Bring the meaning into your heart. Avoid rushing through prayers as if completing an obligation. Slow down and let each word sink in with humility and awe of God. Just like driving at a moderate speed allows better control,

slowing down in prayer allows for deeper awareness of God's presence. If you find yourself rushing, stop, ask for forgiveness, and continue slowly. Studying prayers beforehand can help in understanding their meaning, and eventually, you may wish to memorize them.

Concentrate Your Attention in Prayer
During prayer, the mind may wander. Recognize this distraction but gently bring your focus back to the words. Repeat the part where you lost attention and continue with renewed focus. Sometimes, saying the prayers aloud can help maintain attention. Just as in important conversations, we must give God our undivided focus. The distractions of modern life make it even more necessary to train the mind to focus on heavenly things. Each day, work to improve your attentiveness in prayer.

Don't Rush Into Other Activities After Prayer
When you finish your prayers, take a moment to reflect on their impact. Hold the experience in your heart and treasure it. Allow yourself to carry the sense of God's presence into the rest of your day.

Pray Every Morning and Evening Without Fail
Your prayer life must become a firm and consistent rule, not something done sporadically. Commit to praying each morning and evening without fail. Make it as habitual as daily hygiene routines. Just as brushing your teeth is essential for bodily health, daily prayer is essential for the soul's well-being.

Study Questions

1. Why is it important to have a specific prayer rule rather than approaching prayer informally, and what elements should be included in a prayer rule?

2. How does slowing down during prayer help deepen one's connection with God, and what practical advice is given to avoid rushing through prayers?

3. What challenges can arise when trying to concentrate during prayer, and what strategies are suggested to regain focus when the mind wanders?

4. Why is it important to avoid rushing into other activities immediately after prayer, and how can one benefit from taking a moment of reflection afterward?

5. How can establishing a consistent daily prayer rule become as habitual as personal hygiene routines, and why is this consistency vital for spiritual growth?

Establishing a Rule of Prayer

A prayer rule is the outline of our daily prayer routine. It is important to have a thought out rule. Casually going to your place for prayer and simply talking with God is not the best way to begin to develop your prayer life. We will find that we end up babbling in front of our God. We can take advantage of the centuries of wisdom and being by using proven prayers that will lift us up in our way of communicating with God.

A prayer rule should first specify the place and time of prayer.

Then it should outline the sequence of your prayers and the specific prayers you will say.

Example of a Beginning Daily Prayer Rule

> In the name of the Father, the Son and the Holy Spirit. Amen. Glory to You our God, Glory to You.
>
> **Trisagion Prayer**
> Heavenly King, Comforter, the Spirit of Truth, present in all places and filling all things, Treasury of Goodness and Giver of life: come and abide in us. Cleanse us from every stain of sin and save our souls, O Gracious Lord.
>
> Holy God. Holy Mighty. Holy Immortal Have mercy on us.(3)
>
> Glory to the Father, and the Son and the Holy Spirit, both now and forever and to the ages of ages. Amen
>
> All Holy Trinity, have mercy on us. Lord, forgive our sins. Master, pardon our transgressions. HolyOne, visit and heal our infirmities, for the glory of Your Name.
>
> Lord, have mercy.(3)
>
> Glory to the Father, and the Son and the Holy Spirit, both now and forever and to the ages of ages. Amen

Our Father, Who art in Heaven, hallowed be Thy name. Thy Kingdom come, Thy will be done, on earth as it is in Heaven. Give us this day our daily bread; and forgive us our trespasses, as we forgive those who trespass against us; and lead us not into temptation, but deliver us from evil. For Yours is the Kingdom and the Power and the

Glory of the Father and the Son and the Holy Spirit, both now and forever and to the ages of ages. Amen.

Psalms

Morning Psalms: 3, 38, 63, 88, 103, 143 - Choose one each day
Evening Psalms: 70 and 143 - alternate

In morning only:

Commemorate the Living
Lord have mercy on: The leaders of the church, nation, spiritual fathers and mothers, parents and relative, Old and young, needy, orphans, widows, those in sickness and sorrow, those in captivity or confinement. Remember, strengthen and comfort them and grant them speedy relief and freedom and deliverance. (*add your own names*)

Commemorate the Departed
Remember Your servants who have fallen asleep: our grandparents, parents and family members and friends. Forgive them all their sins committed knowingly or unknowingly and grant them Your Kingdom, a portion of Your eternal blessing and the enjoyment of Your unending life. (*add your own names*)

Psalm 51

*Have mercy on me, O God, according to Thy great mercy;
and according to the multitude of Thy compassions,
blot out my transgression.
Wash me thoroughly from my iniquity, and cleanse me from my sin.
For I realize my iniquity, and my sin is before me continually.*

(Pause and remember your sinfulness)

*Against Thee only have I sinned I and done evil in Thy sight,
that Thou mayest be justified in Thy words
and win when Thou art judged.*

*For, behold, I was conceived in iniquities,
and in sins did my mother desire me.*

*For, lo, Thou lovest truth; the unknown and
secret things of Thy wisdom Thou hast made known to me.*

Thou shalt sprinkle me with hyssop, and I shall be cleansed;

Thou shalt wash me, and I shall become whiter than snow.

*Thou shalt make me hear joy and gladness;
the bones that have been humbled will rejoice.*

*Turn Thy face from my sins, and blot out all my iniquities.
Create in me a clean heart, O God; and renew a right spirit within me.*

Cast me not away from Thy face, and take not Thy Holy Spirit from me.

*Restore to me the joy of Thy salvation,
and confirm me with a princely spirit.*

I shall teach Thy ways to the lawless and the godless will return to Thee.

*Deliver me from blood, O God—O God of my salvation—
and my tongue shall extol Thy justice.*

O Lord, Thou wilt open my lips, and my mouth shall declare Thy praise.

For if Thou hadst desired sacrifice, I would have given it; but burnt offerings do not please Thee.

*The sacrifice for God is a contrite spirit;
a contrite and humble heart God will not despise.*

Gladden Sion, O Lord, with Thy good will; and let the walls of Jerusalem be built. Then Thou wilt be pleased with the sacrifice of righteousness, the oblation and burnt offering.

The Creed (Symbol of Faith)

I believe in one God, Father, Almighty, Maker of heaven and earth, and of all things visible and invisible: And in one Lord Jesus Christ, the only- begotten Son of God; begotten of the Father before all ages; Light from Light, True God from True God, begotten, not made, of One Essence with the Father, through Whom all things were made: Who for us men, and for our salvation, came down from Heaven, and was incarnate by the Holy Spirit and the Virgin Mary, and became Man: And was crucified for us under Pontius Pilate, and suffered and was buried: And He rose on the third day according to the Scriptures: And ascended into Heaven, and sits at the right hand of the Father: He will come again with glory to judge the living and the dead; His Kingdom shall have no end: And in the Holy Spirit, the Lord, the Creator of the Life, Who proceeds from the Father, Who with the Father and the Son is equally worshipped and glorified, Who spoke by the Prophets: And in One, Holy, Catholic and Apostolic Church. I confess one Baptism for the remission of sins. I look for the Resurrection of the Dead; And the life of the Age to come. Amen.

Lesser Doxology

Glory to God, who has shown us the Light! Glory to God in the highest, and on earth, peace, good will toward men! We praise You! We bless You! We worship You! We glorify You and give thanks to You for Your great glory! O Lord God, Heavenly King, God the Father Almighty! O Lord, the Only-begotten Son, Jesus Christ, and the Holy Spirit! O Lord God, Lamb of God, Son of the Father, Who take away the sins of the world, have mercy on us! You, Who take away the sins of the world, receive our prayer! You, Who sit on the right hand of the Father, have mercy on us! For You alone are holy, and You alone are Lord. You alone, O Lord Jesus Christ, are most high in the glory of God the Father! Amen! I will give thanks to You every day and praise Your Name for ever and ever. Lord, You have been our refuge from generation to generation! I said, "Lord, have mercy on me. Heal my soul, for I have sinned against You!" Lord, I flee to You, Teach me to do Your will, for You are my God. For with You is the fountain of Life, and in Your light shall we see light. Continue Your lovingkindness to those who know You. Vouchsafe, O Lord, to keep us this day without sin. Blessed are You, O Lord, the God of our fathers, and praised and glorified is Your Name for ever. Amen. Let Your mercy be upon us, O Lord, even as we have set our hope on You. Blessed are You, O Lord; teach me Your statutes. Blessed are You, O Master; make me to understand Your commandments. Blessed are You, O Holy One; enlighten me with your precepts. Your mercy endures forever, O Lord! Do not despise the works of your hands! To You belongs worship, to You belongs praise, to You belongs glory: to the Father and to the Son and to the Holy Spirit, now and ever and unto ages of ages. Amen.

Morning Prayer of Metropolitan Philaret

Lord, give me the strength to greet the coming day in peace. Help me in all things to rely on Your holy will. Reveal Your will to me every hour of the day. Bless my dealings with all people. Teach me to treat all people who come to me throughout the day with peace of soul and with firm conviction that Your will governs all. In all my deeds and words guide my thoughts and feelings. In unexpected events, let me not forget that all are sent by you. Teach me to act firmly and wisely, without embittering and embarrassing others. Give me the physical strength to bear the labors of this day. Direct my will, teach me to pray, pray in me. Amen.

or Evening Prayer

O Lord, God our Father, if during this day I have sinned in word, deed or thought forgive me in Your goodness and love. Grant me peaceful sleep; protect me from all evil and awake me in the morning that I may glorify you, Your Son and Your Holy Spirit now and forever and ever. Amen.

(Here you may add your own private prayers using your own words or some of the Prayers found in an Orthodox Prayer Book.)

Jesus prayer—repeat 100 times.
Lord Jesus Christ , Son of God, Have mercy on me a sinner.

Reflection
Reflect quietly on the tasks of the day and prepare yourself for the difficulties you might face, asking God to help.

Dismissal
Glory to the Father and to the Son and to the Holy Spirit, now and ever and unto ages of ages. Amen.

Through the prayers of our holy Fathers, Lord Jesus Christ our God, have mercy on us and save us. Amen.

Conclusion: The Lifelong Journey of Prayer
Orthodox prayer is not about perfection, but about growth and relationship. Prayer is a lifelong journey, where the believer moves from the external act of speaking words to an intimate experience of God's presence. Through discipline, concentration, and perseverance, the believer grows in communion with God, and prayer becomes a means of spiritual transformation. The Orthodox Christian is called not just to pray, but to be transformed by prayer, seeking to experience the Kingdom of God within and to unite with Christ in all things.

Study Questions

1. Create a Daily Prayer Rule

Chapter 10

Fasting in the Orthodox Christian Tradition: A Spiritual Discipline

"While getting filled up does a favor for the stomach, fasting returns benefits to the Soul. Be encouraged, because the doctor has given you a powerful remedy... venturing into the Soul to kill sin."
Saint Basil the Great

Fasting is an ancient and deeply rooted practice in the Orthodox Christian tradition. It is not just a ritual of abstaining from food but a spiritual discipline aimed at transforming the soul, strengthening the will, and cultivating a deeper union with God. This comprehensive practice, while involving bodily restraint, is fundamentally about redirecting the heart and mind toward God. It is seen by the Church Fathers as essential for our spiritual growth.

In this chapter we discuss the nature of fasting, its purpose and dual benefits. This is followed by the Church guidelines on how to fast.

Nature of Fasting

The Purpose of Fasting

The primary purpose of fasting is to bring us into closer union with God, aligning our will with His. Jesus Christ, in His teachings, calls us to be perfect as our Father in heaven is perfect (Matthew 5:48). Fasting helps us to refine and strengthen our will, enabling us to live in accordance with God's divine will (Matthew 6:10). While fasting involves abstention from certain foods, its true purpose transcends the physical act, focusing on disciplining the soul to draw closer to God and avoid distractions from worldly desires.

Fasting as an Ascetic Discipline

Fasting is described as an ascetic discipline, which engages in spiritual warfare against ego-centric passions. These passions, which often arise from automatic, subconscious responses influenced by temptation, can distract us from living a life aligned with God's will. Fasting provides an opportunity to free the soul from these distractions, empowering the individual to make deliberate choices that reflect spiritual growth. It develops watchfulness, allowing us to notice and combat temptations more effectively, thus fostering a closer relationship with God.

The Spiritual Benefits of Fasting

Fasting purifies the soul by detaching us from materialism and worldly pleasures. It encourages dependence on God, reminding us that we need Him for everything. Through fasting, when combined with prayer and repentance, we open our hearts to grace, healing, and transformation. The discipline also helps us master our passions—such as greed, gluttony, and laziness—which otherwise hinder spiritual growth. By disciplining the body, fasting makes it easier to align the will with God's higher purposes.

Fasting and Control of Desires

One of the most fundamental reasons for fasting, according to the Church Fathers, is that hunger for food is one of our most basic and powerful passions. If we can learn to control our appetite for food, it becomes easier to control other desires, such as lust and greed. St. Gregory of Sinai categorizes eating into three stages: abstinence (remaining slightly hungry), adequacy (eating just enough), and overindulgence (excessive eating). Overindulgence leads to gluttony, which opens the door to other vices, such as lust and greed. Through fasting, we learn to control these desires, ultimately achieving spiritual freedom and alignment with God's will.

Fasting in a Modern Society

In a consumer-driven society, where food is often seen as a source of comfort and indulgence, fasting can be a particularly challenging discipline. Modern society's convenience and the constant availability of food can easily lead to overconsumption. This has contributed to alarming obesity rates, with about 20% of children and 35% of adults in the U.S. being obese. The root of these issues is often a lack of self-control, exacerbated by advertisements and societal pressure. The teachings of James 1:14 remind us that we are often drawn away by our own desires, making fasting a crucial practice for reclaiming self-discipline and spiritual focus.

Scriptural Foundation of Fasting

Fasting is a practice deeply rooted in Scripture. In the Old Testament, Moses fasted for forty days and nights (Deuteronomy 9:9), the prophet Jonah used fasting as a means of repentance (Jonah 3:7), and Daniel combined fasting with prayer as a way to seek God's will (Daniel 9:3-4). In the New Testament, Jesus Himself fasted for forty days and forty nights (Matthew 4:2), setting an example for His followers. He also taught that certain spiritual battles, such as casting out demons, require both prayer and fasting (Matthew 17:21). Jesus also emphasized that fasting should be done with the right intention, not for public display, but to seek God in secret (Matthew 6:17-18).

Fasting and the Apostles

The Apostles carried forward the practice of fasting as a central part of Christian life. The Apostle Paul frequently mentions fasting in his writings, not only as a personal discipline but also as a communal activity in the Church. In Romans 14:20, he urges believers not to destroy the work of God for the sake of food. Fasting was also linked to key decisions in the early Church. For example, in Acts 13:2-3, the Apostles fasted and prayed before sending Barnabas and Saul for mission work. Similarly, Paul's own spiritual life was marked by fasting, sacrifice, and prayer, showing the depth of commitment required for a life devoted to God.

The Church Fathers on Fasting
The Church Fathers provided extensive teachings on the significance of fasting. St. Athanasius, for example, wrote that fasting purifies the soul and the body, curing spiritual ills and even casting out demons. St. John Cassian emphasized that fasting, along with prayer and self-denial, is a path to spiritual perfection, though not an end in itself. These early Christian writers understood fasting as a way to grow closer to God, purify the soul, and prepare for greater union with the divine.

Modern Understanding of Fasting
While fasting has always been seen as a spiritual discipline, its physical benefits are becoming more widely recognized. Studies on intermittent fasting have shown that it can reduce the risk of chronic diseases such as type 2 diabetes, heart disease, and even certain cancers. Fasting has also been linked to improved mental clarity and cognitive function. Harvard psychiatrist John Ratey, for instance, found that fasting led to increased activity in the brain's motor cortex, improving mental alertness. Fasting, therefore, not only benefits the soul but also promotes physical well-being.

More than Food
Saint Basil as well as Saint John Chrysostom tells us that true fasting is not just about food but includes refraining from sin, judging others, and cultivating love and forgiveness. It should not become a burden or source for pride. It is much more than a rule. It's a spiritual discipline to heal our soul.

Study Questions

1. What is the primary purpose of fasting in the Orthodox Christian tradition, and how does it contribute to a deeper union with God?

2. How does fasting serve as an ascetic discipline and help in the battle against ego-centric passions, such as greed, gluttony, and laziness?

3. What does St. Gregory of Sinai teach about the stages of eating, and how does controlling our appetite for food help in mastering other desires?

4. How does the practice of fasting in modern society differ from the traditional understanding of fasting, and what challenges does contemporary culture present to this spiritual discipline?

5. What role does fasting play in the Scriptures, and how did Jesus, the Apostles, and the Church Fathers model fasting as an essential part of the Christian life?

How to Fast

Fasting in the Orthodox tradition involves abstention from various foods, including meat, dairy, and oil, depending on the fasting period. There are several important fasting periods throughout the year:

Key Fasting Periods in the Orthodox Church

Great Lent: The most significant fasting period, lasting 40 days (plus Holy Week) in preparation for Pascha (Easter). It involves strict fasting from meat, dairy, fish, oil, and wine.

Holy Week: The week leading up to Pascha, where fasting is particularly strict, focusing on total abstinence from food and drink until the Paschal Feast.

The Nativity Fast (Advent): From November 15 to December 24, this period prepares the faithful for the Feast of the Nativity of Christ, with abstention from meat, dairy, and other animal products.

The Apostles' Fast: Beginning after Pentecost, this fast lasts until the Feast of Saints Peter and Paul (June 29). It varies in length, depending on the date of Pascha.

The Dormition Fast: From August 1-14, fasting in honor of the Assumption of the Virgin Mary.

Other Fasting Days: Fasting on Wednesdays and Fridays is a weekly discipline, especially in remembrance of Christ's betrayal (Wednesday) and crucifixion (Friday). Additional fast days occur before major feasts like Christmas and Theophany (January 6).

Practical Guidelines

Weekly Fasts

Wednesdays and Fridays: In memory of Christ's betrayal and crucifixion, Orthodox Christians abstain from meat, dairy, fish, olive oil, and wine, unless it's a feast day.

Fasting Seasons

Great Lent: The strictest fast, lasting 40 days before Pascha, with abstention from meat, dairy, fish, wine, and olive oil, except on specified feast days.

Nativity Fast (November 15 - December 24): Preparation for Christ's birth, gradually stricter as Christmas approaches.

Apostles' Fast: Between the Sunday after Pentecost and June 29, with variable duration.

Dormition Fast (August 1–14): Preparation for the feast of the Dormition of the Theotokos.

One-Day Fasts:

Exaltation of the Holy Cross (September 14).

Eve of Theophany (January 5).

Beheading of St. John the Baptist (August 29).

Observe how this schedule helps you become a participant in the Gospel.

Dietary Guidelines

There are differing levels recommended that involve abstention from:
- Meat and meat products.
- Dairy and eggs.
- Fish (allowed on specific feast days).
- Wine and olive oil (allowed on weekends and certain feast days during fasting seasons).

What to Eat

Fruits, vegetables, legumes, grains, nuts, and seafood like shellfish.

Feast Days During Fasts: Some fasting seasons include feast days (e.g., Annunciation, Palm Sunday) where fish, wine, and olive oil are permitted.

Exceptions to the Rules

Health Conditions: Those with medical needs, such as pregnant women, children, or the elderly, are encouraged to adapt fasting practices with the guidance of a spiritual father.

Pastoral Guidance: Fasting is a personal journey and should be tailored to one's spiritual growth.

The Spirit of Fasting
Fasting is not about rigid adherence to dietary laws but about cultivating repentance, love, and humility. Pairing fasting with increased prayer, confession, communion, and almsgiving completes its purpose.

Fasting in the Orthodox Church: Spiritual and Physical Discipline
Fasting is an essential part of Orthodox Christian life, serving as a discipline to combat the passions and open the door to spiritual renewal through the Holy Spirit. It is not about following a set of rules but about realigning our attitudes towards food and the body, helping us grow spiritually and move toward theosis, or union with God. Fasting, therefore, is not a punishment but a constructive therapy for the soul. It helps us walk the path toward greater spiritual maturity and deeper intimacy with our Creator.

How to Begin
To begin a fasting routine it is generally recommended to begin to develop the habit of fasting on Wednesdays and Fridays like the early Christians. Since meat is now such a prominent part of our diet, begin to abstain from meat on these days. Then once you have mastered this yyou can develop a more strict fast by abstaining from all dairy, eggs, wine. and oil.

Conclusion
Fasting is much more than a dietary restriction; it is a profound spiritual discipline that engages the entire person—body, mind, and soul. It is a path toward self-control, purity, and a deeper relationship with God. Whether we are fasting for repentance, spiritual growth, or as an act of obedience, the ultimate goal is always the same: to become more Christ-like and experience the transformative power of God's grace in our lives. Through fasting, we strengthen our will, free ourselves from worldly attachments, and draw closer to God, who is the source of true peace, joy, and fulfillment.

Study Questions

1. What are the key fasting periods in the Orthodox Church, and how do they prepare the faithful for major feasts such as Pascha and the Nativity of Christ?
2. What is the practice for every week?
3. How does fasting in the Orthodox Christian tradition go beyond dietary restrictions, and what is the deeper spiritual purpose of fasting when paired with prayer, confession, and almsgiving?
4. How do you plan to begin fasting routine in your daily life?

Chapter 11

Orthodox Worship: A Comprehensive Overview

This chapter provides a thorough exploration of Orthodox worship, highlighting its spiritual significance, historical development, and practical structure. It begins by examining worship as a participation in the divine life of God, emphasizing its transformative nature and its role in uniting believers with Christ and the heavenly hosts. The chapter then traces the historical roots of Orthodox worship, from Old Testament practices to the early Christian gatherings that shaped the liturgical traditions preserved today.

The study also delves into the liturgical cycles, including the daily, weekly, and annual rhythms of prayer and celebration that structure the spiritual life of the faithful. Special attention is given to the Divine Liturgy, which stands as the central act of Orthodox worship, offering a profound encounter with Christ through the Eucharist. The structure and significance of the Liturgy are explored, from the preparatory Proskomide to the distribution of Holy Communion.

Throughout this chapter, the theological, historical, and practical dimensions of Orthodox worship are presented to provide a comprehensive understanding of how worship serves as the foundation of the Church's life and the path to communion with God.

Worship as Participation in the Divine Life of God

Orthodox worship stands at the very heart of the Church's spiritual life, serving as a means by which believers encounter and participate with God, and glorify His name. It transcends mere ritual, offering a transformative and mystical experience that bridges heaven and earth. Through the interplay of prayer, sacraments, and the liturgical cycles, Orthodox worship provides a foretaste of the heavenly kingdom, inviting the faithful to participate in the divine life of God.

At its core, Orthodox worship is an act involving reverence and awe, honoring God as the source of all life, goodness, and truth. It acknowledges His supreme authority and expresses gratitude for His mercy and acts of salvation. Worship unites believers with God and brings them into His divine presence, participating in their prayers with those of the saints, and angels. This involvement in divine life reaches its pinnacle in the Divine Liturgy, where the Church on earth participates in the eternal heavenly liturgy. Through worship, the faithful are sanctified, gradually conformed to the image of Christ, and aligned with God's will as revealed in Holy Scripture and Tradition. Additionally, worship is a proclamation of the Gospel, bearing witness to the truth of God's Kingdom and the hope of resurrection.

Historical Roots of Orthodox Worship

The origins of Orthodox worship can be traced back to the Old Testament. Before the time of Moses, worship primarily consisted of sacrifices and prayers offered in open spaces. With Moses came the establishment of the Tabernacle, and later the Temple, which introduced a more structured form of worship led by priests and Levites. During His earthly ministry, Jesus affirmed the sanctity of worship, emphasizing its focus on the Heavenly Father and underscoring the importance of order and reverence.

Following Christ's ascension, the Apostles established early Christian gatherings, known as ecclesia, where believers assembled to worship. Bishops, priests, and deacons were consecrated to lead these gatherings, and over time, the structure of Christian worship was formalized under the guidance of the Holy Spirit and the teachings of the Church Fathers. This structure has been faithfully preserved in the Orthodox Church, ensuring the continuity of worship as a sacred and transformative encounter with God.

Study Questions

1. How does Orthodox worship transcend mere ritual and serve as a transformative and mystical experience for believers?

2. What is the significance of the Divine Liturgy in Orthodox worship, and how does it connect believers with the heavenly Kingdom and the eternal liturgy?

3. How do the historical roots of Orthodox worship, from Old Testament sacrifices to early Christian gatherings, shape the structure and sanctity of worship in the Orthodox Church today?

The Divine Liturgy: Heaven on Earth

The Divine Liturgy is the central act of Orthodox worship, where heaven and earth meet in a profound and mystical way. It is not merely symbolic but a transformative event in which the bread and wine are changed into the Body and Blood of Christ. Through this Eucharistic celebration, believers are united with Christ and the heavenly kingdom, experiencing a foretaste of eternal life.

As described by the emissaries of Prince Vladimir in 987:
> "We knew not whether we were in heaven or on earth. For on earth, there is no such beauty, and we are at a loss how to describe it. We only know that God dwells there among men..."

The Divine Liturgy transcends time and space, inviting the faithful to participate in the eternal heavenly worship. It involves the real presence of the Holy Spirit and Christ, making it a profound encounter and participation with the divine. Often referred to as the "liturgy of the angels," it is an act of unending praise to God, uniting the faithful with the angelic hosts. This unity is beautifully expressed in the hymn "Holy, Holy, Holy," echoing the heavenly worship described in Isaiah.

The saints also join in this worship, as they are living members of the Church in heaven. In Orthodox worship, believers do not pray alone but are united with the saints and angels in offering prayers and intercessions, forming a "great cloud of intercession" before God. This unity underscores the communal and eternal nature of the Divine Liturgy, drawing all of creation into a profound act of worship.

The Divine Liturgy traces its origins to Christ's institution of the Eucharist at the Last Supper, where He commanded, *Do this in remembrance of Me* (Luke 22:19). Following His Ascension, the first Christians gathered to break bread and pray, as described in Acts 2:42. Over time, under the guidance of the Holy Spirit and the teachings of the Church Fathers, the structure of the Liturgy was formalized. Today, the Orthodox Church primarily uses the Liturgy of St. John Chrysostom, developed in the 4th century, while preserving the essential elements instituted by Christ.

The Main Goal

The Divine Liturgy is the sacred meeting point between heaven and earth, where the faithful are drawn into the very life of the Holy Trinity. It is not merely a service but a profound and mystical encounter with Jesus Christ who is truly present, offering Himself to the faithful for their sanctification, healing, and union with Him.

Surrounding the altar, the angelic hosts minister invisibly, singing with the saints who join with the heavenly choir. The faithful are not spectators but are active participants in this divine mystery, standing in the company of the heavenly assembly, their prayers ascending as incense before the Throne of God. The Liturgy is a foretaste of the eternal Kingdom, where the barriers of time and space dissolve, and believers physically as well as spiritually receiving His life-giving Body and Blood, being transformed by His divinity. It is here that the earthly Church participates with the unceasing worship in heaven, becoming joined with Christ, amidst the angels, and the saints in an eternal hymn of love and glory.

Structure of the Divine Liturgy

As we enter the Church we enter into an area called the Narthex. This is a transition space from a busy world of all kinds of worlds cares to one focused on spiritual cares. Here believers leave the busy world outside and prepare for participation in a heavenly banquet. They set aside their worldly cares to focus on the presence of God.

Most faithful will begin this transition by lighting a candle and offering prayers for whoever they desire. They will then venerate the icons that are placed there. As they enter the nave of the Church where the service takes place they will offer a pray to be enlightened by the Holy Spirit. They enter with an inner peace and a feeling of love for God.

The Divine Liturgy consists of three main parts: the Proskomide, the Liturgy of the Catechumens, and the Liturgy of the Faithful.

Proskomide

This preparatory service takes. place in a side altar and involves preparing bread and wine brought by parishioners, symbolizing the "first fruits" of human labor for the consecration that will follow. In ancient times even before Christianity people offered the first fruits their crops or animals. The bread that has been baked prayerfully contains a seal baked into the top of the loaf. The main section in this seal is called the lamb which will be transformed into the Body of Christ. The chalice is filled with wine that has all been brought by the faithful. Prayers or offered for both the living and the dead and a particle for each person is added to the paten or plate that contains the parts that have been cut out. Once completed the paten and chalice are covered and blessed then are set aside, prepare for the time in the liturgy when these gifts will be offered and brought to the altar in a solemn procession.

Liturgy of the Catechumens
This is considered the beginning of the Divine liturgy. The Proskomedi was completed previously. This section includes prayers, hymns, and Scripture readings, aimed at turning the hearts of the faithful toward God. It begins with a Litany where the Deacon or Priest lead the congregation in a series of prayers. Following these prayers there is a procession called the Small Entrance, The priest offers a prayer calling the angels to join us to escort the Gospel representing Christ. Priest blesses the entrance and we sing, "Come let us worship and bow down before Christ our God." Then the Gospel is placed on the altar. Next the Trisagion Hymn ("Holy God, Holy Mighty, Holy Immortal") allowing us to join in the heavily choir glorifying God. Then there is an Epistle reading followed by reading form the Gospel. At this point the priest will offer a sermon to help the faithful gathered to properly understand what has been read and offer ideas on how to apply it to their daily lives. This part of the service prepares the faithful for a deeper participation in the mysteries of faith.

Liturgy of the Faithful
This is the heart of the Divine Liturgy, encompassing a Great Entrance, the recitation of the Creed, the Anaphora (offering prayer), the Epiclesis (invocation of the Holy Spirit), and Holy Communion.

At the start of this portion of the service, a special cloth called the antimension is opened and placed on the altar where the consecration will occur. This cloth is adorned with an icon of Christ being taken down from the Cross, surrounded by depictions of the four Evangelists and inscriptions referencing the Passion of Christ. In the early days of Christianity, when services were held in catacombs, this cloth was spread over the tomb of a martyr. Similarly, modern Orthodox altars contain relics of martyrs. The antimension also bears the signature of the local bishop, authorizing the service.

The Great Entrance follows, where the gifts prepared during the Proskomide are brought in a solemn procession through the congregation and placed on the altar. These gifts are offered to God and then changed into the Body and Blood of Christ. During the procession, the faithful pray:

> "Remember us all, Lord God, in Your Kingdom, now and forever, and unto the ages of ages."

After the Great Entrance, another litany is offered by the deacon or priest, calling on everyone to pray for:

- For the Gifts presented
- For a peaceful and sinless day
- For a guardian angel
- For forgiveness of sins
- For all that is good for our souls
- A life completed in peace and penitence.
- A Christian end to life.
- Committing ourselves and each other to Christ.

The faithful then proclaim their faith by reciting the Creed together. The priest invites all to stand with fear and awe as they prepare to present the Holy Gifts in peace, echoing Christ's command:

> *Therefore, if you bring your gift to the altar, and there remember that your brother has something against you, leave your gift there before the altar, and go your way. First, be reconciled to your brother, and then come and offer your gift* (Matthew 5:23-24).

The service continues with the anaphora, a prayer of offering, and reaches its climax in the Epiclesis, where the priest solemnly invokes the Holy

Spirit to change the bread and wine into the Body and Blood of Christ. The priest prays:

> "Your own gifts we offer to You on behalf of all and for all. We offer to You this reasonable and unbloody sacrifice, and we beg You, we ask You, we pray You:
>
> Send forth Your Holy Spirit upon us and upon these gifts here presented, and make this bread the Precious Body of Your Christ, and that which is in this chalice the Precious Blood of Your Christ, transforming them by Your Holy Spirit."

The precise moment of transformation is a divine mystery, but the faithful believe the Holy Spirit accomplishes this during this prayer.

The divine gifts are then prepared for distribution. The Lamb (the portion of bread cut during the Proskomide that is now the Body of Christ) is broken, and pieces are placed into the chalice. Boiling water, known as zeon, is added to the chalice, symbolizing the warmth of the Holy Spirit. After preparatory prayers, the clergy partake in Holy Communion.

The faithful are then called to receive:
"With the fear of God, with faith, and with love, draw near."

Those who have properly prepared come forward reverently to receive what is now the actual Body and Blood of Christ. They receive it from the chalice on a spoon.

After Communion, the priest prays for those who have received:
Save Your people and bless Your inheritance. (Psalm 28:9)

Prayers of thanksgiving follow, and the service concludes with a dismissal and the distribution of antidoron (blessed bread). Though not Holy Communion, antidoron is received with reverence and serves as a blessing.

Preparation for Holy Communion
Receiving Holy Communion requires spiritual preparation through repentance, prayer, and fasting. Believers approach the Eucharist with reverence and love, ensuring they are in a proper spiritual state. It is assumed that the faithful have been observing the fasting guidelines and have recently confessed their sins to a priest. Fasting is required from midnight before Communion, abstaining from all food and drink.

Frequent participation in Communion
Frequent participation in Holy Communion is strongly encouraged, as it is essential for the life of the soul. Christ Himself commanded this participation, affirming the Eucharist's significance for eternal life:

> 1. By the command of our Lord: Jesus said, *And the bread that I will give is My flesh, which I will give for the life of the world* (John 6:51).
>
> *Most assuredly, I say to you, unless you eat the flesh of the Son of Man and drink His blood, you have no life in you* (John 6:53).
>
> When He gave this mystery to His disciples, Jesus did not make it optional, but instead commanded, *Take, eat... Drink of it, all of you...* (Matthew 26:26-28).
>
> 2. By the Acts and Canons of the Holy Apostles and the Sacred Councils, as well as the testimonies of the Church Fathers.
>
> 3. By the words, order, and celebration of the Divine Liturgy, which emphasize the Eucharist as the culmination of Christian worship.
>
> 4. By the nature of Holy Communion itself, as the Body and Blood of Christ is the source of spiritual nourishment and eternal life.

The Apostles, councils, and Church Fathers strongly emphasized the importance of frequent participation in Holy Communion. In the Book of Acts, we read how the early Christians embraced this practice:

> *And they continued steadfastly in the Apostles' doctrine, in fellowship, in the breaking of bread, and in prayers* (Acts 2:42).

The canons of the Holy Apostles also stress the necessity of Communion:

> "If anyone does not receive Communion when the offering is made, let him declare the reason; and if it is legitimate, let him be excused. But if he does not declare it, let him be excommunicated" (Canon 8).
>
> "Any of the faithful who enter and listen to the Scriptures but do not stay for the prayers and Holy Communion are to be excommunicated, as causing disorder in the Church" (Canon 9).

The goal of the Divine Liturgy itself is Holy Communion. During the invitation to receive the Eucharist, the priest calls the faithful:
"With the fear of God, with faith, and with love, draw near."

After Communion, the faithful give thanks, proclaiming:
"Let our mouths be filled with Your praise, O Lord… for You have deemed us worthy to partake of Your holy, immortal, and immaculate Mysteries."

Saints and Church Fathers have extolled the profound spiritual benefits of the Eucharist:

St. Basil the Great teaches that the Eucharist strengthens the faithful, helps them grow in virtue, and deepens their union with God.

St. Gregory the Theologian writes:
"When the most sacred Body of Christ is received and eaten in a proper manner, it becomes a weapon against those who war against us, it returns to God those who had left Him, it strengthens the weak, it causes the healthy to be glad, it heals sickness, and it preserves health. Through it, we become meek and more willing to accept correction, more long-suffering in our pains, more fervent in our love, more detailed in our knowledge, more willing to obey, and keener in the workings of the charismata of the Spirit."

Frequent participation in Holy Communion is not only a command of Christ but also a vital means of spiritual nourishment, sanctification, and growth in the life of the faithful.

The Eucharist is not merely a symbolic act but the true participation in the life of Christ.

The Transformative Power of Worship
Orthodox worship is a profound expression of the Church's faith, drawing believers into the life of the Holy Trinity. Through worship, the Church sanctifies the faithful, equips them for a life in communion with God, and prepares them for eternal life. It proclaims the reality of God's Kingdom and invites all to partake in the joy and peace of His divine presence. Worship renews the soul, strengthens hope, and fosters a deeper relationship with God and the Church community.

Study Questions

1. What is the significance of the Divine Liturgy as a means of communion with God in Orthodox worship?
2. How does the Orthodox Church view the transformative nature of the Eucharist, particularly the real presence of Christ in the bread and wine?
3. What is the role of the saints, angels, and heavenly hosts in the Divine Liturgy, and how does this contribute to the communal nature of Orthodox worship?
4. How does the Divine Liturgy transcend time and space, and what is its connection to the eternal heavenly worship?
5. What are the main components of the Divine Liturgy, and what is the purpose of each part in bringing the faithful into closer union with God?
6. How does the Proskomide prepare the bread and wine for the Eucharist, and what does it symbolize in the context of the Divine Liturgy?
7. Explain the significance of the Great Entrance and the prayers offered during it in the Liturgy of the Faithful.
8. Why is the Epiclesis, or invocation of the Holy Spirit, a central part of the Divine Liturgy, and how does it relate to the transformation of the bread and wine?
9. What does the participation of the faithful in Holy Communion signify, and why is it essential for spiritual nourishment and growth?
10. How do the actions and words of the priest during the Divine Liturgy emphasize the goal of uniting the faithful with Christ and preparing them for eternal life?

The Liturgical Cycles

Orthodox worship is deeply rooted in its liturgical cycles, which include the daily, weekly, and annual rhythms of prayer and celebration.

The daily cycle of services begins with Vespers (evening prayer), Compline (before sleep), the Midnight Service, Matins (morning prayer), and the Four Hours, each marking significant moments of the day and aligning the faithful with the mysteries of Christ's life and Passion. Matins is often followed by a Divine Liturgy.

The weekly cycle assigns specific themes to each day:

>Sunday: Celebrates Christ's Resurrection.
>
>Monday: Honors the Holy Bodiless Powers (angels and archangels).
>
>Tuesday: Commemorates the prophets, especially St. John the Forerunner.
>
>Wednesday: Reflects on the Cross and Judas' betrayal.
>
>Thursday: Remembers the Holy Apostles and Hierarchs.
>
>Friday: Venerates the Cross and recalls the Crucifixion.
>
>Saturday: Dedicates remembrance to all saints and the departed.

The annual liturgical cycle includes major feast days celebrating the lives of Christ and the Theotokos, such as Christmas, Pascha (Easter), and Pentecost. Fasting seasons, including Lent and the Nativity Fast, prepare believers for these celebrations through repentance and spiritual renewal.

>September 8 Nativity of the Theotokos
>
>September 14 Elevation of the Holy Cross
>
>November 21 Presentation of the Theotokos
>
>December 25 Christmas
>
>January 6 Epiphany (The Baptism of Christ)
>
>February 2 Presentation of the Lord
>
>March 25 Annunciation
>
>Sunday before Easter Palm Sunday

40 Days after Easter Ascension of the Lord
50 Days after Easter Pentecost
August 6 Transfiguration of our Lord
August 15 Dormition of the Theotokos

Study Questions

1. How do the daily, weekly, and annual liturgical cycles in the Orthodox Church structure the faithful's spiritual life and align them with the mysteries of Christ's life and Passion?

2. What is the significance of the specific themes assigned to each day of the week in Orthodox worship, and how do they help deepen the believer's understanding of Christ and the Church's teachings?

Chapter 12

Repentance: A Journey Back to God

Repentance lies at the heart of the Christian life. It is more than merely acknowledging sin—it is a transformative journey that leads us back to communion with God, restoring the loving relationship for which we were created. Drawing on the wisdom of Scripture and the Church Fathers, this article explores the nature of repentance, the meaning of sin, and the profound message of the Parable of the Prodigal Son.

In this chapter we begin with a clarification of the need for repentance and the nature of spiritual warfare. Next we discuss the parable of the Prodigal Son and model of repentence taught by Jesus. Then the way of repentence is outlined. In the final section we describe the preparation and the actual sacrament of Confession.

Need for Repentance

The Christian Calling
As Christians, we are called to a life seeking union with Christ, destined for eternal life in His Kingdom. Realizing this goal depends on a living faith in the Father, Son, and Holy Spirit—a faith characterized by desire, zeal, and love for God. True love for God leads us to follow His commandments and strive to become like Him. Yet, in our human imperfection, we often "miss the mark," falling short of this divine calling.

Spiritual Warfare
Spiritual warfare refers to the ongoing struggle that every Christian faces in resisting the temptations, passions, and sinful inclinations that separate them from God. It is understood not as a physical battle but as a battle within the soul, where divine grace competes with the effects of sin. The Orthodox Church teaches that this warfare involves both inner and outer struggles: the inner battle against our disordered desires (passions) and the outer battle against external temptations and demonic influences.

Key aspects of Spiritual warfare
Battle Against Passions
In Orthodoxy, passions are seen as disordered desires that lead the soul away from God. These include gluttony, lust, anger, pride, and greed. Spiritual warfare involves the continuous effort to resist these passions and redirect the heart and mind toward God. Through prayer, fasting, repentance, and other spiritual disciplines, believers actively combat the passions, seeking to purify the soul and align it with God's will.

> **Guarding the Heart and Mind**
> Spiritual warfare is also a battle for the heart and mind. Orthodox Christians are taught to be vigilant, or "watchful" (nepsis), guarding their thoughts, emotions, and actions. By recognizing harmful impulses early, they can redirect them before they lead to sinful actions. This watchfulness helps to prevent the passions from taking root and overpowering the soul. The heart, as the center of

the person's spiritual being, is crucial in this battle; purity of heart is necessary to experience God's presence.

Resistance to the Enemy

The Orthodox Church teaches that the Devil and his demons actively seek to lead believers astray, using temptations, doubts, and distractions to draw them away from God. St. Paul, in his epistle to the Ephesians (6:10-18), describes the "armor of God" as essential in this spiritual battle. This armor includes truth, righteousness, faith, salvation, and the Word of God—all of which protect and strengthen the believer. Orthodox Christians understand that by actively resisting temptation and remaining steadfast in faith, they can overcome the influence of the enemy.

Cooperation with Divine Grace

Orthodox spiritual warfare is not about fighting in isolation. It involves cooperation with God's grace, which empowers the believer to resist temptation and overcome sin. Through the sacraments, especially the Eucharist and Confession, Orthodox Christians receive the strength to engage in spiritual warfare. Prayer and the Jesus Prayer ("Lord Jesus Christ, Son of God, have mercy on me, a sinner") are also powerful tools in the believer's arsenal, helping to keep the soul focused on God.

The Goal of Theosis (Union with God)

The ultimate goal of spiritual warfare is not just resisting sin, but growing in holiness and being transformed into the likeness of Christ. This process, known as theosis, is central to Orthodox spirituality. Spiritual warfare, therefore, is not only about battling sin but about allowing God's grace to transform the believer's life, drawing them closer to Him and ultimately into communion with God.

As St. Paul writes in Romans 7:15-24:

What I will to do, that I do not practice; but what I will not to do, that I do.

Like St. George, who is depicted slaying a dragon, we are engaged in a spiritual war. The Christian life is a continual struggle against sin, temptation, and our fallen nature. All are sinners—we all fall short of

God's glory, and this battle is ongoing. Repentance is part of our daily struggle to return to God, seeking His mercy and strength to overcome our weaknesses.

Spiritual warfare in the Orthodox Christian tradition is a continual, internal struggle against sin, the passions, and the forces of darkness. It requires vigilance, humility, prayer, and a reliance on divine grace. Through this struggle, the believer is called to grow in holiness, resist temptation, and ultimately be transformed into the image of Christ, fulfilling the Christian calling to union with God.

Understanding Sin

The Greek word for sin is ἁμαρτία (hamartia), which means "missing the mark" or "falling short" of God's standard. In Orthodox Christianity, hamartia refers to any action, thought, or state of being that deviates from God's will and purpose for humanity. It is not simply about breaking laws but about the rupture of a loving relationship with God. Sin is a failure to live in communion with God, caused by self-centeredness, pride, and disobedience.

Sin is not like receiving a parking ticket and paying a fine—it is the rupture of a loving relationship with God. Any sin, no matter how small, separates us from Him due to our self-centeredness and ingratitude. As St. Symeon the New Theologian teaches:

"The person who thinks he does not need to keep all the commandments, but keeps some while neglecting others, should realize that if he neglects just one of them, he will forfeit everything."

Scripture reinforces this truth:
> *Whoever relaxes one of these commandments ... shall be called least in the Kingdom of Heaven* (Matthew 5:19), and,

> *Not everyone who says to me 'Lord, Lord,' shall enter the Kingdom of Heaven, but he who does the will of my Father* (Matthew 7:21).

Sin affects us, not God. As St. Paul says, "The wages of sin are death"—a spiritual death that results from our free choice to turn away from God. Yet, God's love is unwavering, and His invitation for us to return to Him remains open.

Study Questions

1. How does the Orthodox Church understand repentance as a transformative journey, and how does it differ from simply acknowledging sin?

2. What is the role of spiritual warfare in the life of an Orthodox Christian, and how do the passions and external temptations influence this battle?

3. How does the Orthodox view of sin as a rupture in our relationship with God differ from seeing sin merely as breaking laws or moral rules?

4. What does St. Symeon the New Theologian mean when he says that neglecting just one commandment leads to forfeiting everything, and how does this concept relate to the importance of repentance?

The Parable of the Prodigal Son

A life of repentance is a life lived in love for God. It is an ongoing process of transformation and renewal, rooted in humility and grace. The Parable of the Prodigal Son (Luke 15:11–32) offers profound insights into the nature of repentance and God's response to our return.

Archimandrite Nektarios beautifully summarizes the parable's significance:

> "If all the Gospels were lost and only the Parable of the Prodigal Son were to remain, this alone would be sufficient to reveal God's infinite love for mankind."

The Parable

In the story, the younger son demands his inheritance, symbolizing humanity's tendency to take God's gifts for granted while ignoring the Giver. He squanders his inheritance in a "far country," representing the spiritual separation caused by sin. He leaves to live a life aligned with the values of another land, abandoning those of his father's house. In this life, he "wasted his possessions with prodigal living," living according to his own will without regard for his father's desires. This exemplifies that such separation breaks a loving relationship with God. It is not like breaking a law. When we realize this condition, it should make us weep.

The story continues: "But when he had spent all, there arose a severe famine in that land, and he began to be in want. Then he went and joined himself to a citizen of that country, and he sent him into his fields to feed swine." In his desperation, he depends on this foreign land, even becoming a citizen of it. Yet, he gains little benefit: "He would gladly have filled his stomach with the pods that the swine ate, and no one gave him anything." He begins to see that this path will not meet his needs. He humbles himself, grasping at anything, but finds no relief.

This parable teaches us to reflect on our own journeys away from God. Like the Prodigal Son, we too often leave the embrace of God and embrace modern culture instead. Striving for worldly benefits, we ignore the teachings of Scripture, mistakenly thinking this will lead to the "good life." We fail to recognize the reality of our creation—that what we truly seek is a close relationship with God, not worldly values.

When we separate from God, does He abandon us completely? No! He never stops loving us. God is not affected by our sins, but we are. Our separation is our own doing, and without repentance, we risk losing eternal life in Paradise.

Returning to the Father

Coming back to the parable we see the turning point where the prodigal son is awakened to his error.

> But when he came to himself, he said, 'How many of my father's hired servants have bread enough and to spare, and I perish with hunger! I will arise and go to my father, and will say to him, "Father, I have sinned against heaven and before you, and I am no longer worthy to be called your son. Make me like one of your hired servants.

The son recognizes his error, admits his sin, and resolves to change. This is the essence of repentance: humility, acknowledgment of our unworthiness, and a desire to become like a hired servant, in another words, obedient to his father's will. Repentance is about realizing our error with humility and taking action to change one's life, and returning to God seeking forgiveness and help.

The father's response is extraordinary:
> When he was still a great way off, his father saw him and had compassion, and ran and fell on his neck and kissed him.

With great joy, the father orders his servants to bring the best robe, a ring, and sandals, and to prepare a feast to celebrate, saying,
> This my son was dead and is alive again; he was lost and is found.

This illustrates the unconditional love God has for all of us. No matter how far we fall, He is waiting for our return, ready to welcome us back with open arms, a kiss, and a celebration.

He doesn't want us to fear punishment when we repent; He is continually calling us to repent and change our ways, so that our lives align with what He teaches us, reflecting the divine image in which we were created.

This parable teaches that repentance is not about punishment, but about restoration. God is merciful and rejoices when we seek forgiveness, welcoming us with open arms and celebrating our return.

Study Questions

1. How does the Parable of the Prodigal Son illustrate the nature of sin and separation from God, and what does the son's journey symbolize in our own spiritual lives?

2. What is the significance of the Prodigal Son's decision to "come to himself" and recognize his error, and how does this reflect the essential aspects of repentance in Orthodox Christianity?

3. How does the father's response to the son's return in the parable reveal God's unconditional love and mercy, and what does it teach us about God's attitude toward repentance?

4. In what ways does the Parable of the Prodigal Son show that repentance is not about fear of punishment, but about healing, restoration, and returning to communion with God?

5. What lessons can we learn from the Prodigal Son's recognition of his unworthiness and his desire to become like one of the father's hired servants, and how does this relate to the humility required in repentance?

The Way of Repentance

Repentance is central to the Christian journey and involves four key steps:

1. Realization of Sin: Acknowledging our wrongs with the words, "I have sinned." This first step requires self-awareness and honesty, recognizing how we have deviated from God's will.
2. Humility: Confessing, "I am not worthy." Repentance requires a humble recognition of our inadequacy before God, understanding that we do not deserve His grace but seeking it nonetheless.
3. Commitment to Change: Declaring, "Make me one of your hired servants." This is the turning point where we choose to change, desiring to live differently, in accordance with God's will, and willing to accept whatever position He deems fit in His household.
4. Action: Returning to the Father, as the Prodigal Son did, who "arose and came to his father." Repentance demands action. It is not enough to feel sorrow for sin; we must actively seek God and return to Him through prayer, fasting, and humility.

Repentance is not about paying a fine for breaking a law. It is a profound transformation (metanoia) that renews our baptism, restores our original relationship with God, and brings us back into His household. It is motivated by love, not guilt, and sustained by God's grace. Repentance brings about a complete reorientation of the heart, mind, and soul toward God, changing us from the inside out.

Practical Steps to Repentance

Confession plays a vital role in the journey of repentance. It can be informal, through daily self-examination and personal prayer, or formal, through the Sacrament of Confession with a spiritual father. St. Symeon the New Theologian advises seeking an intercessor and guide capable of restoring us to our baptismal state. True confession is an act of humility, love, and vulnerability. It is not simply listing sins or seeking to alleviate guilt but an authentic revelation of the soul's wounds. Through this act of transparency, we open ourselves to God's healing grace.

Repentance is not about simply making a list of our sins and seeking absolution. It is not like accumulating too many parking tickets and asking for mercy from a judge. Nor is it about relieving the guilt we carry. Repentance is a loving action taken out of abundant love for God. It is the act of revealing the sickness in our soul, humbling ourselves, and laying bare our wounds before God. In doing so, we express our longing for unity with Him, seek forgiveness, and commit to a change in our thinking and actions.

Living a Life of Repentance
Repentance requires more than just words—it must be reflected in action. It calls for ascetic effort, humility, and cooperation with God's grace (synergia). As we grow in awareness of our fallen state, the Holy Spirit illuminates our inner being, helping us recognize how far we have strayed from God's image. With this awareness, we are called to use our free will to realign ourselves with His will.

Repentance is the path to restoring our relationship with God. It is not about fearing punishment but about embracing love, humility, and transformation. The Parable of the Prodigal Son beautifully illustrates this truth—God is always ready to welcome us back with joy and compassion. Let us, like the Prodigal Son, arise and return to our Father, seeking the life only He can give.

The Sacrament of Confession: A Path to Healing and Reconciliation
In the Orthodox Church, Confession (also known as the Mystery of Repentance) is one of the most important sacraments. It is a means by which we seek God's forgiveness for our sins, reconcile with God, and restore our relationship with Him. Confession is not simply about acknowledging wrongdoings, but about experiencing spiritual healing, transforming our hearts, and growing in our relationship with God.

Why Do We Need Confession?
Confession is a way to restore our connection with God. It's important to understand that God loves us deeply and desires to restore our relationship with Him. In fact, the Father is always waiting for us, just like in the parable of the Prodigal Son. God is ready to forgive and heal us, but we must approach Him humbly, acknowledging our mistakes and seeking His mercy.

What Happens During Confession?

In Confession, you come before God, to admit your sins. It's not a session for justifying or excusing them. Instead, you openly and humbly acknowledge your shortcomings and wrongdoings. The priest serves as your witness, listens to your confession, and if so moved by the Spirit offers absolution. This comes from God through an ordained priest.

What Does Confession Do for Us?

Restores Our Relationship with God: When we sin, we create a barrier between ourselves and God. Confession removes this barrier and helps us return to God's loving embrace.

Heals the Soul: Sin wounds the soul, just as a physical injury wounds the body. Confession is a means of spiritual healing, like receiving medicine or treatment for a wound. It helps cleanse the soul and makes it whole again.

Releases Guilt and Shame: One of the main struggles that come with sin is guilt. Confession allows us to confront our mistakes in a safe and loving environment, and through the priest's absolution, we are relieved of the weight of guilt and shame.

Strengthens Our Will to Change: Confession is not just about forgiveness; it is a step toward transformation. By confessing, you commit to change, to turning away from sin and living a life more aligned with God's will. Your spiritual father who is standing with you will offer you guidance to help you eliminate this sinful tendency.

Confession is Not a Judge's Court

It's important to understand that Confession is not a place of judgment. The priest does not condemn you but serves as a helper who is there to guide you toward healing. It's also not about simply getting a "pass" for sins. Confession is a way to honestly face our failings and start anew. It's not a transaction to "pay" for our sins; it's an opportunity to open our hearts to God's mercy and grace.

Study Questions

1. What are the four key steps of repentance, and how do they contribute to the process of spiritual transformation in the life of a Christian?

2. Why is humility such an essential aspect of repentance, and how does it help us align our will with God's during the process of returning to Him?

3. How does the Orthodox understanding of repentance differ from a mere act of acknowledging sin, and why is it considered a loving action rather than a mere act of guilt alleviation?

4. What is the role of Confession in the process of repentance, and how does it help restore the relationship between the believer and God?

5. Why is Confession in the Orthodox Church not seen as a judge's court, and what does this say about the nature of God's mercy and the healing process in the Sacrament of Repentance?

The Preparation for Confession

Before going to our spiritual father for confession, it is crucial to prepare one's heart and mind. Many individuals enter confession unprepared, often expecting the priest to ask questions or affirm their goodness. However, true preparation involves honest self-examination, allowing us to confront our weaknesses and sins, which we often try to hide from others, ourselves, and even from God. As St. Theophan the Recluse emphasizes, one must recognize the depth of their sinfulness to return to God with a contrite heart. He says:

> "You must come to know that you are definitely sinful, and you must know to what degree."

> "A sinner returning to God will be accepted by God if he
> a) admits his sins,
> b) repents of them, and
> c) makes a vow not to sin."

St. Theophan's Preparation Steps:

1. Recall all your obligations in relation to God, your neighbor, and yourself.

2. Go through the Ten Commandments. (Helpful questions are often available online or in prayer books.)

3. Review the Sermon on the Mount (Matthew 5).

4. Read the Epistle of James and the Epistles of Paul, especially Romans 12:9–21 and Ephesians 4.

5. Read the First Epistle of St. John.

Steps for Self-Examination

1. Find a Quiet Place: pray and reflect on your love for God and how well you have lived according to His teachings. Create a sheet of paper with the Commandments of God on one side and your life on the other. Compare your actions, thoughts, and words to the divine standards found in the Commandments.

2. Identify Patterns: Determine the underlying patterns of your sins. Look deeply for the governing passions—those desires

or tendencies that shape and condition your other actions. Discovering these passions reveals the root of your sinfulness.

3. Reflect Deeply: Contemplate each sin and their root until you can see how each was committed according to your own desire. Do not make excuses or justify your actions. Work through this reflection until you can sincerely say, "I am guilty of this and that." As you reflect, you will begin to feel burdened and sorrowful. Allow this feeling of regret and repentance to emerge naturally, leading to a heartfelt vow to change (metanoia).

4. Resolve to Return: Like the Prodigal Son, decide to arise and go to your Father, acknowledging your failings and seeking His mercy. Recognize that the path to return to God is not easy. Consider what the Prodigal Son may have wrestled with before deciding to return to his father: fear, shame, or despair. These same struggles may hinder you, but they must be faced with courage and faith in God's mercy.

Questions for Reflection on Relationships
Personal Relationships
Are there unresolved problems in your relationships with others?

Judging Others
Christ commands us: *Do not judge others, so that God will not judge you* (Matthew 7:1). Have you judged others unfairly or harshly?

Scandalizing Others
Reflect on whether your actions or words have led others into sin, especially your children. Scandal may arise from inconsistencies between your words and actions, carelessness, dishonesty, an unruly life, or even a provocative appearance. Christ had compassion for prostitutes, but He rebuked hypocrites harshly, saying, *Woe unto you,* and *The tax collectors and the prostitutes are going into the Kingdom of God ahead of you* (Matthew 21:31).

Reflection on the Self
Sins of the Flesh
Reflect on your thoughts, actions, and attitudes regarding sexual desires. Many believe the Church should adapt to modern values, but is this aligned with God's truth? Avoid either overemphasizing

or neglecting this aspect of sin, and approach it with honesty and balance.

Avarice and Greed

Consider Christ's warning to the rich: "Whoever has two shirts must give one to the man who has none." Christ showed little compassion for those who clung to wealth: *It will be very hard for rich people to enter the Kingdom of Heaven… harder than for a camel to go through the eye of a needle* (Matthew 19:23–24). Do you cling to possessions while ignoring the needs of others?

God's Desire for Repentance

God desires us to recognize our sinful state and actively engage in a life of repentance. It is not our sins that separate us eternally from God but our unwillingness to repent. Pride, which leads us to think we are "good people" without sin, distances us from Him.

We should not fear going to confession. God desires our perfection in His image. Christ never condemned sinners but condemned sin itself. The only sinners Christ rebuked harshly were hypocrites—those who spoke of holiness but did not live it. He criticized the Pharisees for this very reason.

The saints, despite their righteousness, would approach God with humility, asking for His mercy as if they were harlots or thieves. They did not justify themselves or boast of their virtues. Instead, they revealed their wounds, seeking God's healing.

The Individual Nature of Preparation

Each of us lives in unique circumstances and faces different challenges. An Athonite monk offers this perspective: "Someone who has killed ten people may well go to Paradise, whereas someone who has performed ten miracles may go to hell." This illustrates that judgment is based on individual struggles and responses to God's calling.

In confession, we must not only consider what we have done but also what we have failed to do. True preparation is marked by repentance, the path of spiritual growth. The act of repentance and confession is a transformative journey, requiring full acknowledgment of sins, genuine sorrow, and a commitment to change.

Understanding Sinfulness

Sinfulness is not limited to external actions; it extends to our inner disposition. One person may have a severe illness yet feel no pain, while another may suffer greatly from a minor ailment. Similarly, some consciences have become dulled, leaving individuals indifferent to their sins, while others feel intense sorrow over falling short of God's expectations.

Guilt vs. Repentance

Repentance is not driven by guilt. Guilt fosters fear of punishment, portraying God as an angry Father waiting to condemn us. True repentance arises from a contrite heart that seeks to restore the loving relationship with God. As the Psalmist writes:

> *A sacrifice to God is a broken spirit. A broken and humbled heart God will not despise* (Psalm 50 [51]:19).

The Role of the Priest

The priest in confession acts not as a judge but as an intermediary of God's mercy. The priest pronounces absolution, not by his own authority but in the name of the Holy Trinity. Christ instituted this sacrament, saying:

> *Receive the Holy Spirit. If you forgive the sins of any, they are forgiven them* (John 20:22–23).

Confessing before the priest humbles us, curing pride and instilling healthy shame, which helps guard us against future sin. Some may fear their sins will not remain confidential, but the priest is bound by the sacred seal of confession and cannot disclose anything heard.

If we worry excessively about protecting our honor, we must remember that our sin will become evident if it remains unaddressed. Confession restores us to God's grace, allowing us to grow in holiness and find healing for our soul.

Confronting Obstacles and Excuses

Many avoid confession out of shame, fear, or despair, thinking their sins are too great for forgiveness or questioning their own sinfulness or question whether they are truly sinful. However, the Church teaches that no sin is beyond the mercy of God. As St. Ignatius Brianchaninov notes, the power of repentance comes from the boundless grace of God. The key is not to avoid Confession because of fear or guilt but to approach it with humility and a broken spirit knowing the love of God awaits you. Christ's words warn us:

> *Be on your guard, because you do not know the day our the hour when the Son of Man will come* (Matt 25:13).

Study Questions

1. What is the importance of honest self-examination before confession, and how does it prepare us to approach God with a contrite heart?

2. How does St. Theophan the Recluse's advice on preparing for confession help guide us in acknowledging our sins and committing to change?

3. What are some of the fears you may have in going to Confession?

4. Why is repentance considered a transformative journey, and how does it differ from simply feeling guilt or shame for our sins?

The Act of Confession

Confession is not just a recital of sins but a heartfelt expression of repentance. It is essential to confess sins specifically and clearly without justification or excuses. Properly prepared we like the Prodigal son are ready to run to our Spiritual father to open our hearts to God with him as our witness and counselor.

> Be clear about the sin and do not expect the priest to question you.
> Avoid the details or long stories or generalities. Be direct and clear.
> Take full responsibility without justifying yourself or blaming others.
> Do not mention your good deeds or your virtues.
> Do not bring up sins you have already confessed.
> Do not conceal any sins; doing so mocks God.

The Mystery of Repentance and Absolution
When you come for confession, it is often recommended to bring a list of the sins you wish to confess. This helps ensure you do not forget anything in the moment. You will stand before the icon of Christ, with the priest beside you, and make your confession directly to God.

After you confess, the priest offers the prayer of absolution—a powerful moment of divine mercy. This is the moment when your sins are forgiven, and you are restored to full communion with God through the Holy Spirit. Confession is an act of healing, not punishment, reflecting God's profound love and grace. Just as the Prodigal Son was welcomed back by his father with open arms, so too is the repentant sinner embraced by God. The remission of sins is a testament to God's desire for reconciliation and restoration.

Following absolution, the priest may provide guidance or counsel to help you in your spiritual journey. This is often referred to as penance. It is not a punishment but practical advice or actions designed to help you overcome the sinful tendencies you have confessed.

After confession, it is essential to forgive yourself. Burn the written list you used, symbolizing the removal of sin, and carry out the guidance given by the priest with sincerity and effort. Use this advice to make real changes in your life, aligning your actions more closely with God's will.

This sacrament was instituted by Christ Himself. He breathed on His disciples and said:

> *Receive the Holy Spirit. If you forgive the sins of any, they are forgiven them; if you retain the sins of any, they are retained* (John 20:22–23).

He also declared:

> *Whatever you bind on earth will be bound in heaven, and whatever you loose on earth will be loosed in heaven*
> (Matthew 18:17–18; 16:19).

Priests are instruments of God's mercy, not the source of forgiveness. Sins are remitted not through their own authority but in the name of the Holy Trinity. Confession offers a sacred opportunity to be reconciled with God, healed by His grace, and renewed in your spiritual life.

After Confession: A New Beginning

After Confession, the penitent is called to continue the journey of repentance. While the weight of sin may feel lifted, it is important to remember that true repentance involves a constant struggle against sin and a deepening relationship with God. The sacrament is not a one-time event but a continual process of growth, transformation, and renewal. The guidance offered by the priest, often in the form of penance, is meant to assist the penitent in overcoming sinful habits and living a life more aligned with God's will.

Remember also that now you must forgive yourself. God has cleansed and forgiven you. To not forgive yourself is to take on a role higher than God. If you had a paper you brought with you for confession, it is good ritual to take it an burn it putting what happened in the past in the past. Now focus on eliminating the recurrence of such sins.

Conclusion

The Sacrament of Confession is a gift from God for our spiritual healing and growth. It is not merely about acknowledging wrongdoings but about recognizing our sinfulness, confronting our brokenness, and returning to God with humility and love. Through repentance and confession, we experience the remission of sins and the boundless mercy of God, who rejoices at our return.

Like the Prodigal Son, may we arise and return to our Father, seeking the life only He can give.

> "Lord, help us recognize our sins, humble ourselves before You, and strive for a life of repentance and unity with You in Your eternal kingdom. Amen."

Our loving God awaits our return.

Study Questions

1. Why is it important to confess sins specifically and clearly without justifying or excusing ourselves, and how does this demonstrate true repentance?

2. What role does the priest play in the Sacrament of Confession, and how does the absolution offered during the sacrament reflect God's mercy and desire for reconciliation?

3. How does the sacrament of confession serve as a continuous process of spiritual growth and renewal, and how does the guidance given by the priest (penance) contribute to overcoming sinful tendencies?

Chapter 13

Death and the Final Judgment

Orthodox Christianity provides a deeply spiritual and holistic understanding of death, resurrection, and the final judgment. Rooted in Scripture, Holy Tradition, and the teachings of the Fathers, this perspective emphasizes life as a preparation for eternity. With faith, prayer, repentance, and participation in the sacraments, believers can grow in communion with God, preparing their souls for eternal communion with Him. This chapter explores these profound mysteries, illuminating the Orthodox vision of death and the life to come.

We begin by addressing the nature of the spiritual realm, then answer the question: what is death? Following this we address the nature of Paradise and Hell; then the major event to come, the Second Coming of Christ when all will be judged; and finally, the universal resurrection and the nature of our life after death.

The Spiritual Realm

The Orthodox understanding of death and the final judgment begins with an acknowledgment of the spiritual realm. This means accepting a realm that is beyond the physical realm we now live in. God began His creation with this spiritual realm distinct from the material world that is intimately connected to it. It is immaterial, eternal, and transcends the physical laws of time, space, and matter. Within this spiritual realm, the uncreated energies of God—His grace, love, and light—are fully experienced.

Humans, uniquely composed of body and soul, serve as microcosms of both the spiritual and material worlds. This dual nature calls humanity to unite these realms through prayer, worship, and acts of love, actively participating in God's sanctification of all creation. This understanding emphasizes that life on earth is not isolated from the divine but is a continual preparation for eternal communion with God.

For every person, a time will come when they leave the material world and fully participate in the spiritual world. Our earthly life serves as a period of preparation for this eternal existence. Through repentance, participation in the sacraments, and a life rooted in Christ, individuals are called to align their souls with God's will, shaping the soul's ability to enter into and delight in God's eternal presence.

Saint Theophan the Recluse reflects on this profound reality, writing:

> "This world will continue until the fulness of time, or the end of time; at the Resurrection and Judgment, all will receive according to their deeds. Some will descend into hell; others will dwell in Paradise."

The Resurrection and Judgment mark the culmination of history, where Christ's victory over death is fully revealed. In Orthodox theology, the final judgment is not merely a legalistic assessment but a manifestation of each person's relationship with God. Those who have lived in love and communion with Him will experience His presence as light and joy, while those who have rejected Him will experience it as fire and separation.

The spiritual realm, deeply intertwined with earthly life, becomes fully manifest to the soul at the moment of death. This transition marks the beginning of the soul's journey toward eternity, where the realities of the spiritual world are encountered directly.

> ## Study Questions
>
> 1. How does the Orthodox understanding of the spiritual realm shape the view of death and the final judgment? In what ways does earthly life serve as a preparation for eternity?
>
> 2. What role does repentance, prayer, and participation in the sacraments play in preparing the soul for eternal communion with God according to Orthodox teaching?
>
> 3. How does the final judgment reflect a person's relationship with God, and how is this relationship experienced differently by the righteous and the unrighteous?

Understanding Death

Our journey to the spiritual realm involves a major transformation that occurs with death. Death is the moment when the soul separates from the body. St. Paul describes this as *the deliverance of the soul from prison*, (2 Corinthians 5:1–4) and *a departure* (2 Timothy 4:6). St. Peter refers to it as *putting off the body* (2 Peter 1:14), while St. Luke likens it to *sleep* (Acts 13:36).

This separation involves a struggle, as humans were created united as body and soul, an integrated whole. Though death was not part of humanity's original nature, it now serves as a passage into eternal reality.

After this separation, the soul enters a mysterious and unfamiliar realm, much like entering a foreign land. Without a guide, the soul risks being misled, underscoring the necessity of divine assistance. This stage, known in Orthodox theology as the particular judgment, is referenced in Hebrews 9:27: *It is appointed for men to die once, but after this the judgment.* At this juncture, the soul encounters both the forces of good and evil.

For those who have cultivated a loving relationship with God, this journey is lead by the angels, who protect and direct the soul toward Paradise. The soul experiences the fruits of its repentance, love, and communion with God. Conversely, those who have neglected this relationship or have given themselves over to sin may find themselves influenced by demons. These adversaries exploit the passions—disordered desires or habits not mastered during earthly life—to draw the soul away from God and toward Hell.

This process is, in essence, a judgment based on the soul's alignment with God. The soul gravitates naturally toward the state it has chosen in life, either Paradise or Hell. The parable of Lazarus and the rich man (Luke 16:19–31) vividly illustrates this reality. Lazarus, the righteous man, is carried by angels to the bosom of Abraham, while the rich man, unrepentant and self-centered, finds himself in torment. The chasm between the two is described as insurmountable: *Between us and you there is a great gulf fixed* (Luke 16:26).

The Church's liturgical tradition sheds light on this journey with prayers and hymns that affirm hope while acknowledging the reality of judgment. During the Orthodox funeral service, the faithful beseech God:

> Give rest to the soul of Your servant in a place of light, a place of green pasture, a place of repose, where there is no pain, sorrow, or sighing.

Similarly, hymns from the Canon for the Departed beautifully express the Church's theology of death and resurrection. One hymn proclaims:

> I am Your creation, O Lord, and the work of Your hands. Grant me rest in the bosom of Abraham, and number me among the righteous.

These prayers and hymns not only reflect the hope for eternal communion with God but also underscore the soul's dependence on divine mercy. The memorial services and the Church's continual prayers for the departed demonstrate the interconnection between the living and the dead, rooted in love and the hope of salvation.

Orthodox teaching emphasizes that this separation is not an arbitrary punishment but a natural consequence of the choices made during life. The soul's destination reflects its relationship with God, who respects human freedom. The time for repentance and transformation is in this life, as the state of the soul at death may become fixed.

Following the soul's separation from the body, it begins a journey that reveals its eternal destination. This journey leads to one of two states: Paradise, a place of divine communion, or Hell, a state of estrangement from God. The soul's path is shaped by its earthly life and relationship with God.

Study Questions

1. How does Orthodox Christianity describe the soul's journey after death, particularly in relation to the particular judgment and the forces of good and evil?

2. What role do repentance, love, and communion with God play in shaping the soul's destination after death? How does this align with the parable of Lazarus and the rich man in Luke 16:19–31?

3. How do the prayers and hymns of the Orthodox Church, particularly in the funeral service, reflect the Church's understanding of death, judgment, and the hope for eternal communion with God?

Paradise and Hell

Paradise

Paradise is the state where the soul is in full communion with God, characterized by the experience of His love, light, and glory. For those who live in repentance and obedience to God's will, His presence is perceived as joy, peace, and life-giving energy. Paradise is often described as a state of rest and anticipation, where the faithful await the resurrection of the body and the fullness of the Kingdom of God.

For those who have cultivated faith and lived a life of experiencing God and doing His will, death becomes a passage to Paradise, greeted by the embrace of angels. In Orthodox tradition, the Theotokos (Mother of God) plays a vital role as an intercessor, guiding souls to Paradise. As the ultimate intercessor for humanity, she is a source of comfort and hope, embodying divine mercy and maternal care. Her role as the guide and advocate for the faithful is a reflection of her profound relationship with Christ and her continued presence in the life of the Church. This belief is beautifully expressed in Orthodox hymnography, where the faithful sing:

> O most holy Theotokos, save us! Intercede for us who have set our hope in you, that we may inherit the joy of Paradise.

This teaching reminds believers of the Theotokos' active intercession, not only in life but also at the moment of death, offering assurance and support to those who seek her aid.

The Church's funeral hymns reflect the joy of this divine union in Paradise:

> With the saints give rest, O Christ, to the soul of Your servant, where there is no pain, nor sorrow, nor sighing, but life everlasting.

Paradise, therefore, is not merely a place but a condition of being united with God, filled with His grace, and sharing in His divine glory, accompanied by the presence and love of the Theotokos.

While Paradise reflects the joy of union with God, Hell stands in stark contrast as a state of separation from His love.

Hell

In contrast, hell is the state of estrangement from God, where the unrepentant soul resists His love. As Hebrews 12:29 declares, *Our God is a consuming fire.* For the unrepentant, the presence of God—intended to be a source of joy and life—becomes a torment, exposing their sin and rejection of divine love.

Hell is a state where the soul's uncontrolled passions remain unsatisfied, and the divine light of God is experienced as fire rather than warmth. In Orthodox theology, hell is not a punishment inflicted by God but the natural consequence of the soul's refusal to love, repent, and be transformed by God's grace. It is a state freely chosen, shaped by one's earthly life and priorities.

The funeral hymns warn of this reality, urging the living to repent and pray for the departed. One hymn poignantly states:

> I weep and lament when I think upon death, and see our beauty, created in the image of God, lying in the tomb disfigured, without glory or form. O marvel! What is this mystery which has befallen us? Why have we been given over to corruption, and why have we been wedded to death? Truly, as it is written, by the command of God, Who gives rest to the departed.

This reveals the Church's emphasis on repentance and the hope of transformation through God's mercy, even as it acknowledges the tragic reality of separation from Him.

The final separation of souls into Paradise or Hell reaches its ultimate fulfillment at the Second Coming of Christ.

Study Questions

1. How does Orthodox theology describe the state of Paradise and the soul's experience there? What role does the Theotokos (Mother of God) play in guiding souls to Paradise?

2. In what way does Orthodox Christianity view Hell, and how is it different from a punishment inflicted by God? How does the soul's rejection of divine love contribute to its experience in Hell?

3. How do the funeral hymns in the Orthodox Church reflect the contrast between Paradise and Hell? What do they teach about repentance, the state of the soul after death, and the hope of transformation through God's mercy?

The Second Coming of Christ

The Second Coming, or Parousia, marks the culmination of history and the end of the present age. It will involve the return of Jesus Christ in full glory to establish His eternal Kingdom for the righteous faithful. Scripture describes this event as sudden and undeniable, *like lightning* (Matthew 24:27), visible to all and cosmic in scope. Christ will return as the victorious King and Judge, revealing Himself as the *Light of the world* (John 8:12).

The Second Coming will renew the entire cosmos, freeing it from corruption and bringing all creation into harmony with God's will, as St. Paul writes:

> *The creation itself also will be delivered from the bondage of corruption into the glorious liberty of the children of God* (Romans 8:21).

The Renewal of Creation

At the Second Coming, the cosmos will be transformed, fulfilling God's original purpose for humanity and all of creation. In the beginning, God created the world as *very good* (Genesis 1:31), designed to be a dwelling place where humanity, made in His image, could live in perfect communion with Him. The Fall introduced sin and death into the world, corrupting this original harmony and subjecting creation to futility (Romans 8:20).

The Second Coming brings this story to completion, as Christ's return ushers in the restoration of all things. The earth and heavens, once marred by sin, will be renewed, becoming a dwelling place of righteousness:

> *But according to His promise we are looking for new heavens and a new earth in which righteousness dwells* (2 Peter 3:13).

This renewal is not merely a return to the pre-fallen state but a glorification of creation. The entire cosmos will share in the victory of Christ's Resurrection, freed from corruption and death. Humanity, in its resurrected and glorified state, will inhabit this new creation, worshiping God and living in perfect harmony with His will. The liturgical life of the Church reflects this hope, proclaiming:

> Blessed is the Kingdom of the Father and of the Son and of the Holy Spirit, now and ever and unto the ages of ages!

The renewal of creation reveals the fulfillment of God's purpose: a world fully united to Him, where love, peace, and divine glory reign eternally.

Signs of the Second Coming

The Scriptures provide indications of events that will precede the Parousia. These include perilous times, marked by widespread moral decay and spiritual decline. As St. Paul warns:

> *In the last days perilous times will come: men will be lovers of themselves, lovers of money, boasters, proud, blasphemers... lovers of pleasure rather than lovers of God* (2 Timothy 3:1–5).

Another significant sign is the rise of the Antichrist, who will oppose Christ and deceive many. However, the Antichrist will not have the power to compel believers who remain steadfast in faith. St. Paul writes:

> *Let no one deceive you in any way. For that day will not come unless the rebellion comes first, and the man of lawlessness is revealed... The Lord Jesus will kill with the breath of His mouth and bring to nothing by the appearance of His coming* (2 Thessalonians 2:3, 8).

Despite these signs, the exact timing of the Second Coming remains unknown. Jesus Himself teaches:

> *But of that day and hour no one knows, not even the angels of heaven, but My Father only* (Matthew 24:36).

The Apostles echo this teaching. As recorded in Acts, Jesus tells His disciples:

> *It is not for you to know times or seasons which the Father has put in His own authority* (Acts 1:7).

A Call to Watchfulness

The uncertainty surrounding the timing of the Second Coming emphasizes the need for vigilance and spiritual readiness called watchfulness. Jesus warns:

> *Take heed, watch and pray; for you do not know when the time is... And what I say to you, I say to all: Watch!* (Mark 13:33, 37).

This call to watchfulness is not meant to inspire fear but to encourage a life of prayer, repentance, and active communion with God. The Church's liturgical life reflects this anticipation, especially during feast days such as the Ascension and the Last Judgment, when hymns proclaim the hope and awe of Christ's return. For example, in the Liturgy, we confess:

> We proclaim Your death, O Lord, and Your holy Resurrection, and we await Your glorious Second Coming.

Study Questions

1. What is the Orthodox understanding of the renewal of creation at the Second Coming? How does this transformation fulfill God's original purpose for humanity and the cosmos?

2. What signs are described in Scripture that will precede the Parousia, and how do they highlight the need for spiritual vigilance? What role does the rise of the Antichrist play in these signs?

3. Why is watchfulness an essential aspect of preparation for the Second Coming? How does the Church's liturgical life reflect this call to readiness, and how does it guide the faithful in anticipation of Christ's return?

The Universal Resurrection

The universal resurrection will be a simultaneous and transformative event. St. Paul declares:

> *For this perishable nature must put on the imperishable, and this mortal nature must put on immortality* (1 Corinthians 15:53).

At the resurrection, the faithful will be transfigured, their bodies becoming spiritual and heavenly, Jesus. says they will be *like angels* (Luke 20:36). St. Makarios of Egypt says that while everything is immersed in light and fire, yet each person retains their unique identity.

Similarly, St. Cyril of Jerusalem explains:

> *The body after putting on incorruption is changed, as iron, which comes into contact with fire, becomes fire. The body will radiate the glory of God while remaining truly itself.*

The resurrected body, though glorified, will retain continuity with the earthly body. It will be completely restored and glorified. St. Paul likens this to a seed:

> *What you sow is not the body which is to be, but a bare kernel... but God gives it a body as He has chosen* (1 Corinthians 15:37–38).

> *It is sown a physical body, it is raised a spiritual body... Lo! I tell you a mystery... For this perishable nature must put on the imperishable, and this mortal nature must put on immortality* (1 Corinthians 15:44, 51–53).

St. John Chrysostom reinforces this idea, teaching that the resurrected body is not a new creation but one that retains its identity while being glorified. As St. Paul writes:

> *The resurrection will glorify the faithful, making them incorruptible and filled with the Spirit* (1 Corinthians 15:53).

St. Makarios notes:

> All the members are raised and become like fire, but each person remains in his own nature and hypostasis, filled completely with the Spirit.

Liturgical Expressions of the Resurrection
The Church's liturgical tradition beautifully expresses the hope of the resurrection through hymns, particularly during Pascha (Easter) and the Funeral Service. At Pascha, the Church triumphantly sings:

> Christ is risen from the dead, trampling down death by death, and upon those in the tombs bestowing life.

This hymn captures the core of Christian hope: Christ's victory over death and His promise of life to all who follow Him. The Funeral Service also proclaims the resurrection with these words:

> With the saints give rest, O Christ, to the soul of Your servant, where there is no pain, nor sorrow, nor sighing, but life everlasting.

These hymns emphasize that the resurrection is not only an event to anticipate but a present reality that shapes the life of the Church, infusing it with joy and hope.

The Final Judgment
After the Universal Resurrection, all humanity will stand before Christ to give an account of their lives. St. John the Theologian writes:

All that are in the graves shall hear His voice and come forth; those who have done good to the resurrection of life, and those who have done evil to the resurrection of judgment (John 5:28–29).

St. Matthew records this event:

> *When the Son of Man comes in His glory, and all the holy angels with Him, then He will sit on the throne of His glory. All the nations will be gathered before Him* (Matthew 25:31–32).

The judgment will reflect the truth of each person's life, shaped by love and communion with God. At its core, the judgment will center on love—particularly the love shown to others as an expression of love for Christ. As the Lord declares:

> *Inasmuch as you did it to one of the least of these My brethren, you did it to Me* (Matthew 25:40).

The Lord Himself warns:

Not everyone who says to Me, 'Lord, Lord,' shall enter the kingdom of heaven, but he who does the will of My Father in heaven (Matthew 7:21).

This highlights the need for a life of active faith and communion with God, rather than merely intellectual or superficial belief. St. John reminds us:

> And now, little children, abide in Him, that when He appears we may have confidence and not be ashamed before Him at His coming (1 John 2:28).

This underscores that the Final Judgment is a manifestation of divine justice and mercy, rooted in how each person responded to God's commandments and the needs of others during their earthly life.

The Experience of the Righteous
For the faithful, the Final Judgment will be the culmination of their journey toward Theosis—union with God. As St. John writes: *We shall see Him as He is* (1 John 3:2).

This vision of Christ, the ultimate fulfillment of human existence, will bring indescribable joy and peace. The faithful will experience the fullness of God's presence, radiating love, light, and life. This is not merely a reward but the natural outcome of a life lived in communion with God, shaped by repentance, humility, and love.

The liturgical hymns of the Orthodox Church express this hope with clarity and depth. For example, during the Sunday of the Last Judgment, the Church prays:

> When You, O God, shall come to earth with glory, all things shall tremble, and the river of fire shall flow before Your judgment seat; the books shall be opened, and the hidden things disclosed. Then deliver me from the unquenchable fire and make me worthy to stand at Your right hand, O Righteous Judge.

This hymn reveals the awe and hope that characterize the faithful's anticipation of the Final Judgment.

The Experience of the Unrepentant
For those who rejected God's love and lived in estrangement from Him, the Final Judgment will be a moment of truth experienced as torment. The presence of God, which is joy and light for the righteous. For others it will reveal separation from God seen as a consuming fire. As St. Paul writes: *Our God is a consuming fire* (Hebrews 12:29).

This torment is not imposed by God but is the natural consequence of a soul's rejection of His love. The light of Christ, which should bring warmth and peace, instead exposes the soul's separation from Him. This state of being reflects the tragic reality of hell—a condition of eternal separation from God and the fulfillment for which the soul was created.

The parable of the sheep and the goats (Matthew 25:31–46) illustrates this duality, showing how the righteous inherit eternal life while the unrighteous face eternal separation. The Church reminds the faithful that repentance and transformation remain possible in this life, but at the Final Judgment, the soul's choices will be revealed and sealed for eternity.

Theological Perspective
The Final Judgment emphasizes God's respect for human freedom. Each person's eternal state is determined by their response to God's love and their actions in life.

Union with God, the ultimate goal of human life, is offered to all but must be actively sought through faith, repentance, and love. This truth is reflected in the words of St. John Chrysostom:
> The judgment of God is not according to appearances but according to the truth of deeds and the disposition of the soul.

Communion with God as the Goal
The ultimate aim of the resurrection is not merely a new life but a life of perfect communion with God, which is the greatest of all blessings. This communion is the fulfillment of an Orthodox way of life, grounded in repentance, the sacraments, and love for Christ. St. Porphyrios advises:
> We must not approach Christ out of fear of how we will die or what will become of us. Rather, we must open our hearts to Him, as when we tug at a curtain and the sunlight immediately shines in.

For St. Porphyrios, this loving relationship with God dispels fear and draws us into the joy of His presence:
> I didn't want to think about hell or the tollgates. I set them aside. I remembered only the love of God and was glad.

This love and longing for Christ should guide the Christian life, shaping the heart to receive Him fully in the resurrection.

The Christian Hope

The universal resurrection is the cornerstone of Christian hope. Through His Crucifixion and Resurrection, Jesus Christ claimed victory over death, opening the way to new and transfigured life. As St. Paul proclaims:

> *If there is no resurrection of the dead, then Christ is not risen. And if Christ is not risen, then our preaching is empty, and your faith is also empty... For as in Adam all die, even so in Christ all shall be made alive* (1 Corinthians 15:13–15, 20, 22).

The Orthodox way of life, centered on the sacraments, prayer, and repentance, prepares us for this ultimate destiny. As Christians, we await the resurrection with faith, hope, and the assurance of Christ's victory over death.

A Call to Readiness

The Final Judgment is not only a future event but also a call to live with vigilance and love in the present. The Lord warns:

> *Watch therefore, for you know neither the day nor the hour in which the Son of Man is coming* (Matthew 25:13).

But, the Lord Himself warns:

> *Not everyone who says to Me, 'Lord, Lord,' shall enter the kingdom of heaven, but he who does the will of My Father in heaven* (Matthew 7:21).

This highlights the need for a life of active faith and communion with God, rather than merely intellectual or superficial belief. St. John reminds us:

> *And now, little children, abide in Him, that when He appears we may have confidence and not be ashamed before Him at His coming* (1 John 2:28).

The Orthodox way of life—centered on prayer, the sacraments, and acts of mercy—prepares the soul to meet Christ with confidence and joy. The Church's teachings and liturgical life remind us that the Final Judgment is not merely a moment of reckoning but the fulfillment of God's divine plan to bring all creation into perfect harmony with Him.

Living in Preparation

The Orthodox spiritual life is a journey toward Theosis—union with God. This lifelong process requires intentional effort, supported by the grace of God. Believers are called to:

- Pray Daily and Participate in the Sacraments: Regular prayer nurtures a personal relationship with God, while the sacraments, especially the Eucharist, unite believers with Christ and His Church.
- Fast to purify the heart and body, and strengthen one's wilt to act inline with the will of God.
- Read Scripture to deepen understanding of His word and strengthens faith.
- Lead a virtuous life, doing what He taught with love for God and neighbor. This is the essence of Christian living, reflected in acts of kindness, humility, and forgiveness.

These practices guide believers toward a goal of Theosis, where the soul is prepared to enter eternal communion with God. Orthodox Christianity offers a perspective of death filled with hope, pointing to the resurrection and life everlasting.

Conclusion

Orthodox Christianity views death not as an end but as a transition into eternal life. This perspective fills the Christian life with hope, as the faithful are encouraged to cultivate their relationship with God here and now. Eternal life begins in this world with faith based on the Scriptures enhanced through prayer, participation in the sacraments, and acts of love and repentance along with the discipline of fasting.

This journey finds its culmination in the resurrection, where the faithful will be glorified, shining with God's uncreated light, and dwelling in His eternal kingdom. As St. Paul proclaims:

> *If Christ is not risen, then our preaching is empty, and your faith is also empty... But now Christ is risen from the dead, and has become the first fruits of those who have fallen asleep* (1 Corinthians 15:14, 20).

Orthodox Christianity calls all to embrace this hope and live in joyful anticipation of eternal life.

Study Questions

1. How does the Orthodox understanding of the resurrection describe the transformation of the body? What role does St. Paul's analogy of the seed play in explaining this change?

2. What do the hymns from Pascha and the Funeral Service reveal about the Orthodox view of the resurrection? How do these liturgical expressions help shape the hope and joy of the faithful?

3. How does the Final Judgment serve as a manifestation of divine justice and mercy? What role does love, particularly love for others, play in the judgment according to the teachings of Christ?

4. What is the significance of Theosis in the context of the resurrection and the Final Judgment? How does the Orthodox spiritual life, including prayer, sacraments, and acts of mercy, prepare the faithful for eternal communion with God?

Appendices

Appendix A

Ten Questions Inquirers Have About the Orthodox Faith

Question 1: Why Are Icons and Veneration of Saints Important in Orthodox Worship?

In the Orthodox Christian tradition, icons and the veneration of saints are integral to worship and the spiritual life of the faithful. These practices are often misunderstood or seen as unnecessary by those unfamiliar with the Orthodox faith, particularly by those coming from traditions that may have a different approach to sacred images and the honoring of saints. This lesson seeks to explain why icons and the veneration of saints are important in Orthodox worship, offering a scriptural and theological basis for these practices, and referencing the writings of Church Fathers who provide deeper insight into their significance.

The Theological Basis of Icons in Orthodox Worship

Icons are not mere decorations or artistic expressions but are theological symbols that embody profound truths about God, His saints, and His divine economy. In Orthodox Christianity, icons are viewed as a means of participating in the divine reality. They are windows into heaven, revealing the spiritual truths that transcend the material world. The Church Fathers, especially St. John of Damascus, explain that icons are a way to express the Incarnation of Christ.

The Incarnation of Jesus Christ is the cornerstone of Orthodox theology. The belief that God became man in the person of Jesus Christ allows for the use of images because God in His fullness has revealed Himself in human form. Before the Incarnation, God was invisible, and no one could depict Him. However, in the person of Jesus Christ, God took on human nature, which made it possible to represent Him visually.

St. John of Damascus, in his Exposition of the Orthodox Faith (Book IV, Chapter 16), writes:

> I do not worship matter, I worship the Creator of matter, who became matter for my sake… in order to save the matter that He created.

In this context, icons become an expression of the truth of God's revelation in history. They are an acknowledgment of the reality of the Incarnation. Through the use of icons, Orthodox Christians are able to focus on the spiritual truths that underlie the physical world.

The use of icons is grounded in Scripture, particularly in the Old Testament. While the Second Commandment in Exodus 20:4–5 prohibits the making of idols, it does not forbid the creation of all images. The distinction lies between idols, which are false representations of God or gods, and images that are used to glorify the true God. The key difference is that in the Orthodox tradition, icons do not represent a "god" but rather depict the real God, His saints, and events from salvation history. This is a critical distinction.

In the Old Testament, God commanded the construction of the golden cherubim on the Ark of the Covenant (Exodus 25:18–20), and images of cherubim were placed in the Temple (1 Kings 6:23–28). These were not idols but sacred images used in the worship of God. This sets the precedent for the Orthodox use of images in the worship of the true God.

The New Testament also supports the use of icons in Orthodox practice. In John 1:18, the apostle John writes, "No one has ever seen God; the only Son, who is in the bosom of the Father, He has made Him known." Christ, as the visible image of the invisible God (Colossians 1:15), is the fulfillment of the Old Testament representations and provides the foundation for the Orthodox use of icons.

The Veneration of Saints: Honoring the Holy and Faithful

Veneration of saints is another core element of Orthodox worship. Unlike the worship given to God alone, veneration (or dulia) is the honor shown to the saints, who are seen as examples of the faithful. In Orthodox theology, there is a difference between worship (latreia) given to God and honor (dulia) given to saints, which is a form of respect and admiration for their virtuous lives and their closeness to God.

The Orthodox Church believes in the communion of saints, a spiritual bond between the living and the departed members of the Church. The saints, because they are united to Christ, intercede for the faithful before God. This is rooted in biblical understanding, such as in Revelation 5:8, where the prayers of the saints are presented to God. The saints are seen as powerful intercessors who pray for the living, as we read in Hebrews 12:1, where the author speaks of the *cloud of witnesses* who surround the faithful.

St. John Chrysostom, a Church Father, explains:
> We do not worship the saints, but we venerate them as friends of God. Just as when we honor the king's friends, we honor the king himself, so when we venerate the saints, we are honoring Christ.

This intercessory role of the saints is not seen as competing with Christ's mediation, but rather as part of the Christian understanding of the Church as the Body of Christ, where all members, living and dead, are united in Him.

Scriptural Basis for the Veneration of Saints
The veneration of saints has strong scriptural support. In 1 Timothy 2:1–4, Paul urges the faithful to pray for all people, for *kings and all who are in authority*. The Orthodox Church extends this concept to include all saints, who have "authority" in heaven through their close relationship with God. This is consistent with the understanding of the Church as a living entity, with Christ as the Head, and the saints as His body, working together for the salvation of the world.

The Role of Icons and Veneration in Orthodox Worship
Icons and the veneration of saints serve several purposes within Orthodox worship:

Spiritual Focus and Mediation: Icons provide the faithful with visual reminders of divine truths and serve as a means of contemplating the mysteries of the faith. The saints depicted in icons are not just historical figures but present examples of holiness and intercession. Through the veneration of these saints, Orthodox Christians are encouraged to model their own lives after the example of Christ as embodied in the saints.

Participation in the Divine: Icons bring the faithful into a more direct participation in the divine mysteries. In the liturgy, the iconostasis (the icon screen in the church) serves as a spiritual threshold, reminding the faithful that they are entering into the presence of God. By venerating icons, the faithful are joining with the heavenly hosts in worship, as described in Revelation 7:9–10, where saints and angels worship before the throne of God.

Teaching and Catechesis: Icons also function as a form of catechesis, teaching the faithful about key biblical events, the lives of saints, and theological truths. As a visual language, icons convey biblical stories and doctrines in a way that is accessible to all, regardless of literacy or background.

Connection with Tradition: Icons and the veneration of saints connect the faithful with the living tradition of the Church, stretching back to the apostles and the early Church Fathers. These practices are part of the continuity of the Church throughout the centuries and help to maintain the integrity of Orthodox theology and worship.

The Church Fathers on Icons and Veneration
The Church Fathers played a crucial role in defending the use of icons and the veneration of saints. St. Basil the Great (c. 330–379), in his Letter to the Bishops of Egypt, wrote:

> The saints who are honored are not gods, but the servants of God, the holy ones who have pleased Him. We do not worship them, but venerate them because they are honored by God.

St. Theodore the Studite (8th century), a staunch defender of the use of icons, argued that icons are essential for the proper expression of faith, writing:

> The honor given to the image passes over to the prototype.

These Fathers, among many others, emphasized that veneration of icons and saints is not idolatry but a proper expression of Christian worship and devotion.

Conclusion

Icons and the veneration of saints are essential elements of Orthodox Christian worship, rooted in the theological understanding of the Incarnation and the communion of saints. Icons serve as a way to visually represent the divine mysteries and the lives of holy men and women who exemplify Christ's love. Through the veneration of these icons and saints, the faithful are drawn closer to God, participating in the divine life and becoming part of the living Tradition of the Church. The scriptural and patristic foundations for these practices affirm that they are not merely aesthetic or cultural, but central to the Orthodox understanding of worship, spiritual growth, and communion with God.

Question 2: What Does the Orthodox Church Teach About the Virgin Mary?

The Virgin Mary occupies a central and venerated place in the life of the Orthodox Church. She is honored as the Mother of God (Theotokos), a title that encapsulates the unique role she plays in the mystery of the Incarnation. This article provides an in-depth exploration of the Orthodox Church's teachings about the Virgin Mary, drawing from Holy Scripture, the writings of the Church Fathers, and the rich Tradition of the Church.

The Title Theotokos: Mother of God

In Orthodox theology, the title Theotokos (Greek: Θεοτόκος), meaning "God-bearer" or "Mother of God," is the most significant and defining title for the Virgin Mary. This title was officially affirmed at the Council of Ephesus in 431 AD, a crucial event in the development of Orthodox Christology. The doctrine of the Theotokos is based on the belief that Jesus Christ is both fully God and fully man, and as such, His Mother, the Virgin Mary, gave birth to the person of Jesus Christ, who is the Son of God.

Biblical Foundation

The title Theotokos is rooted in the Bible, particularly in the Annunciation narrative in the Gospel of Luke. In Luke 1:35, the angel Gabriel announces to Mary that the Holy Spirit will come upon her and that she will conceive the Son of God:

> "The Holy Spirit will come upon you, and the power of the Most High will overshadow you; therefore, the child to be born will be called holy, the Son of God."

In the Orthodox understanding, by giving birth to Jesus Christ, the Virgin Mary truly becomes the Theotokos, the Mother of God, because the One she bore was not merely a human child, but the God-man, Jesus Christ. As St. Gregory the Theologian writes,

> "What was not assumed is not healed; but that which is united to His Godhead is saved." (Theological Oration 1).

Theological Significance

The affirmation that Mary is the Theotokos protects the integrity of the doctrine of the Incarnation. If Mary is the Mother of Jesus Christ, and Jesus is truly God, then Mary must be the Mother of God, preserving the truth that Christ is fully divine and fully human. Theologically, this avoids any form of Nestorianism, which would separate the divine and human natures of Christ into two distinct persons.

The Virgin Mary, as the Theotokos, is seen as the symbol of the Church itself, as the Church gives birth to Christ through the sacramental life and the preaching of the gospel.

The Immaculate Conception and Original Sin

The Orthodox Church does not accept the Roman Catholic doctrine of the Immaculate Conception, which teaches that Mary was conceived without original sin. While the Orthodox Church does believe that Mary was sanctified and blessed by God, it does not hold that she was preserved from original sin from the moment of her conception.

The Orthodox Understanding

The Orthodox Church teaches that Mary, while born with the inherited condition of original sin like all humanity, was chosen by God to be the vessel through which the Savior of the world would be born. This selection does not imply that she was sinless from birth, but rather that she was *full of grace* (Luke 1:28) and free from personal sin. The grace of God acted in her life to purify her and to prepare her for the role of Mother of God.

In the Orthodox view, Mary's holiness is not inherent by nature but is a result of her willing cooperation with God's grace. Her "yes" to God's will, as expressed in her fiat, *Behold the handmaid of the Lord; be it unto me according to thy word* (Luke 1:38), is what makes her a model of perfect obedience to God's will. Her immaculate purity, therefore, is not an automatic privilege of her conception but a result of her faith and submission to God.

Church Fathers on Mary's Purity
St. John of Damascus, one of the most influential Church Fathers, teaches that Mary was "purified from all defilement," and that she was "worthy of bearing God because of her holy and virtuous life." He does not explicitly endorse the Immaculate Conception but emphasizes her purity and obedience to God's call.

St. Gregory Nazianzus also speaks of Mary as being "without sin" not by her own power but through God's grace, and St. Irenaeus of Lyons describes Mary as the "New Eve" who, unlike the first Eve, consented to God's will and gave birth to the Savior.

Mary's Role in Salvation History
In Orthodox theology, the Virgin Mary is seen as playing a vital and cooperative role in the economy of salvation. While Christ alone is the Savior of mankind, Mary's "yes" to the angel's message allows the divine plan of salvation to unfold.

The New Eve
One of the most important theological insights the Orthodox Church draws from Mary is her role as the "New Eve." In contrast to the first Eve, who through her disobedience brought sin into the world, the Virgin Mary, through her obedience, became the instrument of the salvation of humanity. St. Irenaeus, in his work Against Heresies, states:

> The knot of Eve's disobedience was untied by Mary's obedience; for what the virgin Eve had bound by her unbelief, the virgin Mary loosed by her faith.

This parallel between Eve and Mary is central in understanding Mary's role in salvation history. As Eve was the mother of all the living, so Mary is the spiritual mother of all who are reborn in Christ.

Intercessor and Advocate
In addition to being the Theotokos, Mary is regarded as an intercessor for all Christians. In Orthodox prayer, Mary is often invoked to intercede on behalf of the faithful, particularly in times of need. The Orthodox Church believes that Mary, as the Mother of God, has a special relationship with her Son, Jesus Christ, and, as such, her prayers are powerful.

The hymn "Akathist to the Theotokos," a central part of Orthodox devotion, expresses the Church's deep veneration for Mary and calls upon her intercessions: "Rejoice, O full of grace, the Lord is with you." Mary is seen not as a deity but as a human who enjoys a special relationship with God, one that allows her to intercede for the faithful.

The Dormition and Assumption of Mary
The Orthodox Church teaches that, at the end of her earthly life, the Virgin Mary was taken up bodily into heaven, an event known as the Dormition (Greek: Κοίμησις) of the Theotokos. This event is celebrated on August 15th, and it signifies Mary's full participation in the resurrection of her Son, Jesus Christ. While the Orthodox Church does not teach the same concept of Assumption as the Roman Catholic Church (which emphasizes that Mary was assumed into heaven without experiencing death), the Dormition is understood as a "falling asleep" that leads to her being received into heaven.

This event is a prefiguration of the final resurrection of the body and is seen as a sign of hope for all believers that they, too, will be resurrected at the end of time. The Orthodox liturgy praises Mary for her purity and obedience, and her Dormition is seen as a glorious end to a life lived in perfect conformity to God's will.

Mary's Role in Orthodox Worship
Mary holds a prominent place in Orthodox worship. She is invoked in many prayers, hymns, and liturgical rites, and her icon is central to the worship of the Orthodox Church. Her image is often displayed in the church, not for the purpose of worshiping her, but as a representation of her role in the salvation of mankind and her unique position in the life of the Church.

The feast days dedicated to the Virgin Mary, such as the Annunciation (March 25), the Dormition (August 15), and the Nativity of the Theotokos (September 8), are significant occasions in the Orthodox liturgical calendar. These feasts celebrate key moments in Mary's life and her role in the plan of salvation. During the Divine Liturgy, hymns such as the Akathist Hymn and the Magnificat (Luke 1:46-55) are sung, extolling her virtues and her role in God's redemptive work.

Conclusion
In the Orthodox Church, the Virgin Mary is much more than a historical figure or a passive vessel for the Incarnation of Christ. She is venerated as the Theotokos, the Mother of God, who played an indispensable role in the fulfillment of God's plan of salvation. Her purity, faith, and obedience to God's will make her the ultimate model for all Christians. The Orthodox Church teaches that Mary is a human being who was filled with God's grace, and through her, Christ entered the world to redeem humanity.

In honoring the Virgin Mary, the Orthodox faithful do not worship her as a deity, but rather revere her as the most honored of all creation, who through her obedience became the instrument by which God took flesh for the salvation of the world. Her intercession continues to be a source of comfort and hope for the faithful as they strive to follow her example of faith and devotion to God.

Question 3
Why Do Orthodox Christians Pray to Saints and the Virgin Mary? Isn't That Idolatry?

The question of why Orthodox Christians pray to saints and the Virgin Mary is a common one, particularly from those unfamiliar with the practice or coming from traditions that view such acts as bordering on idolatry. This question touches on key theological issues such as the nature of prayer, the role of saints and the Virgin Mary, and the distinction between veneration and worship. The Orthodox Church's approach to these practices is deeply rooted in Scripture, Tradition, and the writings of the Church Fathers, and it is important to clarify why praying to saints and Mary is not considered idolatry in the Orthodox Christian faith.

Understanding Prayer in Orthodox Christianity
Before addressing why Orthodox Christians pray to saints and the Virgin Mary, it is essential to understand the nature of prayer itself in Orthodox theology. Prayer in the Orthodox Church is not just a means of petitioning God but also an expression of the relationship between the believer and the entire body of Christ, which includes both the living and the dead. In the Orthodox understanding, all Christians, whether living on earth or in heaven, are united as one body in Christ. This belief is rooted in the biblical teaching of the Communion of Saints, which asserts that all members of the Church are connected in a spiritual bond through Christ, the Head of the Church (Ephesians 1:22–23).

Prayer in the Orthodox Church is primarily directed to God, the Father, the Son (Jesus Christ), and the Holy Spirit. However, Orthodox Christians also ask the saints, especially the Virgin Mary, to intercede on their behalf, much like they would ask a fellow believer for prayers. The distinction between asking for intercession and offering direct worship is a key point that distinguishes Orthodox Christian practice from idolatry.

Veneration of Saints and Mary: Distinction from Worship
One of the most important concepts to understand is the difference between *latreia* (worship) and *dulia* (veneration). According to Orthodox theology, worship (*latreia*) is due to God alone, while veneration (*dulia*) is the honor shown to saints, angels, and the Virgin Mary. This distinction is crucial because it helps to explain why praying to saints and the Virgin Mary is not idolatry.

The Worship of God Alone
The Orthodox Church makes a firm distinction between the worship due to God and the honor given to saints. The first commandment of the Decalogue, *You shall worship the Lord your God and Him only shall you serve* (Matthew 4:10), is central to Orthodox theology. The Church teaches that worship, which includes adoration, sacrifice, and reverence, is directed solely toward God. No creature, be it saint, angel, or Mary, is worthy of worship in the same way God is.

The Veneration of Saints

While saints are honored and their intercession sought, the Orthodox Church does not teach that the saints are to be worshipped. Saints are viewed as models of Christian virtue and faith, and their lives are honored because they have shown the way to holiness. The Orthodox faithful ask the saints to pray for them because the saints, being in the presence of God, are in a unique position to intercede on behalf of others.

In the words of St. John Chrysostom, a key figure in early Orthodox theology:

> We do not worship the saints, but we venerate them as friends of God. Just as when we honor the king's friends, we honor the king himself, so when we venerate the saints, we are honoring Christ.

The saints are not seen as divine beings, but rather as human beings who, through their cooperation with God's grace, achieved holiness. This understanding is rooted in Scripture, where the apostle James writes, *The prayer of a righteous person is powerful and effective* (James 5:16). Since saints are righteous and holy, their prayers on behalf of others are considered powerful and effective.

The Veneration of the Virgin Mary

The Virgin Mary, as the Mother of God (*Theotokos*), occupies a unique position in Orthodox Christianity. While Orthodox Christians venerate her with great honor and devotion, this veneration is distinct from worship. Mary is honored as the one who gave birth to Jesus Christ, the Savior of the world. Her special role in salvation history is celebrated, but Orthodox Christians do not believe that she is divine or worship her as such.

The veneration of the Virgin Mary includes asking for her intercession, just as one would ask a fellow believer to pray for them. This practice is based on the biblical principle of the Communion of Saints, where all Christians, both living and deceased, are united in Christ and can intercede for one another (Revelation 5:8). The Orthodox Church teaches that Mary, as the Mother of God, has a special relationship with her Son, and thus, her intercession is considered especially powerful.

In the words of St. John of Damascus, a great defender of Orthodox doctrine regarding the Virgin Mary:

> We do not worship Mary as God, but we honor her as the Mother of God, for she bore the Word of God in her womb.

Biblical and Patristic Foundation for Praying to Saints and Mary

The Orthodox practice of praying to saints and the Virgin Mary is deeply rooted in both the Bible and the writings of the Church Fathers. Here are some key biblical and patristic arguments in support of these practices:

Biblical Basis

- Intercession of Saints: The idea of seeking the prayers of others, including saints, is scripturally supported. In Revelation 5:8, we read that the saints in heaven offer the prayers of the faithful on earth to God: "And when He had taken the scroll, the four living creatures and the twenty-four elders fell down before the Lamb, each holding a harp, and golden bowls full of incense, which are the prayers of the saints." This passage suggests that the prayers of the saints are a means by which the faithful on earth are supported in their spiritual lives.

- The Communion of Saints: The concept of the Communion of Saints, which teaches that all Christians are spiritually united in Christ, is reflected in Hebrews 12:1, which speaks of the *great cloud of witnesses* surrounding us. These "witnesses" are understood to be the saints who, having already attained salvation, are still engaged in caring for the spiritual well-being of the Church on earth.

- Mary's Role: In Luke 1:28, the angel Gabriel greets Mary as *full of grace,* and in Luke 1:42–43, Elizabeth calls her *blessed among women* and acknowledges her special role in salvation. In Luke 1:48, Mary herself prophesies, *For behold, henceforth all generations will call me blessed.* This biblical testimony provides the foundation for the Orthodox veneration of Mary.

Patristic Support

- St. Basil the Great: St. Basil the Great, an early Church Father, defended the practice of asking the saints to pray for us, explaining that it is a sign of the unity of the Church: "Just as we ask the living

to pray for us, so too we ask the saints who are in heaven to pray for us, for they are alive in Christ."
- St. John Chrysostom: As mentioned earlier, St. John Chrysostom emphasized the difference between worship and veneration, stating that the veneration of the saints is a way of honoring God's work in their lives, and through their intercession, the faithful are brought closer to Christ.
- St. Cyril of Alexandria: St. Cyril wrote in defense of the honor given to the Virgin Mary, stating that "She who gave birth to the Savior is rightly honored by all generations, not as a goddess, but as the true Mother of God."

The Role of Saints and Mary in the Life of the Church
In Orthodox Christianity, saints and the Virgin Mary play a crucial role in the spiritual life of the believer. The saints are seen as examples of holiness and faithfulness, and their lives serve as models for Orthodox Christians to emulate. The prayers of the saints are believed to bring strength, comfort, and encouragement to the faithful as they journey toward salvation.

The Virgin Mary, as the Mother of God, is particularly revered for her role in the Incarnation and for her obedience to God. Orthodox Christians seek her intercession, trusting that she, as the Mother of Christ, has a special role in helping bring them closer to her Son.

Conclusion
Praying to saints and the Virgin Mary is not idolatry in the Orthodox Church because it is a form of veneration, not worship. Worship is reserved for God alone, while the saints and Mary are honored as models of faith, holiness, and intercession. Orthodox Christians ask for their prayers, trusting that, as members of the Body of Christ, the saints are actively involved in the salvation of the faithful. This practice is deeply rooted in Scripture and the writings of the Church Fathers, who consistently emphasize the distinction between worship and veneration. By seeking the intercession of the saints and the Virgin Mary, Orthodox Christians express their belief in the Communion of Saints and their desire to grow closer to God.

Question 4
How Does the Orthodox Church Understand the Atonement and the Role of Christ's Death on the Cross?

The question of the atonement—the understanding of Christ's death on the cross and its significance for salvation—is a central issue in Christian theology. It is often a point of divergence between various Christian traditions, particularly between the Orthodox Church and many Protestant denominations. In this lesson, we will explore the Orthodox Church's understanding of the atonement, drawing from Holy Scripture, the writings of the Church Fathers, and the deep theological insights that have shaped Orthodox doctrine over the centuries.

The Orthodox View of Atonement: A Healing of Humanity

The Orthodox Church understands the death of Christ on the cross as a cosmic and transformative event that is primarily concerned with the healing and restoration of humanity, rather than simply as a legal transaction. In this view, the atonement is not a matter of satisfying a divine legal debt or appeasing God's wrath (as in many Western Protestant theories of atonement), but rather a profound act of love through which Christ restores fallen humanity to communion with God.

Christ as the Divine Physician

In Orthodox theology, humanity's fall into sin resulted in separation from God and spiritual death. Christ's death on the cross is seen as the remedy for this condition, which the Orthodox Church views as a process of healing rather than a transaction. Christ is the Divine Physician who heals the wounds of sin, liberates humanity from death, and restores our relationship with God. This is deeply tied to the Orthodox understanding of salvation, which is not just a legal declaration but a process of spiritual healing and transformation.

The concept of Christ as the Divine Physician is grounded in Scripture. In Luke 5:31–32, Christ Himself says, *It is not the healthy who need a doctor, but the sick. I have not come to call the righteous, but sinners to repentance.* Similarly, in 1 Peter 2:24, it says, *He Himself bore our sins in His body on the tree, that we might die to sin and live to righteousness.*

This idea of healing and restoration is further emphasized in the teachings of the Church Fathers. St. Irenaeus of Lyons, one of the earliest Church Fathers, described Christ's work as the restoration of humanity to its original, pre-fallen state. He writes in *Against Heresies*:

> The Word of God became man in order to heal the disobedience of man, and to restore the image of God that had been lost in the fall.

The Restoration of the Image of God

The Orthodox Church teaches that Christ, as the God-man, came to restore the image of God in humanity that was marred by sin. Humanity was created in God's image and likeness (Genesis 1:26–27), but sin distorted this image. Christ, by becoming fully human and fully divine, enables humans to regain the fullness of their created nature. His death on the cross is seen as a key moment in this restoration, as it breaks the power of sin and death that hold humanity captive.

In the words of St. Athanasius of Alexandria, one of the most significant early Church Fathers,

> *He became what we are in order to make us what He is.* This profound truth underscores the Orthodox view of salvation as a process of deification (*theosis*), where human being1s are restored to their original purpose of becoming partakers in the divine nature (2 Peter 1:4).

Christ's Death and Victory Over Death and Sin

In Orthodox theology, Christ's death on the cross is not viewed as a mere substitutionary act that satisfies divine wrath, but rather as a victory over the powers of sin, death, and the devil. Christ's death is seen as the culmination of His divine mission to conquer evil and restore creation to its original, intended state.

The Ransom Theory

One of the earliest and most important interpretations of Christ's death in the Orthodox tradition is what is often called the "ransom theory." This understanding holds that Christ's death was a ransom paid to Satan or the forces of evil to free humanity from their power. In this view, humanity had been enslaved by sin and death, and Christ's death on the cross was the price that was paid to release humanity from this bondage.

This interpretation is not meant to imply that God was somehow obliged to Satan, but rather that Christ's death represented the ultimate victory over the forces that had held humanity captive. Christ, being sinless and divine, was able to defeat death and the devil, and His resurrection sealed this victory. St. Gregory of Nyssa, a Church Father, wrote:

> The Word of God entered into the realm of death, and by the very fact that He is life, He abolished death. He entered into the domain of death, and by His entrance, He destroyed it.

This view is closely tied to the Orthodox emphasis on Christ's resurrection, which is seen as the definitive victory over the power of death. In the Paschal hymns of the Orthodox Church, Christ's death and resurrection are celebrated as the triumph of life over death, light over darkness, and good over evil.

Christ's Death as the Destruction of Death

The Orthodox Church teaches that Christ's death on the cross destroyed death itself. In His death, Christ experienced the full extent of human suffering and separation from God. But His death was not the end—through His resurrection, He conquered death and opened the way for all humanity to be resurrected in Him. The Apostle Paul writes in 1 Corinthians 15:54–57:

> Death is swallowed up in victory. O death, where is your victory? O death, where is your sting? The sting of death is sin, and the power of sin is the law. But thanks be to God, who gives us the victory through our Lord Jesus Christ.

Christ's death is therefore not just about paying a penalty for sin, but about destroying the power of sin and death once and for all. In Orthodox theology, salvation is not merely about forgiveness of sins, but about overcoming the ultimate consequences of sin—spiritual death and separation from God.

The Role of Christ's Death in the Orthodox Understanding of Atonement

The Orthodox Church teaches that the atonement is a multifaceted event that involves Christ's entire life, death, and resurrection. It is not just a singular event focused on the cross, but a process in which Christ, through His incarnation, passion, and resurrection, restores humanity to its intended purpose of communion with God.

Atonement as a Process of Deification

For the Orthodox Church, the goal of the atonement is not just to clear a legal debt but to enable humanity to share in the divine life. The term theosis (deification) is central to this understanding of salvation. Christ's death on the cross, combined with His resurrection, opens the way for human beings to become partakers in the divine nature. Through His death and resurrection, Christ transforms humanity from the image of sin to the image of holiness.

St. Athanasius, in his famous work On the Incarnation, explains: "The Son of God became man so that we might become God."

This is not to suggest that humans become gods in the literal sense, but that they are brought into union with God through the grace of the Holy Spirit. Christ's death on the cross is thus not just an act of propitiation but the means by which human beings are made capable of entering into a transformative relationship with God.

The Cross as the Triumph of Love

In Orthodox theology, Christ's death is understood as the ultimate act of divine love. John 15:13 teaches, *Greater love has no one than this: to lay down one's life for one's friends.* Christ, through His sacrificial death on the cross, reveals the depth of God's love for humanity and opens the door for humans to respond to this love through faith and repentance.

In the words of St. Maximus the Confessor, a key Orthodox theologian:
> The cross is the great victory and the great mystery, by which the love of God is made manifest.

Christ's death on the cross is a revelation of God's love for humanity, and it is through this love that the believer is healed, restored, and brought into communion with God.

Conclusion

In summary, the Orthodox Church understands the atonement as the act of healing, restoring, and transforming humanity through the death and resurrection of Jesus Christ. Christ's death on the cross is not primarily seen as a payment for sin or as an appeasement of divine wrath, but as the means by which Christ defeats the powers of sin, death, and the devil. Through His death and resurrection, Christ restores the broken relationship between humanity and God and opens the way for human beings to be deified, becoming partakers of the divine nature.

In Orthodox theology, salvation is a process of transformation that is made possible by Christ's victory over death, and the cross stands as the ultimate symbol of this victory and divine love. The death of Christ is central to Orthodox understanding of the atonement, but it is inseparable from His resurrection, which completes the work of salvation and offers the hope of eternal life to all believers.

Question 5
What is the Orthodox Understanding of the Pope and Papal Primacy? How Does the Orthodox Church Understand the Nature and Authority of the Church?

The relationship between the Orthodox Church and the papacy is one of the most significant theological differences between the Orthodox and Roman Catholic Churches. The question of the Pope and papal primacy has been a source of division since the Great Schism of 1054. In this article, we will explore the Orthodox understanding of the Pope's role and primacy, along with the Orthodox Church's view of the nature and authority of the Church.

The Orthodox Understanding of the Pope
In the Orthodox Church, the Pope is seen as the bishop of Rome and, like all bishops, he holds a place of honor and respect within the global Church. However, the Orthodox Church does not accept the Roman Catholic doctrine of papal primacy, which holds that the Pope has universal jurisdiction over the entire Church, with authority over all other bishops, including those of the Orthodox Church.

The Role of the Pope in the Early Church
The Orthodox Church acknowledges that the bishop of Rome has a special place in the history of Christianity due to Rome's importance as the capital of the Roman Empire and its association with Saint Peter, whom Catholics view as the first Pope. The Orthodox Church

recognizes that Peter was a significant figure in the early Church, but it does not accept that Peter's primacy was passed on to his successors in an absolute or universal sense.

The Orthodox view holds that the early Church recognized a conciliar model of governance in which all bishops were seen as equal in authority, with no single bishop holding universal jurisdiction over the entire Church. In the first centuries of Christianity, while the bishop of Rome held a place of honor, this honor was not equivalent to the papal authority claimed by the Roman Catholic Church today.

The Role of the Pope in the Orthodox Church Today
The Orthodox Church continues to respect the bishop of Rome as the leader of the Church of Rome but does not grant him authority over the entire Orthodox Church. The Orthodox Church operates with a conciliar model, where authority is shared among the bishops of the various local Churches, each of which is independent and self-governing.

In the Orthodox tradition, the Pope is not considered the head of the universal Church. Instead, the head of each autocephalous (independent and self-governing) Orthodox Church is a primate (e.g., the Patriarch of Constantinople, the Archbishop of Athens, etc.), and these primates work together in a conciliar manner, representing the unity of the Church. Each local Church is considered fully apostolic and complete, and no single bishop or patriarch has authority over all of them.

Papal Primacy vs. Conciliarity in the Orthodox Church
The Roman Catholic doctrine of papal primacy holds that the Pope is the supreme and final authority on matters of faith and practice, and his decrees are binding on the entire Church. This belief is based on interpretations of Scripture, particularly Matthew 16:18–19, where Jesus says to Peter, *You are Peter, and on this rock I will build my Church.*

In contrast, the Orthodox Church rejects the idea that the Pope holds universal and supreme authority over all Christians. While the Orthodox Church does accept that Peter was the chief of the apostles and that Rome held a special place due to Peter's association with the city, it believes that this primacy is not a universal, absolute authority. Rather, the authority of all bishops is equal, and the Church as a whole is governed by councils, not by a single individual.

The Orthodox Church teaches that the fullness of the Church's authority is embodied in the collective body of bishops who meet in Ecumenical Councils, which are convened to address matters of doctrine, practice, and discipline. These councils are considered to be the highest authority in the Church, with the consensus of the bishops representing the voice of the Church as guided by the Holy Spirit.

The most famous example of conciliarity in action is the seven Ecumenical Councils, which were convened to address key theological questions, including the nature of Christ and the relationship between the Father, Son, and Holy Spirit. These councils are considered authoritative in Orthodox theology, and no single bishop, including the Pope, can override the decisions of an Ecumenical Council.

The Nature and Authority of the Church in Orthodox Theology
In Orthodox Christianity, the Church is understood to be the mystical Body of Christ, through which Christ continues His presence in the world. The Church is not an institution or organization in a human sense, but the living, breathing community of those who are united in Christ through the sacraments and the teachings of the apostles.

The Church as the Body of Christ
The Orthodox Church believes that Christ is the Head of the Church, and all members of the Church are His body (Ephesians 1:22–23). This means that Christ is the source of all authority in the Church, and the authority of the Church is rooted in Christ Himself, not in any individual leader. Bishops, priests, and deacons are ordained to serve the Church and administer the sacraments, but their authority is always exercised in communion with the rest of the Church and under the guidance of the Holy Spirit.

The Orthodox understanding of the Church emphasizes the importance of unity in faith and practice. The Church is called to preserve the truth as handed down from the apostles, and this truth is revealed through Scripture, Holy Tradition, and the life of the Church. The Church is also called to be a visible expression of Christ's love and salvation, offering the sacraments, preaching the gospel, and fostering the life of prayer.

The Role of the Bishops

In Orthodox theology, bishops are seen as the successors of the apostles. Each bishop, in communion with the other bishops, is responsible for preserving the faith and shepherding the faithful. The authority of a bishop is not absolute but is always exercised in connection with the other bishops. Bishops are called to maintain the unity of the Church, preserve the teachings of the apostles, and guide the faithful in the ways of holiness.

In the Orthodox Church, the concept of "synodality" (or conciliarity) plays a key role in the governance of the Church. The bishops of a particular region, or of the entire Orthodox world, meet in synods or councils to make decisions on matters of doctrine and practice. This synodal structure ensures that authority is shared among the bishops and that no single bishop has the power to impose his will upon the entire Church.

The Role of the Ecumenical Patriarch of Constantinople

While the Orthodox Church does not recognize the Pope as the supreme authority, it does recognize the special role of the Ecumenical Patriarch of Constantinople. The Ecumenical Patriarch is considered "first among equals" (Latin: primus inter pares) among the Orthodox bishops. This means that while the Ecumenical Patriarch does not have universal authority over the entire Church, he holds a position of honor and is a symbol of the unity of the Orthodox Church.

The Ecumenical Patriarch's role is primarily to serve as a spokesperson for the Orthodox Church and to call and preside over synods and councils. However, his authority is not absolute, and he exercises his leadership in communion with the other Orthodox patriarchs and bishops.

Conclusion: The Orthodox Church's View of Authority and the Papacy

In summary, the Orthodox Church recognizes the Pope as the bishop of Rome and honors the historical and symbolic significance of his position. However, the Orthodox Church rejects the Roman Catholic doctrine of papal primacy, which grants the Pope universal and supreme authority over the entire Church. Instead, the Orthodox Church operates with a conciliar model of governance, where authority is shared among the bishops, and the Church's leadership is exercised through Ecumenical Councils.

The Orthodox Church understands its nature as the mystical Body of Christ, where Christ is the Head and the bishops are His earthly representatives, serving the Church and guiding the faithful. The authority of the Church is grounded in Christ Himself, and the Church's unity is maintained through shared belief in the apostolic faith, the sacraments, and the guidance of the Holy Spirit. The role of the Ecumenical Patriarch of Constantinople is one of honor and leadership in preserving the unity of the Church, but he does not exercise universal authority over all Christians.

For Catholic inquirers, it is important to understand that the Orthodox Church does not deny the importance of the papacy in the history of the Church, but it offers a different understanding of papal authority, emphasizing the conciliar and communal nature of the Church's leadership.

Question 6 What is the Orthodox Position on Purgatory?

The concept of purgatory, as it is understood in Roman Catholic theology, is a point of theological difference between the Roman Catholic Church and the Orthodox Church. The Roman Catholic Church teaches that purgatory is a temporary state of purification for those who die in God's grace but still need to be purified before entering heaven. In contrast, the Orthodox Church does not have a distinct doctrine of purgatory as it is defined in Catholic theology. However, the Orthodox Church does believe in the existence of a post-death purification process, though it is understood differently.

In this article, we will explore the Orthodox Church's perspective on life after death, purification, and how this compares to the Roman Catholic understanding of purgatory.

The Orthodox Understanding of the Afterlife

In Orthodox Christianity, life after death is seen as a transition into the fullness of life in Christ. The Orthodox Church teaches that after death, the soul undergoes an intermediate state, which is not purgatory as defined by Catholicism, but rather a state of waiting for the final judgment and the resurrection of the dead.

The Immediate Post-Death State

The Orthodox Church teaches that immediately after death, the soul is separated from the body and enters into a state of awareness of its eternal destiny. In this intermediate state, the soul experiences either peace and joy or torment and separation from God, depending on its relationship with Christ and the choices made during life. The soul awaits the final resurrection, when the body will be reunited with the soul, and all will stand before the judgment seat of Christ.

In Orthodox theology, there is a distinction between the "particular judgment" and the "final judgment." The particular judgment occurs immediately after death and is an individual judgment of the soul's eternal fate. The final judgment will occur at the end of time, when all the dead are resurrected, and the righteous will enter into eternal life while the wicked are separated from God.

The Importance of the Final Judgment

While the immediate post-death state is important in Orthodox theology, the final judgment is the definitive moment when each person's eternal fate is sealed. The soul's experience in the intermediate state is seen as a reflection of its relationship with God and the degree of transformation it has undergone. Those who are in a state of grace and communion with God may experience a foretaste of heaven, while those who are separated from God may experience a foretaste of hell.

The Orthodox View on Purification After Death

While the Orthodox Church does not have a specific doctrine of purgatory, it does believe in the possibility of post-death purification. This is often discussed in terms of the "soul's purification" or the "final purification" that occurs after death, but it is not seen as a permanent, separate state like the Catholic understanding of purgatory.

The Concept of Post-Death Purification

The Orthodox Church teaches that some souls may require a period of purification after death before they are able to enter the fullness of God's presence. This purification is not understood as a punishment for sins, but rather as a cleansing process, as souls are transformed and purified from any remaining attachment to sin or imperfection that may prevent them from fully experiencing the glory of God.

This process is not tied to a specific place or temporary state, as in the Catholic doctrine of purgatory, but is understood to be a dynamic experience of transformation. The soul is purified through God's grace, and this transformation occurs through the power of prayer, especially the prayers of the living, as well as through God's mercy and love.

The Role of Prayer and Almsgiving for the Departed
The Orthodox Church places significant importance on the prayers for the dead. These prayers are not seen as changing the eternal fate of the departed, but rather as helping to purify the soul and bring it closer to God's grace. The Church prays for the souls of the departed in its liturgical services, particularly during the Divine Liturgy and in specific prayers for the deceased, such as the Memorial Services (Panikhida). Orthodox Christians also practice almsgiving and acts of mercy for the deceased, as it is believed that these acts can help facilitate the soul's purification.

The prayer of the Church is understood as part of the communion of saints, where the faithful on earth, the living and the dead, are united in Christ. The prayers of the Church are offered as a means of strengthening the soul in its journey toward God. The Church does not believe that the soul's destiny can be altered after death, but that the prayers of the living can help strengthen and purify the soul's condition in preparation for the final resurrection.

In the Liturgy of the Departed, for example, prayers are offered asking God to forgive the sins of the departed and to grant them rest in the light of His presence. This is an expression of the Orthodox belief in the ongoing relationship between the living and the dead within the context of Christ's redemptive work.

The Orthodox Church's Understanding of Sin and Purification
Orthodox theology does not view sin merely as a legal infraction to be paid for, but as a condition that distorts the human person and separates them from God. The purification process is understood as the healing of this separation and distortion. Through Christ's death and resurrection, the power of sin and death is overcome, and the soul is healed, restored, and made whole.

The Healing Nature of God's Grace

In the Orthodox view, purification after death is not a matter of paying a penalty, but rather of healing the soul from the effects of sin. God's grace, which is active in the life of the believer, continues after death and works to cleanse and restore the soul. This grace is not a punishment, but a healing force that prepares the soul for union with God.

The concept of theosis (deification) plays a key role in the Orthodox understanding of salvation. Theosis is the process by which a person is transformed into the likeness of God, participating in His divine nature. While the soul may experience a period of purification after death, the ultimate goal is for the soul to be fully united with God in His divine glory.

St. Gregory of Nyssa, a prominent Church Father, writes:
> For the soul is not punished for its sins in the afterlife, but rather, it is purified, so that it may become worthy of the glory of God.

This understanding emphasizes that salvation is a process of healing and restoration, not merely of punishment and retribution.

The Orthodox Church's Rejection of the Catholic Doctrine of Purgatory

The Orthodox Church does not accept the Catholic doctrine of purgatory, which teaches that souls are temporarily purified in a state of suffering before entering heaven. In Catholicism, purgatory is often understood as a place where the faithful undergo purification for the temporal consequences of sin, and it is associated with a form of suffering as the soul is cleansed.

In contrast, the Orthodox Church does not teach that souls are in a specific place of suffering after death. While the Orthodox Church believes in the possibility of purification, this is understood as a process of transformation that takes place under God's mercy and grace. The idea of purgatory as a temporary state of suffering does not have a place in Orthodox theology.

Instead, the Orthodox Church focuses on the ultimate victory over sin and death through Christ's resurrection and the healing and restoration of the soul through God's grace. The purification process is seen as part of the soul's journey toward union with God, and it is not separated into a distinct and punitive state like purgatory.

Conclusion: The Orthodox Approach to Purification After Death
The Orthodox Church does not have a doctrine of purgatory as it is understood in Roman Catholic theology. Instead, the Church teaches that after death, the soul enters an intermediate state of awareness and awaits the final judgment and resurrection. While some souls may require purification after death, this purification is seen as a process of healing, not a punishment. The Orthodox Church emphasizes the ongoing role of prayer, especially the prayers of the living, in aiding the purification of the soul.

The Orthodox Church believes that the ultimate goal of salvation is the union of the soul with God, through His grace and mercy, in the process of theosis. The purification of the soul is understood as part of this journey of healing and restoration, in preparation for eternal life in the presence of God.

For Orthodox Christians, salvation is not just about the forgiveness of sins, but about the transformation of the human person into the likeness of God. This process continues after death, and the prayers and intercessions of the living can help guide the departed souls toward this final union with God.

Question 7 How Does the Orthodox Church View the Immaculate Conception of the Virgin Mary?

The doctrine of the Immaculate Conception of the Virgin Mary is a key teaching in the Roman Catholic Church, which holds that Mary was conceived without original sin. This doctrine was dogmatically defined by Pope Pius IX in 1854, and it has been a central part of Catholic Mariology. However, the Orthodox Church does not accept the doctrine of the Immaculate Conception in the same way. While the Orthodox Church honors and venerates the Virgin Mary as a most blessed and pure woman, the understanding of her purity and sinlessness differs significantly from the Catholic teaching of the Immaculate Conception.

In this section, we will explore how the Orthodox Church views the Immaculate Conception, its theological underpinnings, and the Church's understanding of the Virgin Mary's holiness.

The Orthodox Church's Understanding of Mary's Purity

The Orthodox Church holds the Virgin Mary in the highest regard and venerates her as the Theotokos (God-bearer), the Mother of God, who is most holy and pure. However, the Orthodox Church does not accept the Roman Catholic teaching that Mary was conceived without original sin, a doctrine known as the Immaculate Conception.

The Purity of Mary: A Process of Sanctification

The Orthodox Church teaches that Mary was conceived in the same way as all human beings, born with original sin as a result of humanity's fall from grace in the Garden of Eden. However, what sets Mary apart is that from the moment of her conception, God's grace was abundantly present in her life. She was sanctified by God's grace and chosen by Him to bear the incarnate Word, Jesus Christ.

The Orthodox Church believes that Mary's holiness and purity are not the result of a unique, preemptive act of divine intervention that prevents original sin at the moment of her conception (as in the Catholic doctrine), but rather are the result of her faithful cooperation with God's grace. Throughout her life, Mary lived a life of perfect obedience and submission to God's will, and this was the cause of her purity.

In Orthodox thought, purity is not an inherent quality but is rather a result of God's grace and the person's cooperation with it. St. Gregory Palamas, a significant theologian in the Orthodox Church, explains that Mary's sanctification was a continuous process, wherein she freely received God's grace and remained sinless due to her constant openness to God's will.

The Immaculate Conception:
Catholic Doctrine vs. Orthodox Understanding

The doctrine of the Immaculate Conception asserts that Mary was preserved from original sin from the very moment of her conception by a special act of God's grace, ensuring that she was without sin throughout her life. This doctrine was dogmatically defined by the Catholic Church in 1854, and it is closely tied to the Catholic view of original sin and its transmission.

In contrast, the Orthodox Church does not have a doctrine of the Immaculate Conception. The Orthodox view holds that Mary, like all humans, was born with original sin, but that she was sanctified by God in preparation for her role as the Mother of God. The Orthodox Church believes that the grace of God is freely given to all, and Mary's special holiness came from her faithful and sinless response to God's call.

The Orthodox Church also rejects the notion that Mary's sinlessness was a necessity for her to bear Christ. The Orthodox view is that Christ, being fully God and fully man, did not need a sinless vessel for His incarnation. The focus of the Orthodox faith is not on Mary's sinlessness but on her role as the one who bore God incarnate. St. John of Damascus, an important Church Father, writes:

"We do not worship the Virgin as a goddess, but we honor her as the Mother of God, who bore the Word of God in her womb, and by her intercession, we are brought closer to Christ."

Mary's Role as the *Theotokos*
While the Orthodox Church does not accept the doctrine of the Immaculate Conception, it emphasizes the extraordinary role of the Virgin Mary as the *Theotokos*, or God-bearer. The Orthodox Church believes that Mary was chosen by God to bear the Savior of the world, and this makes her the most blessed and exalted of all human beings. The Orthodox veneration of Mary is not as a deity but as the most perfect and faithful servant of God.

Mary's role as the *Theotokos* is central to Orthodox Christology. By saying "yes" to the angel Gabriel's message at the Annunciation (Luke 1:38), Mary became the instrument through which the Word of God was made flesh. This act of willing obedience to God is seen as the highest example of human faith and devotion. The Orthodox Church celebrates Mary's role in salvation history by honoring her as the Mother of God, and through her, all Christians are invited to partake in the grace of God.

The Orthodox Church teaches that Mary's purity and holiness are seen in her willing acceptance of God's plan and her life of faithful obedience to His will. She is venerated as a model for all Christians to follow, especially in her humility, faith, and trust in God.

The Orthodox Understanding of Sin and Holiness

The doctrine of the Immaculate Conception is tied to a particular understanding of sin and holiness that differs from the Orthodox perspective. In Roman Catholic theology, original sin is seen as a stain that affects human nature, which must be removed in order for a person to be fully united to God. In this view, the Immaculate Conception preserves Mary from original sin in order to make her a fit vessel for Christ.

In contrast, the Orthodox Church teaches that original sin is not a stain that can be washed away by a specific act of divine intervention, but rather a condition that affects the entire human race. Original sin is the result of humanity's disobedience and separation from God, and all human beings, except for Christ and the Virgin Mary, are born with this condition. However, in the Orthodox Church, the emphasis is placed on the transformative power of God's grace to heal and restore humanity.

For the Orthodox, holiness is not about being sinless from birth, but rather about responding to God's grace through repentance and obedience. Mary's purity is understood as the result of her perfect cooperation with God's grace throughout her life, not because she was conceived without original sin. This understanding emphasizes the process of theosis (deification), by which humans become partakers in the divine nature, growing in holiness through communion with God.

The Veneration of Mary in Orthodox Theology

Despite not accepting the doctrine of the Immaculate Conception, the Orthodox Church venerates the Virgin Mary as the most holy and exalted of all saints. She is honored above all other saints because of her unique role in salvation history as the Mother of God. In the Orthodox liturgical tradition, the Virgin Mary is frequently invoked in prayers, hymns, and feasts.

Key feast days in honor of the Virgin Mary in the Orthodox Church include:

- The Annunciation (March 25): Celebrating the moment when the Archangel Gabriel announced to Mary that she would bear the Son of God.
- The Nativity of the Theotokos (September 8): Celebrating Mary's birth as the one chosen to bear Christ.
- The Dormition of the Theotokos (August 15): Celebrating Mary's death and her assumption into heaven.

Orthodox Christians see Mary as a powerful intercessor before God. Her purity and faithfulness make her an example for all believers, and her intercession is sought in prayer. The Orthodox Church teaches that Mary, by her intercession, helps to bring the faithful closer to her Son, Jesus Christ.

St. John Chrysostom, an early Church Father, states:
> Let us honor the Mother of God, who bore the Word of life, so that through her intercession, we may obtain mercy from her Son and God.

Conclusion: The Orthodox View of the Virgin Mary and the Immaculate Conception

In conclusion, the Orthodox Church reveres the Virgin Mary as the Theotokos, the Mother of God, and acknowledges her special holiness and purity. However, the Orthodox Church does not accept the Roman Catholic doctrine of the Immaculate Conception, which teaches that Mary was conceived without original sin. Instead, the Orthodox Church believes that Mary was born with original sin, like all human beings, but that she was sanctified by God's grace and lived a life of perfect obedience and purity, making her worthy to bear the Savior of the world.

The Orthodox veneration of Mary is centered on her role as the Mother of God, her example of faith and obedience, and her special relationship with Christ. The Orthodox Church emphasizes that holiness is not about an absence of sin from birth, but about cooperating with God's grace and growing in holiness through faith, repentance, and communion with God. Thus, while the Immaculate Conception is not a doctrine held by the Orthodox Church, Mary is nonetheless revered as the most holy and blessed of all human beings.

Question 8 How Does the Orthodox Church Address Doctrinal Development Over Time?

The issue of doctrinal development—how Christian doctrine evolves over time—is one that has been addressed differently by various Christian traditions. In the Orthodox Church, the approach to doctrinal development is distinctive and rooted in the Church's understanding of the nature of revelation, the preservation of the apostolic faith, and the authority of the Church. While the Orthodox Church acknowledges that its understanding of certain theological concepts may deepen or become clearer over time, it maintains that doctrinal development must always remain faithful to the original deposit of faith passed down from the apostles.

In this article, we will explore the Orthodox Church's approach to doctrinal development, focusing on the relationship between Tradition, Scripture, and the role of the Church in preserving and articulating the faith.

The Unchanging Nature of the Apostolic Faith

The Orthodox Church believes that the core of Christian doctrine is rooted in the apostolic faith, which was handed down directly by Jesus Christ to the apostles and from them to their successors. This faith, as revealed in the Scriptures and passed on through the Church's Tradition, is considered unchanging and eternal. The Orthodox Church teaches that the Gospel is the same today as it was in the time of the apostles, and it is preserved in its fullness within the life of the Church.

Orthodox theologians often emphasize the principle of *the faith once for all delivered to the saints* (Jude 1:3). This means that the core doctrines of the Christian faith—such as the nature of God, the person of Christ, salvation, and the sacraments—are established and unchangeable. The Orthodox Church does not accept the idea of doctrinal development that introduces new teachings that contradict the original apostolic faith. Any development in doctrine must be seen as a deeper understanding or clarification of existing truths, not as the introduction of entirely new concepts.

The Role of Tradition in Doctrinal Development

In the Orthodox Church, Holy Tradition plays a central role in preserving and transmitting the apostolic faith. Tradition, in the Orthodox sense, is not merely the cultural or historical practices of the Church, but the living transmission of the faith, including Scripture, liturgical practices, the writings of the Church Fathers, and the ongoing life of the Church. Tradition is viewed as a dynamic process that is continually at work within the Church, guided by the Holy Spirit, ensuring that the fullness of the Christian faith is preserved and faithfully passed down from generation to generation.

While the Orthodox Church believes that the doctrines of the faith do not change, it also believes that the understanding of these doctrines can develop over time. This development is not about introducing new doctrines, but rather about the Church's ongoing reflection on the revelation of God and the application of that revelation to new contexts. The development of doctrine in the Orthodox Church is thus always viewed as a deepening or unfolding of the original apostolic faith, not as a departure from it.

The Role of Ecumenical Councils in Doctrinal Development
In the Orthodox Church, doctrinal development is closely tied to the authority of the Ecumenical Councils. The Ecumenical Councils were gatherings of bishops from across the Christian world, convened to address pressing theological issues and clarify important aspects of the faith. These councils are seen as the highest authority in the Orthodox Church when it comes to matters of doctrine and faith.

The Orthodox Church recognizes seven Ecumenical Councils, which took place between the fourth and eighth centuries. These councils addressed key theological debates, such as the nature of Christ (the Council of Nicaea in 325), the relationship between the Father, Son, and Holy Spirit (the Council of Constantinople in 381), and the nature of grace and free will (the Council of Chalcedon in 451). The decisions made at these councils were not innovations but were understood as clarifications of the apostolic faith, guided by the Holy Spirit.

The decisions of the Ecumenical Councils are considered binding for all Orthodox Christians, as they represent the collective wisdom of the Church's bishops, guided by the Holy Spirit, in discerning and preserving the truth of the faith. The Orthodox Church does not accept councils or doctrinal developments that are not recognized as Ecumenical or that do not conform to the original apostolic faith.

The Difference Between Doctrinal Development and Doctrinal Innovation

A key distinction in Orthodox theology is the difference between doctrinal development and doctrinal innovation. The Orthodox Church does not reject the idea that the understanding of doctrine can develop over time, but it insists that this development must be faithful to the original revelation and the teachings of the apostles. In this sense, the development of doctrine is always seen as a process of "deepening" rather than changing the essential truths of the faith.

On the other hand, the Orthodox Church rejects any doctrinal innovation that introduces teachings or practices that are not consistent with the apostolic faith and Tradition. For example, the Orthodox Church does not accept the Roman Catholic doctrine of papal infallibility, as it believes this teaching was not part of the original apostolic faith and was introduced long after the apostolic period.

The Orthodox Church also rejects innovations that were introduced during the Protestant Reformation, such as the doctrine of sola scriptura (Scripture alone) or the denial of the sacraments. The Orthodox Church believes that these innovations are contrary to the fullness of the apostolic faith as preserved in the Church's Tradition.

The Living Tradition of the Church

The Orthodox Church understands doctrinal development as part of the living Tradition of the Church. This means that the Church does not rely solely on past formulations of doctrine, but also continues to reflect on and articulate the truth of the faith in response to new questions, challenges, and circumstances. However, this ongoing reflection is always done in the context of preserving the core teachings of the faith, which are considered unchangeable.

For example, while the Orthodox Church does not accept the concept of papal supremacy, it has continually reflected on the role of the bishop of Rome and his relationship to the rest of the Church. The Orthodox

Church acknowledges the primacy of honor given to the bishop of Rome, but this honor is not understood as implying universal jurisdiction or infallibility, which were later doctrines developed in the Western Church.

In this sense, the Orthodox Church believes that the Holy Spirit continues to guide the Church through its bishops, theologians, and the faithful. The Church is seen as a living organism that grows in understanding and faith, but without departing from the original deposit of faith.

The Role of the Church Fathers in Doctrinal Development
The writings of the Church Fathers are crucial in the Orthodox understanding of doctrinal development. The Fathers, who lived in the first few centuries of the Church, are seen as authoritative witnesses to the apostolic faith. Their writings serve as a guide to understanding the Scriptures and the teachings of the apostles, and their interpretations of doctrine are considered an essential part of the living Tradition of the Church.

In the Orthodox Church, the writings of the Church Fathers are not seen as equivalent to Scripture, but they are highly revered as an expression of the faith handed down by the apostles. The Orthodox Church looks to the Fathers to help interpret Scripture, to clarify doctrinal issues, and to provide guidance on how to live out the Christian faith in different historical contexts.

The writings of the Church Fathers are a key source of authority in the Orthodox Church, and their teachings continue to influence Orthodox theology and practice today. The Fathers help ensure that doctrinal development remains faithful to the original apostolic deposit and that the Church's understanding of doctrine is consistent with the Tradition of the early Church.

Theological Reflection and Cultural Context
The Orthodox Church also recognizes that theological reflection and the articulation of doctrine take place within specific cultural and historical contexts. The Church must respond to the challenges and questions that arise in different times and places, but this must always be done in a way that is consistent with the apostolic faith.

For example, in the early Church, theological reflection was primarily concerned with the nature of Christ and the Trinity, as the Church grappled with various heresies. In later centuries, the Church's focus shifted to questions of the Church's authority, liturgy, and sacraments, as new theological challenges arose. Today, the Orthodox Church continues to reflect on how to live out the Christian faith in a modern world, but always within the framework of the unchanging truths of the Gospel.

Conclusion: Doctrinal Development in the Orthodox Church
In summary, the Orthodox Church views doctrinal development as a deepening of understanding rather than a change in doctrine. The Church believes that the core truths of the faith, as handed down from the apostles, are unchanging and eternal. Doctrinal development is understood as the Church's ongoing reflection on and articulation of these truths, guided by the Holy Spirit, in response to the needs of the faithful and the challenges of new contexts.

The Orthodox Church emphasizes the centrality of Holy Tradition, the authority of the Ecumenical Councils, and the writings of the Church Fathers in preserving and articulating the faith. Doctrinal innovation that departs from the apostolic faith is rejected, and any development must always be consistent with the original deposit of faith. The Orthodox Church, therefore, believes that the unchanging truth of the Gospel is preserved in the life of the Church, which continues to grow in understanding while remaining faithful to its origins.

Question 9   How Does the Orthodox Church Address the Problem of Evil and Suffering?

The problem of evil and suffering is one of the most challenging theological and philosophical issues in any religious tradition, and it is no less difficult for the Orthodox Church. Evil and suffering raise profound questions about the nature of God, the meaning of human life, and the existence of a benevolent and omnipotent Creator. While the Orthodox Church does not offer a simple or definitive answer to the problem, it provides a framework for understanding evil and suffering through its theology of free will, the Fall of man, and the hope of redemption in Christ.

In this section, we will explore how the Orthodox Church addresses the problem of evil and suffering, focusing on key theological concepts such as the role of free will, the consequences of the Fall, the mystery of suffering, and the hope of redemption through Christ.

The Role of Free Will in the Problem of Evil
In Orthodox Christianity, evil is often understood as the result of the misuse of human free will. The Church teaches that God created humans with free will—an essential gift that allows individuals to choose between good and evil. This gift of free will is integral to the nature of love and relationship. Without freedom, love would not be genuine, and the possibility of sin and evil would not exist.

The Orthodox Church does not view God as directly responsible for evil; rather, evil arises when human beings choose to turn away from God and His goodness. This misuse of free will leads to sin, which results in both moral and natural evil. In this view, evil is not something that God created but something that comes into the world as a result of human choice and rebellion against God.

In the book of Genesis, we see that the first humans, Adam and Eve, were given the freedom to choose to obey God or to follow their own desires. They chose disobedience, and as a result, evil and suffering entered the world. The Orthodox Church teaches that while God allowed the possibility of evil through the gift of free will, He does not cause or will evil. Instead, evil is a consequence of human choices that oppose God's goodness.

St. Irenaeus, one of the early Church Fathers, writes:
> God, in His wisdom, gave freedom of choice to man, so that man, in exercising his free will, might come to know God's goodness and to choose God freely, not by coercion.

The Fall and Its Consequences
The Orthodox Church holds that the first humans, Adam and Eve, were created in a state of grace and harmony with God, the natural world, and each other. This state of original righteousness is sometimes called the "original paradise." However, when Adam and Eve disobeyed God by eating the forbidden fruit, they introduced sin and death into the

world. This event, known as the Fall, had far-reaching consequences for humanity and the world.

The Fall is understood in the Orthodox Church not just as a historical event, but as a symbolic representation of the human tendency to choose autonomy from God, and the result of that choice—alienation, suffering, and death. The Fall fractured the original harmony and led to a world filled with suffering, disease, and death.

While humanity inherited the effects of the Fall (i.e., death, suffering, and a propensity for sin), the Orthodox Church does not teach the concept of "original guilt," as some Western Christian traditions do. Rather, it teaches that all human beings inherit the consequences of Adam and Eve's sin, including a fallen nature and the potential for sin, but they are not personally guilty of Adam's sin.

In this way, suffering in the world is understood as a result of human disobedience to God's will and the disruption that sin caused to the created order. However, the Orthodox Church also emphasizes that suffering is not meaningless but can serve as a context for spiritual growth and healing.

The Mystery of Suffering
While the Orthodox Church acknowledges the reality of evil and suffering, it does not claim to have a complete understanding of why suffering exists. The mystery of suffering is an important aspect of Orthodox theology, and the Church does not offer simple explanations. Instead, it encourages believers to approach suffering with humility, recognizing that human understanding is limited, and that suffering is a complex and multifaceted phenomenon.

In Orthodox thought, suffering is often seen as a result of living in a fallen world. It is also viewed as a consequence of the choices made by individuals or society. However, the Orthodox Church teaches that suffering is not without purpose or meaning. In fact, suffering is seen as a potential means of purification and spiritual growth.

The Orthodox Church believes that suffering can lead to personal transformation if one responds to it with faith, prayer, and trust in God's providence. Through suffering, one can learn humility, patience, and dependence on God. The Church teaches that the goal of life is not to escape suffering but to find meaning in it through union with Christ, who Himself experienced suffering and death.

In the life of the saints, we see numerous examples of individuals who endured suffering with faith and hope, finding in it a means of spiritual purification and deepening their relationship with God. The most profound example of this is Christ Himself, who took on human suffering and death in order to redeem humanity.

St. Paul, in his second letter to the Corinthians, writes:
> *We are afflicted in every way, but not crushed; perplexed, but not driven to despair; persecuted, but not forsaken; struck down, but not destroyed* (2 Corinthians 4:8–9).

In this passage, St. Paul suggests that suffering, when faced with faith, can become a means of growth and transformation.

Christ's Suffering and the Redemption of the World

In Orthodox theology, Christ's death on the cross is the key to understanding the problem of evil and suffering. Christ's suffering and death are seen as the ultimate act of love and sacrifice, through which God entered into human suffering and took on the consequences of sin and death.

The Orthodox Church teaches that Christ, as both fully God and fully man, experienced the full range of human suffering, including betrayal, rejection, pain, and death. Through His suffering, He sanctified human suffering and gave it meaning. The cross becomes the means by which God redeems the world and defeats the power of evil and death.

In Christ's Passion, death, and resurrection, the Orthodox Church sees the ultimate victory over sin and suffering. Christ's resurrection is the key to understanding the ultimate defeat of evil. The Church teaches that through Christ's victory over death, the hope of eternal life is given to all who unite themselves with Him. This is the Orthodox understanding of salvation: it is not merely a matter of forgiveness of sins but the complete healing of humanity and the creation itself.

Christ's suffering is not seen as pointless or arbitrary but as a means of conquering evil and restoring creation to its intended purpose. The resurrection of Christ is seen as the first fruits of the new creation, a world where evil and suffering no longer have the final word.

The Hope of Redemption: The Final Victory Over Evil
The Orthodox Church teaches that while suffering and evil are real, they are not the final reality. The hope of the Orthodox Christian is that Christ's second coming will bring the final victory over evil, suffering, and death. In the eschatological vision of the Orthodox Church, all things will be made new, and suffering will be wiped away.

Revelation 21:4 is often cited in Orthodox theology to emphasize this hope:
> *He will wipe every tear from their eyes. There will be no more death or mourning or crying or pain, for the old order of things has passed away.*

The ultimate answer to the problem of evil and suffering is not found in an explanation but in the hope of the resurrection and the restoration of all things in Christ. Orthodox theology teaches that suffering, when united to Christ, can be redeemed and transformed. The final victory over evil will be achieved when God's Kingdom is fully realized, and all of creation is restored to its original goodness and harmony.

Conclusion: Living with the Mystery of Suffering
The Orthodox Church does not offer easy answers to the problem of evil and suffering, but it offers a profound understanding of suffering as part of the human condition. Suffering is recognized as a result of the Fall and human choices, but it is also seen as a potential means of spiritual growth and union with God. The ultimate solution to the problem of evil is found in Christ's suffering, death, and resurrection, through which He conquers death and offers the hope of eternal life.

Orthodox Christians are called to approach suffering with faith and hope, trusting that God is with them in their pain and that, through Christ, suffering will be ultimately overcome. The Church encourages believers to endure suffering with patience and to unite their sufferings with Christ, who has sanctified and redeemed human suffering.

In this way, suffering is not without meaning, but becomes a part of the journey toward salvation and the restoration of all things in Christ.

Question 10   What Role Does Reason and Science Play in the Orthodox Faith?

In the Orthodox Christian tradition, reason and science are generally seen as complementary to, rather than in conflict with, faith. The Orthodox Church holds that both faith and reason are gifts from God, and that truth can be found in both the revealed Word of God (Scripture and Tradition) and the created world. Orthodox theology does not see any inherent contradiction between the teachings of the Church and scientific discoveries. Rather, it teaches that science and reason can deepen our understanding of the natural world, while faith provides the spiritual and moral framework within which human beings are called to live.

This section will explore the relationship between reason, science, and Orthodox faith, focusing on key aspects such as the role of reason in understanding the faith, the Church's stance on scientific inquiry, and how both science and faith contribute to human flourishing.

The Role of Reason in the Orthodox Faith

In Orthodox Christianity, reason is regarded as a gift from God, and it is seen as an essential tool in the pursuit of truth. Reason allows humans to understand the natural world, engage in theological reflection, and explore the mysteries of the universe. The Orthodox Church does not reject reason or intellect but upholds them as part of God's design for human beings, made in His image. Orthodox theology emphasizes the use of reason in understanding divine revelation, but it also teaches that reason must be guided by faith, particularly when it comes to the mysteries of the divine and salvation.

Faith and Reason as Complementary

The Orthodox Church does not see a division between faith and reason. Rather, faith and reason are viewed as two complementary ways of approaching truth. Faith, as understood in the Orthodox tradition, is trust in God's revealed Word and in the truths of the Church, whereas reason is the intellectual capacity to understand, interpret, and apply that truth in everyday life. Orthodox theology teaches that while faith is necessary to understand the mysteries of God, reason is a vital tool in helping us live out that faith.

This complementary relationship between faith and reason is reflected in the writings of many Church Fathers, including St. Gregory of Nyssa, who saw reason as a means of understanding the divine order and St. John of Damascus, who defended the compatibility of Christian faith with human reason.

In his Exposition of the Orthodox Faith, St. John of Damascus writes:

> Reason is given to us by God, and it is through reason that we come to understand the natural world and its Creator. But it is through faith that we come to understand the deeper mysteries of God.

Thus, in the Orthodox worldview, reason is not an adversary to faith but a tool that helps illuminate the truths of faith. Reason and faith are meant to work together to help individuals live in harmony with God's creation.

Science and the Orthodox Church: Harmony Between Faith and Discovery

The Orthodox Church has a long history of engagement with science, and it views scientific discovery as a means of exploring God's creation. The Orthodox Church has no official doctrine that opposes scientific inquiry, and many Orthodox theologians have seen the study of the natural world as a way of contemplating the greatness and beauty of God. In fact, the Orthodox Church recognizes that science, when pursued with humility and in accordance with moral principles, can serve the greater good and enhance human life.

Creation as God's Work

In Orthodox theology, creation is understood as the work of God, and the natural world is considered a revelation of God's glory. The Orthodox Church teaches that all of creation is "good" (Genesis 1:31), and that humans are called to care for it and understand it. This perspective creates a harmonious relationship between faith and science: the natural world, as studied by science, reflects the Creator's design and wisdom.

Science and faith are seen as complementary tools for understanding the universe. While science seeks to understand the "how" of the world through empirical observation and experimentation, faith addresses the "why" by providing meaning and purpose to the created order. The

Orthodox Church acknowledges that scientific discoveries, especially in fields such as physics, biology, and astronomy, can help us to better understand the intricate and marvelous nature of God's creation.

The Relationship Between Faith and Scientific Discoveries
Throughout history, many Orthodox thinkers have embraced the compatibility of science and faith. For example, the Orthodox Church does not reject the theory of evolution, but instead sees it as one of the ways that God may have worked through the natural world to bring about the diversity of life. The Church teaches that God is the Creator of all things, and that the process of creation, whether it is through evolutionary processes or direct creation, is ultimately in God's hands.

St. Gregory Palamas, a 14th-century Orthodox theologian, emphasized that while reason and science can bring us closer to understanding the created world, they cannot fully explain the divine mysteries. Reason can guide us in our understanding of how things work in the material world, but it cannot comprehend the fullness of God's nature or His purposes for creation. This is where faith and divine revelation play a crucial role.

The Orthodox Church does not see science as a threat to its teachings but as a complementary source of knowledge. Scientific discoveries are seen as uncovering the beauty and order that God has created in the world. The Church encourages the study of science, as long as it is done with the understanding that ultimate truth comes from God.

Reason and Science in the Context of Human Flourishing
In Orthodox thought, the pursuit of knowledge and understanding through reason and science is ultimately directed toward human flourishing. The goal of human life, according to the Orthodox Church, is not just intellectual achievement but spiritual growth and communion with God. Science and reason, when pursued within a moral and ethical framework, can serve the well-being of humanity by promoting knowledge that benefits society and supports the holistic development of the human person.

Science in Service of Humanity
The Orthodox Church teaches that science, when aligned with ethical principles, can serve as a powerful tool for improving the human condition. Medical science, for example, is seen as a means of healing and alleviating human suffering. The Church has historically supported

the development of hospitals, schools, and other institutions of learning, seeing them as part of its mission to care for the body and soul of humanity.

At the same time, the Orthodox Church also cautions against the idolization of science or reason. Science and technology must always be used for the common good and should be tempered by moral and spiritual considerations. For instance, scientific advancements in fields such as genetics, artificial intelligence, and environmental studies must be guided by principles of love, justice, and stewardship of the earth, in line with the Orthodox understanding of human responsibility toward creation.

Ethical Considerations in Scientific Progress
The Orthodox Church teaches that scientific progress must always be accompanied by ethical reflection. Just as reason must be guided by faith, scientific progress must be guided by moral principles. The Orthodox Church has a rich tradition of moral theology that speaks to issues such as the sanctity of life, the dignity of the human person, and the care of creation. These principles help provide a framework for making ethical decisions in the realm of science and technology.

In recent times, the Orthodox Church has expressed concern over certain scientific advancements, such as cloning, genetic manipulation, and environmental degradation, which it views as potentially harmful to human dignity and the natural order. The Church calls for ethical reflection in these areas and encourages the faithful to consider the moral implications of scientific progress.

The Mystery of God and the Limits of Reason
While the Orthodox Church embraces the use of reason and science, it also acknowledges that there are limits to human understanding. The mysteries of God and His divine will are beyond the full comprehension of the human mind. The Church teaches that while reason and science can help illuminate many aspects of the created world, they cannot fully grasp the mysteries of salvation, the nature of God, or the ultimate purpose of human life.

The Orthodox Church emphasizes the importance of humility in both reason and scientific inquiry. As much as human beings are capable of reason, they are also reminded of the limitations of human knowledge. In this sense, reason is always subject to faith, which provides the deeper, spiritual understanding of the universe and the divine plan for humanity.

In the words of St. Gregory the Theologian:
> The more we know, the more we recognize that there is infinitely more to know, and that we are dependent on God for our understanding.

This acknowledgment of the limits of human reason points to the Orthodox belief in the transcendent mystery of God, who is beyond human comprehension, even as He is intimately involved in the world He created.

Conclusion: The Harmonious Relationship Between Faith, Reason, and Science

In summary, the Orthodox Church views reason and science as valuable tools that can help deepen our understanding of the world, while always recognizing their limits in addressing spiritual truths. Faith and reason are seen as complementary aspects of the human quest for truth, with science providing insight into the created world and faith offering the ultimate understanding of human existence, divine revelation, and the nature of God.

The Orthodox Church encourages the pursuit of knowledge, including scientific discovery, as long as it is pursued with ethical reflection, humility, and a recognition of God's sovereignty. Reason and science, when used correctly, are seen as part of God's plan for human flourishing, serving the good of humanity and promoting a deeper understanding of both the natural world and the divine. Faith, however, remains the ultimate guide for understanding the meaning and purpose of life, and it calls us to recognize the mystery of God that transcends all human knowledge.

Appendix B

Books for Inquirers

Here is a list of recommended books for inquirers exploring the Orthodox Christian faith. These books are grouped by topic and cater to Protestant, Catholic, and atheist backgrounds, addressing common questions, theological concerns, and spiritual practices.

Introductory Books on Orthodoxy

The Orthodox Way by Bishop Kallistos Ware
    A classic and accessible introduction to Orthodox theology, spirituality, and worldview.

The Orthodox Church by Bishop Kallistos Ware
    A historical and theological overview of the Orthodox Church and its teachings.

Introducing the Orthodox Church: Its Faith and Life
    by Anthony M. Coniaris
    A concise and approachable book for newcomers to Orthodoxy.

Everywhere Present: Christianity in a One-Storey Universe
    by Stephen Freeman
    Explains the Orthodox understanding of the sacramental worldview.

Orthodox Dogmatic Theology by Michael Pomazansky
    A concise and easily readable summary of the important doctrine of the Orthodox Church.

Welcome to the Orthodox Church: An Introduction to Eastern Christianity by Frederica Mathewes-Green (Author)

For the Life of the World by Protopresbyter Alexander Schmemann
    Fr. Alexander Schmemann explains in this classic how the Orthodox approach to the world stems from the liturgical life of the Church.

The Orthodox Faith, Worship, and Life by Hieromonk Gregorios
    A comprehensive Catechism of the Holy Orthodox faith based upon the Nicene-Constantinopolitan Creed.

Thinking Orthodox: Understanding and Acquiring the Orthodox Christian Mind by Eugenia Scarvelis Constantinou, Ph.D.
    Orthodox Christianity is based on preserving the mind of the early Church, its phronema. What his it and how it can be acquired, and expressed in true Orthodox practice.

Journey to Reality: Sacramental Life in a Secular Age, by Zachary Porcu
    To fully understand Orthodox doctrine and practice, we have to unlearn an entire secular worldview and become participants in a sacramental worldview instead—a worldview that embraces reality as it truly is. This provides a guide to this process.

The Mountain of Silence: A Search for Orthodox Spirituality, by Kyriakos C. Markides
    An acclaimed expert in Christian mysticism offers a fascinating look at the Greek Orthodox approach to spirituality.

The Path to Salvation: A Manual of Spiritual Transformation by Saint Theophan the Recluse
    With the ancient patristic model he speaks to contemporary people, linking them to the original Christian impetus and revealing to them the way into the Heavenly Kingdom.

Books for Protestant Inquirers

Thirsting for God in a Land of Shallow Wells by Matthew Gallatin
    Written by a former Protestant, this book explains why he embraced Orthodoxy and how Orthodoxy fulfills spiritual hunger.

Rock and Sand: An Orthodox Appraisal of the Protestant Reformers and Their Teaching by Josiah Trenham
    A respectful critique of Protestant theology and how Orthodoxy offers a fuller expression of the Christian faith.

Becoming Orthodox: A Journey to the Ancient Christian Faith by Peter E. Gillquist
    A personal journey of a Protestant pastor and his congregation into Orthodoxy.

Orthodoxy and Heterodoxy: Orthodox Christianity and Non-Orthodox Doctrine by Fr. Andrew Stephen Damick
> Discover how Orthodox Christianity and non-Orthodox doctrine differ and why it matters to your spiritual journey. (This updated version was recorded 2015-2016.) A fuller treatment of these topics, with material not included in the podcast, is found in the book by the same name.

The Way, by Clark Carlton

Books for Catholic Inquirers

Two Paths: Orthodoxy & Catholicism: Rome's Claims of Papal Supremacy in the Light of Orthodox Christian Teaching by Michael Whelton (Author), Dr. Herman A. Middleton (Editor)
> A clear comparison of Orthodox and Catholic theology and practices. For layman and scholar alike, Whelton's work is the best and fullest work dealing with this topic from an Orthodox perspective

The Primacy of Peter: Essays in Ecclesiology and the Early Church edited by John Meyendorff
> Discusses Orthodox views on papal primacy and ecclesiology.

The Mystical Theology of the Eastern Church by Vladimir Lossky
> A deep dive into Orthodox theology, with contrasts to Western Christian thought.

Books for Atheist Inquirers

The Experience of God: Being, Consciousness, Bliss by David Bentley Hart
> A philosophical defense of the Christian understanding of God, addressing modern atheistic arguments.

On the Incarnation by St. Athanasius (translated by C.S. Lewis, with an introduction)
> A profound exploration of why God became man, written by one of the Church Fathers.

Spiritual Life and Prayer

Way of the Ascetics by Tito Colliander
   A practical and accessible guide to Orthodox spirituality and asceticism.

Our Thoughts Determine Our Lives by Elder Thaddeus of Vitovnica
   A modern Orthodox classic on the power of thoughts and inner peace.

Wounded by Love: The Life and Wisdom of Elder Porphyrios
   The teachings of a modern Orthodox saint on love, humility, and the life in Christ.

Art of Prayer: an Orthodox Anthology

Beginning to Pray by Metropolitan Anthony Bloom

The Mountain of Silence: A Search for Orthodox Spirituality by Kyriakos C. Markides
   An expert in Christian mysticism travels to monasteries high in the Trodos Mountains of Cyprus giving us a fascinating look at the Greek Orthodox approach to spirituality that will appeal to modern seekers.

History and Tradition

The Apostolic Fathers: Early Christian Writings
   Writings of the first Christian leaders after the apostles, offering insights into early Church practices.

The Roots of Christian Mysticism by Olivier Clément
   Explores the spiritual and theological foundations of the early Church.

The Jesus We Missed: The Surprising Truth About the Humanity of Christ by Fr. Patrick Henry Reardon
   A reflection on Christ's humanity in light of Orthodox theology.

Divine Liturgy

For the Life of the World by Alexander Schmemann
   Explains how Orthodoxy views life, worship, and the world as sacramental and meaningful.

The Heavenly Banquet: Understanding the Divine Liturgy by Fr. Emmanuel Hatzidakis
   In depth, yet easy to follow, written in simple, understandable language, this book will aid Catechists.

A Commentary On the Divine Liturgy by St. Nicholas Cabasilas

Contemporary Issues and Apologetics

Christianity and Modernity by Fr. Seraphim Rose
   Addresses modern challenges to the Christian faith from an Orthodox perspective.

Against the Modern World: Traditionalism and the Secret Intellectual History of the Twentieth Century by Mark Sedgwick
   Discusses how Orthodox tradition addresses contemporary spiritual crises.

Truth Matters, Life Matters More by Hank Hanegraaff
   A former Protestant apologist explains his journey to Orthodoxy and its relevance in today's world.

The Bible and Orthodox Interpretation

The Bible and the Holy Fathers for Orthodox by Johanna Manley
   A study guide combining Scripture readings with commentary from the Church Fathers.

Orthodox Study Bible
   Includes the Septuagint Old Testament and commentary based on Orthodox Tradition.

Scripture and Tradition in Orthodoxy by Sebastian Brock
   Explains the interplay between Scripture and Holy Tradition in the Orthodox Church.

Lives of the Saints

Saint Iakovos Tsaltikis: The Garden of the Holy Spirit by Stylos Papadopoulos
Saint John of Kronstadt by I. K. Surely
Saint Netarios: The Saint of our Century by Sotos Chrondropoulos
St Porphyrios: Wounded by Love
Saint Paisios of Mount Athos by Elder Isaac

Iconography

The Theology of the Icon by Leonid Ouspensky
> The most comprehensive introduction available to the history and theology of the icon,

The Art of the Icon: A Theology of Beauty by Evdokimov
> This book illuminates traditional teachings on both Iconography and the spiritual significance of the subject of beauty within the Orthodox East.

Iconostasis by Pavel Florensky
> This book explores in highly original terms the significance of the icon: its philosophic depth, its spiritual history, its empirical technique.

Appendix C

Websites, Blogs, and You Tube Channels for Inquirers

Here are some of the best websites, blogs and Youtube channels for learning about the Orthodox faith, offering reliable resources for inquirers, catechumens, and anyone interested in Orthodox Christianity.

Websites, Blogs and You Tube channels for Inquirers

Official and Comprehensive Resources

Greek Orthodox Archdiocese of America (GOARCH)
>Includes detailed explanations of Orthodox beliefs, feast days, sacraments, and the Bible.

>Provides multimedia resources like videos, sermons, and podcasts.
>https://www.goarch.org/

Orthodox Church in America (OCA)
>Offers extensive resources on Orthodox theology, liturgy, saints, and Church history.

>Features a Q&A section for inquirers and a well-organized library of articles.
>https://www.oca.org/

Antiochian Orthodox Christian Archdiocese
>Focuses on the Orthodox Christian life, with resources on fasting, prayer, and spiritual practices.

>Offers links to liturgical texts and pastoral guidance.
>https://www.antiochian.org/home

Saint George Greek Orthodox Cathedral — Our Faith
>website of the Greek Orthodox church in Greenville SC.
>saintgeorge.church.org

Educational and Apologetics Websites

Orthodox Wiki
> A collaborative encyclopedia covering Orthodox theology, saints, history, and practices.
>
> Accessible for beginners and detailed enough for deeper study.
> https://orthodoxwiki.org/Main_Page

Ancient Faith Ministries
> A hub for Orthodox podcasts, blogs, books, and live programming.
>
> Features series like "Orthodoxy Live" and "Journey to Orthodoxy."
> https://www.ancientfaith.com/

Journey to Orthodoxy
> Focused on conversion stories from Protestants, Catholics, and others.
>
> Offers explanations of Orthodox teachings and practical advice for inquirers.
> https://journeytoorthodoxy.com/

Roots of Orthodoxy
> Dedicated to showcasing Orthodox Christianity by interviewing priests from all over the United States
> https://www.youtube.com/@RootsofOrthodoxy

Trisagion Films
> Presenting tangible theology through original videos and articles, all to the glory of God. We cover aspects of Orthodox worship and practice, pilgrimage, the lives of the saints, iconography and the sacred arts, and recordings of homilies, interviews, and special events.
> https://www.trisagionfilms.com/

Scripture and Liturgy

Search the Scriptures
> Offers background information on the Orthodox Study Bible and its approach to Scripture.
> Includes links to resources for deeper engagement with the Bible.
> https://orthodoxbiblestudy.info/

Digital Chant Stand
> Provides access to Orthodox liturgical texts, including services, hymns, and prayers.
>
> Great for exploring the richness of Orthodox worship.
> https://dcs.goarch.org/goa/dcs/dcs.html

Spiritual Life and Practices

Orthodox Prayer
> Many resources on Orthodox Prayer
> https://orthodoxprayer.org/

Missionary and Outreach Sites

Orthodox Christian Mission Center (OCMC)
> Focused on Orthodox missions around the world.
>
> Offers insights into the global Orthodox Church and its outreach efforts.
> https://www.ocmc.org/

Conversion Stories and Resources

The Orthodox Christian Network (OCN)
> Provides podcasts, articles, and videos that explain Orthodoxy in an accessible way.
> Includes content for inquirers and seekers of all backgrounds.
> https://faith.myocn.net/

Youth and Family-Oriented Resources
    Orthodox Pebbles
    Offers creative and interactive resources for teaching children about the Orthodox faith.
    Includes crafts, lessons, and activities related to feast days and traditions.
    https://orthodoxpebbles.com/
Y2AM: Be the Bee
    A project by the Greek Orthodox Archdiocese designed for young adults and teens.
    Features short videos explaining aspects of Orthodox spirituality in an engaging way.
    https://www.y2am.org/be-the-bee

Good blogs

Blogs for Orthodox Inquirers

Ancient Faith Blogs
    Website: Ancient Faith Blogs
    A collection of blogs by Orthodox writers addressing faith, theology, culture, and everyday life.
    https://blogs.ancientfaith.com/

Orthodox Way of Life
    Articles about how to live the Orthodox Christian faith
    https://orthodoxwayoflife.blogspot.com

YouTube Channels for Orthodox Inquirers

Be the Bee
    Channel: Be the Bee
    Hosted by Steven Christoforou, this channel explains Orthodox theology and spirituality in short, engaging videos.
    Great for beginners and young adults.
    Key topics: prayer, sacraments, living a Christ-centered life.

Ancient Faith Ministries
Channel: Ancient Faith Ministries
Features interviews, talks, and discussions on Orthodox theology, history, and contemporary issues.
Includes content from popular podcasts like Orthodoxy Live and Lord of Spirits.
https://www.youtube.com/@AncientFaithMinistries

Fr. Josiah Trenham - Patristic Nectar Films
Channel: Patristic Nectar Films
Features in-depth talks by Fr. Josiah Trenham on Orthodox theology, biblical studies, and contemporary issues.
Great for serious theological engagement.
https://www.youtube.com/@PatristicNectarFilms

Father Spyridon Bailey
Channel: Father Spyridon Bailey
Focuses on spiritual teachings and reflections on Orthodox life and practice.
Particularly valuable for those transitioning from atheism or Protestantism.
https://www.youtube.com/@FatherSpyridonROCOR

Orthodox Talks (Fr. Kosmas)
Channel: Orthodox Talks by Fr. Kosmas
Long-form lectures addressing Orthodox spirituality, struggles, and theological issues in detail.
Ideal for inquirers wanting deeper teaching on Orthodox topics.
https://www.youtube.com/@orthodoxtalks3541

Jonathan Pageau
Channel: Symbolic World
Explores Orthodox symbolism, philosophy, and culture.
Particularly appealing to inquirers with an intellectual or artistic focus.
https://www.youtube.com/@JonathanPageau

Orthodox Wisdom
   Channel: Orthodox Wisdom
   Features readings and teachings from the Church Fathers and modern Orthodox saints.
   Focused on traditional Orthodoxy and spiritual life.
   https://www.youtube.com/@OrthodoxWisdom

Father Seraphim Aldea
   Channel: Mull Monastery
   Personal reflections and teachings on Orthodox monasticism and spirituality.
   Encourages a contemplative approach to the faith.
   https://www.youtube.com/@mullmonastery

Holy Resurrection
   A YouTube channel of the Holy Resurrection Serbian Orthodox Church in Lebanon PA USA
   https://www.youtube.com/channel/UCLYut6IxIvx5PxwUWMXJz8g

These blogs and YouTube channels offer a mix of:

Practical guidance for living the Orthodox faith. Theological depth for answering tough questions. Personal stories of conversion and spiritual growth. Visual and engaging content for those new to Orthodoxy. These resources cater to various learning styles and interests, helping inquirers deepen their understanding of the Orthodox Church and its teachings.

Appendix D

The Nicene Creed

I believe in one God, Father Almighty, Creator of heaven and earth, and of all things visible and invisible.

And in one Lord Jesus Christ, the only-begotten Son of God, begotten of the Father before all ages; Light of Light, true God of true God, begotten, not created, of one essence with the Father through Whom all things were made. Who for us men and for our salvation came down from heaven and was incarnate of the Holy Spirit and the Virgin Mary and became man. He was crucified for us under Pontius Pilate, and suffered and was buried; And He rose on the third day, according to the Scriptures. He ascended into heaven and is seated at the right hand of the Father; And He will come again with glory to judge the living and dead. His kingdom shall have no end.

And in the Holy Spirit, the Lord, the Creator of life, Who proceeds from the Father, Who together with the Father and the Son is worshipped and glorified, Who spoke through the prophets.

In one, holy, catholic, and apostolic Church.

I confess one baptism for the forgiveness of sins.

I look for the resurrection of the dead, and the life of the age to come.

Amen.

Πιστεύω εἰς ἕνα Θεόν, Πατέρα παντοκράτορα, ποιητὴν οὐρανοῦ καὶ γῆς, ὁρατῶν τε πάντων καὶ ἀοράτων.

Καὶ εἰς ἕνα Κύριον Ἰησοῦν Χριστόν, τὸν Υἱὸν τοῦ Θεοῦ τὸν μονογενῆ, τὸν ἐκ τοῦ Πατρὸς γεννηθέντα πρὸ πάντων τῶν αἰώνων· φῶς ἐκ φωτός, Θεὸν ἀληθινὸν ἐκ Θεοῦ ἀληθινοῦ, γεννηθέντα οὐ ποιηθέντα, ὁμοούσιον τῷ Πατρί, δι' οὗ τὰ πάντα ἐγένετο. Τὸν δι' ἡμᾶς τοὺς ἀνθρώπους καὶ διὰ τὴν ἡμετέραν σωτηρίαν κατελθόντα ἐκ τῶν οὐρανῶν καὶ σαρκωθέντα ἐκ Πνεύματος Ἁγίου καὶ Μαρίας τῆς παρθένου καὶ ἐνανθρωπήσαντα.

Σταυρωθέντα τε ὑπὲρ ἡμῶν ἐπὶ Ποντίου Πιλάτου καὶ παθόντα καὶ ταφέντα. Καὶ ἀναστάντα τῇ τρίτῃ ἡμέρᾳ, κατὰ τὰς Γραφάς. Καὶ ἀνελθόντα εἰς τοὺς οὐρανοὺς καὶ καθεζόμενον ἐκ δεξιῶν τοῦ Πατρός. Καὶ πάλιν ἐρχόμενον μετὰ δόξης κρῖναι ζῶντας καὶ νεκρούς, οὗ τῆς βασιλείας οὐκ ἔσται τέλος.

Καὶ εἰς τὸ Πνεῦμα τὸ Ἅγιον, τὸ κύριον, τὸ ζωοποιόν, τὸ ἐκ τοῦ Πατρὸς ἐκπορευόμενον, τὸ σὺν Πατρὶ καὶ Υἱῷ συμπροσκυνούμενον καὶ συνδοξαζόμενον, τὸ λαλῆσαν διὰ τῶν προφητῶν.

Εἰς μίαν, ἁγίαν, καθολικὴν καὶ ἀποστολικὴν Ἐκκλησίαν. Ὁμολογῶ ἓν βάπτισμα εἰς ἄφεσιν ἁμαρτιῶν. Προσδοκῶ ἀνάστασιν νεκρῶν, καὶ ζωὴν τοῦ μέλλοντος αἰῶνος.

Acknowledgments

Fr. Charles expresses his deepest gratitude to his family for their unwavering love and support. He is especially thankful to his priest, Fr. Tom Pistolis, for his patience and trust in allowing him the great responsibility of catechizing so many new members of the Orthodox faith. He also extends heartfelt appreciation to His Eminence Metropolitan Alexios, who ordained him and has always embraced him with love, and to his spiritual father, Fr. Iakovos of the Holy Mountain, whose guidance has been a light along his spiritual path.

Author Biography

Fr. Deacon Charles was ordained as a permanent deacon in 2007. He holds a Masters degree in Orthodox Theology from Balamand University in Lebanon and a Ph.D. in Adult Learning and Change. Additionally, he has a Masters degree in Engineering and has held executive positions in major business organizations. He was also a partner in a consulting firm focused on applying values for organizational development. For a number of years, he founded an intentional community seeking to cultivate a life lived in harmony with nature and spirit alongside like-minded individuals.

Today, he leads Adult Catechism classes and other adult learning programs at the Saint George Greek Orthodox Cathedral in Greenville South Carolina, mentors inquirers into the Orthodox faith in an online program, and assists the parish priest as needed.

Fr. Charles has been married for 61 years to his wife, Kathy, whose Greek heritage played a significant role in leading him to the Orthodox faith. They have been blessed with two children and four wonderful granddaughters.